# GLUTEN-FREE DIET

## A Comprehensive Resource Guide

### DEDICATION

To my dad,
whose innovative spirit taught me that
anything was possible,
and to my mom,
whose support and encouragement
helped make our dreams a reality.

## Shelley Case

**B.Sc. (Nutrition & Dietetics), RD**

**Registered Dietitian**

# Gluten-Free Diet – A Comprehensive Resource Guide

by
Shelley Case, B.Sc. (Nutrition & Dietetics), RD, Registered Dietitian

Revised Edition – April 2002
Second Printing – July 2003

**Copyright © 2001 by**
Shelley Case, B.Sc. (Nutrition & Dietetics), RD, Registered Dietitian

**Published by**
**Case Nutrition Consulting**
1940 Angley Court
Regina, Saskatchewan
Canada  S4V 2V2
Phone/FAX: 306-751-1000

www.glutenfreediet.ca
E-mail: info@glutenfreediet.ca

**Canadian Cataloguing in Publication Data**

Case, Shelley

Gluten-free diet – a comprehensive resource guide

Includes index.
ISBN 1-894022-79-3

1. Gluten-free diet – Handbooks, manuals, etc.  2. Gluten-free diet – Recipes.  I. Title.

RM237.86.C37 2002              613.2'6              C2002-910464-5

**Cover Design by**
Brian Danchuk, Brian Danchuk Design
Regina, Saskatchewan

Page design and formatting by Iona Glabus

**Designed, Printed and Produced in Canada by:**
Centax Books, A Division of PW Group
Publishing Director – Margo Embury
1150 Eighth Avenue, Regina, Saskatchewan, Canada  S4R 1C9
(306) 525-2304                        FAX: (306) 757-2439
centax@printwest.com                www.centaxbooks.com

# ABOUT THE AUTHOR

A Registered Dietitian, Shelley earned a Bachelor of Science degree in Nutrition and Dietetics from the University of Saskatchewan and completed her Dietetic Internship at the Health Sciences Centre in Winnipeg. For the past 22 years Shelley has helped thousands of people change poor eating habits and manage a variety of disease conditions through good nutrition. She specializes in nutrition counseling for gastrointestinal disorders such as celiac disease, food allergies and intolerances, heart disease and diabetes.

**Shelley M. Case**
Registered Dietitian

Shelley is a frequent guest speaker on television and radio. She has also delivered numerous lectures and workshops to the general public, physicians and other health professionals, as well as organizations and associations. In 1997 she established her own nutrition consulting business and offers a variety of services to individuals, organizations and businesses. These services are customized to meet her client's unique needs.

Highlights of Shelley's career include: Acting Director and Teaching Dietitian at the Southern Saskatchewan Metabolic and Diabetes Education Centre in the Regina General Hospital; Marketing Dietitian and Outpatient Dietitian for Nutrition and Food Services in the Regina Health District. She has been President of the Saskatchewan Dietetic Association (SDA) and has dedicated many hours in support of that organization including author of the Diabetes and Hypoglycemia Sections of the SDA Diet Manual. Shelley has also co-authored the Celiac Disease Section in the *Manual of Clinical Dietetics* – 6th Edition (American Dietetic Association and Dietitians of Canada), as well as sections of the Canadian Celiac Association's *Celiac Disease Needs a Diet for Life Handbook* and *A Guide for the Celiac Diabetic*.

Continuing to be involved in the Dietitians of Canada, Shelley serves on the Medical Advisory Boards of the Celiac Disease Foundation, Gluten Intolerance Group and Canadian Celiac Association, and the Advisory Boards of *Gluten-Free Living* magazine and *Living Without* magazine. She is very active in her community and church. A committed volunteer, she has chaired numerous conferences and special events. She is also an accomplished musician and enjoys playing piano and electric keyboard. Shelley lives with her husband and two children in Regina, Saskatchewan, Canada.

# TABLE OF CONTENTS

# TABLE OF CONTENTS

# INTRODUCTION TO
# *THE GLUTEN-FREE DIET —*
# *A COMPREHENSIVE RESOURCE GUIDE*

This Guide was written for those who have been medically diagnosed as having Celiac Disease (CD) or Dermatitis Herpetiformis (DH) and must follow a strict gluten-free diet for life. Physicians, dietitians, chefs and food service staff will also find this a useful resource. Managers of grocery, health food and specialty food stores can use this Guide to assist in purchasing new products.

*The Gluten-Free Diet – A Comprehensive Resource Guide* is intended to provide practical information about the gluten-free diet, including nutritional aspects, meal planning, shopping, recipes, brand names of gluten-free products available, directory of companies and other resources. For more specific information on CD and DH contact the Celiac Support organizations listed on page 157.

The information which follows has been exhaustively researched from sources believed to be reliable and representative of the best current opinions on the subject at the time of printing. The author does not endorse any product listed in this Guide. Inclusion of brand name products is strictly for information purposes.

It should be noted that manufacturers of regular commercial food products often change the ingredients or suppliers of their ingredients used in their products. **Carefully reading labels on a regular basis** and contacting the company (if in doubt) **is of utmost importance** to ensure that products have remained gluten-free. Please notify the author if you learn that information in this Guide has changed, so that it can be included in future revisions.

In conclusion, I would like to sincerely thank all those who assisted me in so many ways during the development and production of this Guide over the last four years. A special thank you to **Carie Romanuik** for typing the numerous drafts for 13 months; **Enid Young**; **Marion Zarkadas,** M.Sc.(Nutrition), RD.; **Cynthia Kupper,** RD, CD, Executive Director, Gluten Intolerance Group (GIG); **Tricia Thompson**, M.S., RD; **Mavis Molloy**, RDN; **Dr. Connie Switzer**, M.D., FRCP (C), Chair, Professional Advisory Board, Canadian Celiac Association; **Ann Whelan,** Editor, *Gluten-Free Living* magazine; **Carol Fenster,** PhD, Savory Palate, Inc.; **Kelly Jackson** and **Jan Chernus,** Bob's Red Mill Natural Foods, Inc.; **Steven Rice,** Authentic Foods; **Marilyn and Chuck Withers,** Liv-N-Well Distributors; **Bette Hagman**; **Carolyn Townley-Smith; staff from Canadian Food Inspection Agency, Health Canada, FDA and USDA** for all their assistance, advice and ongoing encouragement. A special bouquet to **Iona Glabus** and **Margo Embury** of Centax Books for all of their hard work and incredible dedication to making this Guide a reality and success. To **my family**, words cannot express my gratitude for all of your support, patience, encouragement and love!

Shelley Case, B.Sc. (Nutrition & Dietetics), RD
Registered Dietitian

# CELIAC DISEASE AND DERMATITIS HERPETIFORMIS

## CELIAC DISEASE

**Celiac Disease (CD)** is a genetically based, life-long autoimmune disorder in which the absorptive surface of the small intestine is damaged by a substance called gluten. This results in malabsorption (the inability of the intestine to absorb nutrients) of carbohydrates, fat, protein, vitamins and minerals which are needed for good health. A wide range of symptoms may be present which may vary greatly from one person to another.

**These symptoms may occur singly or in combination in children and adults:**
- **Diarrhea, sometimes constipation (often both)**
- **Abdominal pain, bloating and gas**
- **Nausea and vomiting**
- **Weight loss**
- **Chronic fatigue and weakness**
- **Iron deficiency with or without anemia**
- **Vitamin and mineral deficiencies**
- **Mouth ulcers**
- **Bone/joint pain**
- **Depression**
- **Lactose intolerance**
- **Easy bruising of the skin**

**Additional symptoms in children:**
- **Severe irritability**
- **Distended abdomen**
- **Failure to thrive**
- **Delayed puberty**
- **Dental enamel defects**
- **Concentration/learning difficulties**

Diagnosis of CD is often very difficult because of the broad range of symptoms that can vary from mild to severe. Also, some people are asymptomatic (i.e., have no major symptoms) in spite of gluten-sensitivity. There are specific blood screening tests such as IgA endomysial and IgA tissue transglutaminase antibodies. However, the only definitive test for diagnosing CD is a small bowel biopsy. **A gluten-free diet should never be started before the blood tests and biopsy are done as this can interfere with making the correct diagnosis.** Celiac disease is considered to be the most underdiagnosed common disease today, affecting 1 in every 130-200 people in North America. New research indicates that Celiac disease is twice as common as Crohn's disease, ulcerative colitis and cystic fibrosis combined.

**REFERENCES:**
(1) Fasano, A., et al. Prevalence of Celiac Disease in At-Risk and Not-at-Risk Groups in the United States: A large multicenter study. *Arch Intern Med* 2003; 163: 286-292.
(2) Fasano, A. and Catassi, C. Current approaches to diagnosis and treatment of celiac disease: an evolving spectrum. *Gastroenterology* 2001; 120:636-651.
(3) Pietzak, M., et al. Celiac disease: going against the grain. *Nutrition in Clinical Practice* 2001 Dec; 18: 335-344.
(4) Green, P.H.R., et al. Characteristics of adult celiac disease in the USA: Results of a National Survey *Am J of Gastroenterology* 2001; 96 (1): 126-131.
(5) Murray, J.A. The widening spectrum of celiac disease. *Am J Clin Nutr*. 1999; 69: 354-365.
(6) University of Maryland Center For Celiac Research    www.celiaccenter.org

# Dermatitis Herpetiformis

**Dermatitis Herpetiformis (DH)** is another form of celiac disease. It is a chronic skin condition which is characterized by an intense burning and an itching rash. The most common areas affected are the elbows, knees, back of neck and scalp, upper back and the buttocks. Almost all people with DH that have small bowel biopsies will show intestinal mucosal abnormalities. However, many with DH will have no bowel complaints, although, a small percentage may present with bloating, abdominal pain and diarrhea. If the bowel involvement is severe, some individuals may show evidence of malabsorption and malnutrition. Diagnosis for DH is a skin biopsy from unaffected skin next to the lesion.

# Treatment

## Celiac Disease

Once the diagnosis for celiac disease is confirmed, it is essential to follow a **strict gluten-free diet** for life. Additional vitamin and mineral supplements may be necessary to correct the malnutrition. Also, many people may need to eliminate lactose (the natural sugar found in milk) until the damaged bowel is healed (see pages 37-41).

**Long-term effects of untreated celiac disease include:**

- **Vitamin and mineral deficiencies**
- **Osteoporosis**
- **Increased risk (2 to 3 times the normal) of certain types of cancer, especially gastrointestinal malignancies**
- **Gynecological disorders (infertility and miscarriages)**
- **Development of other autoimmune disorders (e.g., Type 1 diabetes, thyroid disease, connective tissue diseases)**

## Dermatitis Herpetiformis

Treatment for dermatitis herpetiformis is a **strict gluten-free diet** for life AND, for some patients, a drug called Dapsone (from the "sulphone family"). Response to the medication can be dramatic (usually 24 to 48 hours). The burning is relieved and the rash begins to disappear.

Following a strict gluten-free diet will result in:

- **Improvement in the skin lesions**
- **Major reduction in drug dosage for those people initially started on Dapsone. After a time it may be possible to discontinue the drug to control the skin rash**
- **The gut function will return to normal.**

**Note:** It is important to receive help from a physician and registered dietitian with expertise in the diagnosis and management of gluten sensitivities. Also, individuals are encouraged to join celiac associations that can provide resources and ongoing support (see page 157).

# THE GLUTEN-FREE DIET

Gluten is the general name for the storage proteins (prolamins) in wheat, rye and barley. These specific prolamins damage the small intestine in people with celiac disease and dermatitis herpetiformis. The actual names of the toxic prolamins are gliadin in wheat, secalin in rye and hordein in barley. Up until 1996, the avenin prolamin in oats was considered to be toxic, however new research indicates that avenin in oats is not harmful. Although corn contains zein prolamin and rice contains orzenin prolamin, these prolamins do not have the toxic effect on the intestine of persons with celiac disease.

Gluten is the substance in flour responsible for forming the structure of dough, holding products together and leavening. While the presence of gluten is evident in baked goods (e.g., breads, cookies and cakes) and pasta, it is often a "hidden ingredient" in many other items such as sauces, seasonings, soups, salad dressings, candy, as well as some vitamins and pharmaceuticals. The challenge for individuals on a gluten-free diet is to avoid these hidden sources.

## GLUTEN-CONTAINING INGREDIENTS TO BE AVOIDED

- Barley
- Bulgur
- Cereal Binding
- Couscous
- Durum*
- Einkorn*
- Emmer*
- Filler
- Farro*
- Graham Flour
- Kamut*
- Malt**
- Malt Extract**
- Malt Flavoring**
- Malt Syrup**
- Oat Bran***
- Oats***
- Oat Syrup***
- Rye
- Semolina
- Spelt (Dinkel)*
- Triticale
- Wheat
- Wheat Bran
- Wheat Germ
- Wheat Starch

\*   Types of wheat
\*\*   Derived from barley
\*\*\*   Many recent studies have demonstrated that consumption of oats (25-60 g/day) is safe for children and adults with celiac disease. However, further studies are needed to determine the long-term safety of oat consumption. Also, the issue of cross contamination of oats with wheat and/or barley remains a concern in North America, therefore, oats are **NOT** recommended by celiac organizations in Canada or the USA.

## INGREDIENTS TO QUESTION*

- Hydrolyzed Plant or Vegetable Protein (HPP/HVP)
- Seasonings
- Flavorings
- Starch
- Modified Food Starch
- Dextrin
- Maltodextrin

\* For specific labeling regulations in USA and Canada for these ingredients see pages 10-19. For web site references for Food Regulations see page 21.

# USA AND CANADIAN LABELING REGULATIONS

## DEFINITION OF TERMS:

**Ingredient:** "Ingredient" means an individual unit of food that is combined as an individual unit of food with one or more other individual units of food to form an integral unit of food that is sold as a prepackaged product (e.g., baking powder is the "ingredient" in a cookie).

**Component:** "Component" means an individual unit of food that is combined as an individual unit of food with one or more other individual units of food to form an "ingredient" (e.g., baking powder is the "ingredient" and it is made up of four "components" [1. sodium or potassium bicarbonate; 2. an acid-reacting material; 3. starch or other neutral material; 4. may contain an anticaking agent]).

## HYDROLYZED PLANT PROTEIN OR VEGETABLE PROTEIN (HPP or HVP)

❖ Hydrolysis involves breaking down the protein by acids or enzymes.

❖ Most hydrolyzed plant proteins are made from corn, soy or wheat but can be made from other protein sources such as peanut.

❖ Hydrolyzed plant proteins are added to a wide variety of foods such as soups, sauces, spice mixtures and gravies.

❖ Partially hydrolyzed plant proteins are used in pharmaceuticals in North America and in foods in Europe, but they are rarely used in foods in North America.

**USA**
(Code of Federal Regulations)

### Sec. 102.22 Protein Hydrolysates

The common or usual name of a protein hydrolysate shall be specific to the ingredient and shall include the identity of the food source from which the protein was derived (e.g., "Hydrolyzed wheat gluten", "hydrolyzed soy protein"). The names "hydrolyzed protein" and "hydrolyzed vegetable protein" are not acceptable because they do not identify the food source of the protein.

**CANADA**
(Food & Drug Regulations)

### B.01.009 (1) #30

Components of ingredients or of classes of ingredients are not required to be shown on a label of foods identified in this section of the Regulations. In this case "Hydrolyzed plant protein" is acceptable and the plant source does not have to be identified.

NOTE: This refers to plant proteins hydrolyzed by methods other than enzymatic (e.g., acid hydrolysis)

### B.01.010 (3) (a) #8

The ingredient or component of an item shall be shown in the list of ingredients by the common name. Hydrolyzed plant protein produced by the enzymatic process must be listed "hydrolyzed" plus the "name of the plant" plus "protein" (e.g., "hydrolyzed soy protein".)

NOTE: At the time of printing this book, recommendations for identifying the plant source of all types of hydrolyzed plant proteins and including it in the common name of the list of ingredients are being considered under the *Schedule of Amendments No. 1220 – Enhanced Labelling of Food Constituents.*

# USA AND CANADIAN LABELING REGULATIONS

## SPICES, HERBS AND SEASONINGS

❖ Canadian and American regulations have some differences in how they define the terms spices, seasonings and herbs (see pages 12 and 13).

❖ Pure spices, herbs and seeds do not contain gluten. Some imitation spices, e.g., imitation black pepper, contain other ingredients such as buckwheat hulls and ground rice in addition to black pepper. The author has not been able to find any companies using wheat as a filler.

❖ When two or more spices are blended together, processors usually list the ingredients on their label:

> e.g., Chili Powder (ground oregano, cumin, garlic and ground chili pepper)
> Curry Powder (ground ginger, fenugreek, cloves, cinnamon, cumin, pepper)

❖ In general terms, "seasonings" are a blend of flavoring agents (e.g., spices, herbs, protein hydrolysates) and are often combined with a carrier (e.g., salt, sugar, lactose, whey powder, milk powder, cereal flours and starches). Gravy mixes, sauces and snack foods often contain wheat flour as the carrier in the seasoning mixture. It should be noted that in Canada and the USA, seasonings, spice or herb mixtures, when used as ingredients in other foods are exempt from a declaration of their components (see pages 12 and 13). However, in the USA, whenever the term seasoning is used in the ingredient statement of a meat or poultry product, its components must be identified as a sublist. (Note: meat and poultry product labeling [if it is 2% or more cooked or 3% or more raw meat or poultry] is under the jurisdiction of the USDA (United States Department of Agriculture). Labeling of all other food products is administered by the FDA (Food & Drug Administration) in the USA and Canadian Food Inspection Agency (CFIA) and Health Canada (HC) in Canada.

**It is important to confirm with the manufacturer that the product containing a seasoning mixture is gluten-free.**

❖ In response to the FDA and CFIA's recommendations for more specific labeling of foods causing allergies and sensitivities, many processors have already made or are in the process of making major changes to the labeling of their ingredients. It is now more common to see components of ingredients being declared on the food label:

> e.g., **Taco Seasoning Mix** (maltodextrin, onion and garlic powder, salt, chili pepper, chili powder, paprika, modified cornstarch, cumin, oregano, hydrogenated soybean oil, spice, color [contains sulfites], silicon dioxide).
>
> **Nacho Cheese Sauce Mix** (Modified milk ingredients, modified tapioca starch, soybean oil shortening, salt, cheese powder blend [Cheddar cheese solids, disodium phosphate, color], monosodium glutamate, dehydrated sweet green peppers, disodium phosphate, modified cornstarch, citric acid, guar gum, lactic acid, jalapeño pepper powder, spice).

# USA AND CANADIAN LABELING REGULATIONS

**USA**
(Code of Federal Regulations)

### Sec.101.22 (2) (a) Spices

The term spice means any aromatic vegetable substance in the whole, broken or ground form, except for those substances which have traditionally been regarded as foods, such as onions, garlic and celery; whose significant function in food is seasoning rather than nutritional; that is true to name; and from which no portion of any volatile oil or other flavoring principle has been removed. Spices include the spices listed in sec.182.10 (such as the following: allspice, anise, basil, bay leaves . . . ). Paprika, turmeric and saffron or other spices which are also colors, shall be declared as "spice and coloring" unless declared by their common name.

### Sec. 170. Food Additives

### Sec. 170.3 (26) Definitions

Herbs, seeds, spices, seasonings, blends, extracts and flavorings, including all natural and artificial spices, blends and flavors.

### Sec. 182.10 Spices and Other Natural Seasonings and Flavorings

Spices and other natural seasonings and flavorings that are generally recognized as safe for their intended use, within the meaning of section 409 of the act, are as follows (83 items are listed by their common name and botanical name).

### Sec. 403 (i) (2)

Spices, flavorings and colors, when used as ingredients in other foods are exempt from a declaration of their components (except for "hypoallergenic foods" Sec. 105.62 – see page 18).

NOTE: There is no specific definition of the term "seasoning". However, sections 101.22, 170.3 and 182.10 refer to spices that act as a "seasoning agent".

# USA AND CANADIAN LABELING REGULATIONS

## SPICES, HERBS AND SEASONINGS CONT'D.

**CANADA**
(Food & Drug Regulations)

### B.01.010 (3) (b) #6

The ingredients or components may be shown in the list of ingredients by the common name. One or more spices, seasonings or herbs (except salt) can also be called "spices," "seasonings" or "herbs".

### B.01.009 (2) #4 & #5

Spice mixtures or seasoning or herb mixtures, when used as ingredients in other foods are exempt from a declaration of their components except for those ingredients or components listed in B.01.009 (3) and (4).

### B.01.009 (3)

Salt, glutamic acid, or its salts, including MSG, hydrolyzed plant protein, aspartame, potassium chloride and any ingredient or component that performs a function in, or has any effect on, that food when present in the preparations or mixture listed in B.01.009 (2) must always be shown by their common names in the list of ingredients to which the preparation or mixture is added, as if they were ingredients of that food.

### B.01.009 (4)

Peanut oil, hydrogenated peanut oil and modified peanut oil when present in the foods listed in B.01.009 (1) and the preparations and mixtures listed in B.01.009 (2) must always be listed by name in the list of ingredients.

### NOTE:

1. There is no specific definition of the term seasoning.

2. The class name "seasoning" is permitted if a seasoning mixture is added to a food at 2% or less of weight of the final product.

3. At the time of printing this book, recommendations for identifying all cereal grains containing gluten when they are present in foods as ingredients or components in the list of ingredients are currently being considered under the *Schedule of Amendments No. 1220 – Enhanced Labelling of Food Constituents*.

# USA and Canadian Labeling Regulations

## FLAVORINGS

❖ Canadian and American regulations have differences in how they define the term flavorings (see pages 14 and 15.)

❖ According to flavor experts from industry and government in Canada and the USA, gluten-containing grains are not commonly used in flavorings (1, 2). However, there are two exceptions:

1. Barley Malt can be used as a flavoring agent and is usually (though not always) listed on the label (1). It might be listed as barley malt, barley malt extract or barley malt flavoring. Some companies may list it as "flavor (contains barley protein)" or occasionally declare it only as "flavor"(2).

2. Hydrolyzed wheat, corn and/or soy protein can be used as "flavor" or "flavor enhancers" in a variety of foods. However, in Canada and the USA, they must be declared as "hydrolyzed proteins" and not hidden on the label as "flavor" or "natural flavor" [B. 01.009 (3) in Canada and Sec. 101.22 (h) (7) in the USA].

**USA**
(Code of Federal Regulations)

**Sec.101.22 Foods; labeling of spices, flavorings, colorings and chemical preservatives**

**(a) (1) Artificial Flavor or Artificial Flavoring:**

Any substance, the function of which is to impart flavor, which is not derived from a spice, fruit or fruit juice, vegetable or vegetable juice, edible yeast, herb, bark, bud, root, leaf or similar plant material, meat, fish, poultry, eggs, dairy products, or fermentation products thereof. Artificial flavor includes the substances listed in Sec. 172.515 (b) and 182.60 [Synthetic flavoring substances and adjuvants] except where these are derived from natural sources.

**(a) (3) Natural Flavor or Natural Flavoring:**

The essential oil, oleoresin, essence or extractive, protein hydrolysate, distillate, or any product of roasting, heating or enzymolysis, which contains the flavoring constituents derived from a spice, fruit or fruit juice, vegetable or vegetable juice, edible yeast, herb, bark, bud, root, leaf or similar plant material, meat, seafood, poultry, eggs, dairy products, or fermentation products thereof, whose significant function in food is flavoring rather than nutritional. Natural flavors include the natural essence or extractives obtained from plants listed in Sec. 182.10, 182.20, 182.40 and 182.50 and substances listed in 172.510 [natural favoring substances and natural substances, e.g., include flowers, roots, herbs, leaves.]

**Sec.101.22 Foods; labeling of spices, flavorings, colorings and chemical preservatives**

**(h) Labeling of a food to which Flavor is added:**

(1) Spice, natural flavor and artificial flavor may be declared as "spice", "natural flavor" or "artificial flavor" or any combination thereof.

**REFERENCES:**

(1) *Gluten Free Living* magazine, Nov/Dec. 2000

(2) Author's personal communication with the Canadian Flavour Manufacturers Association (CFMA), various manufacturers in Canada and the USA, Canadian Food Inspection Agency (CFIA) and Health Canada (HC).

# USA and Canadian Labeling Regulations

## FLAVORINGS CONT'D.

**USA**
(Code of Federal Regulations)

**CANADA**
(Food & Drug Regulations)

(7) Because protein hydrolysates function in foods as both flavorings and flavor enhancers, no protein hydrolysate used in food for its effects on flavor may be declared simply as "flavor", "natural flavor" or "flavoring". The ingredients shall be declared by its specific common or usual name as provided in Sec. 102.22.

### Sec. 403 (i) (2)

Spices, flavorings and colors, when used as ingredients in other foods are exempt from a declaration of their components, except for "hypoallergenic foods " Sec. 105.62 (see page 18).

### B.01.010 (3) (b)

The ingredients or components may be shown in the list of ingredients by the common name.

### #4 "Flavour"

One or more substances prepared for their flavouring properties and produced from animal or vegetable raw materials or from food constituents derived solely from animal or vegetable raw materials.

### #5 "Artificial Flavour", "Imitation Flavour" or "Simulated Flavour"

One or more substances prepared for their flavouring properties and derived in whole or in part from components obtained by chemical synthesis.

### #13 "Name of Plant or Animal Source Plus "Flavour"

One or more substances the function of which is to impart flavour and that are obtained solely from the plant or animal source after which the flavour is named.

### B.01.009 (2) #2, #3 and #10

Flavouring preparations, artificial flavouring preparations and food flavour-enhancer preparations, when used as ingredients in other foods, are exempt from a declaration of their ingredients or components, except for the ingredients or components listed in B.01.009 (3) and (4).

### B.01.009 (3)

Salt, glutamic acid, or its salts, including MSG, hydrolysed plant protein, aspartame, potassium chloride and any ingredient or component that performs a function in, or has an effect on, that food when present in the preparations or mixture listed in B.01.009 (2) must always be shown by their common names in the list of ingredients to which the preparation or mixture is added, as if they were ingredients of that food.

### B.01.009 (4)

Peanut oil, hydrogenated peanut oil and modified peanut oil when present in the foods listed in B.01.009 (1) and the preparations and mixtures listed in B.01.009 (2) must always be listed by name in the list of ingredients.

NOTE: At the time of printing this book, recommendations for identifying all cereal grains containing gluten when they are present in foods as ingredients or components in the list of ingredients are currently being considered under the *Schedule of Amendments No. 1220 – Enhanced Labelling of Food Constituents*.

## STARCHES

| USA (Code of Federal Regulations) | **Sec. 578.100 Starches** The single word "starch" on a food label is considered the common or usual name for starch made from corn; alternatively, the name "cornstarch" may be used. Starches from other sources should be designated by some non-misleading term that indicates the source of such starch, for example, "potato starch", "wheat starch", or "tapioca starch". |
|---|---|
| CANADA (Food & Drug Regulations) | Starches are presently required to be identified by plant source on the food label except cornstarch, which can be called "cornstarch" or just "starch" made from maize. **B.13.011 [S]** cornstarch shall be starch made from maize. |

## MODIFIED FOOD STARCHES

❖ Modified food starches can be made from corn, tapioca, potato, wheat or other starches. However, wheat and other gluten sources are rarely used in North America. Corn is almost always the source, with potato, tapioca or rice used occasionally.

❖ It is very difficult to completely remove all traces of protein during the manufacture of food-grade starch. (1) Wheat starch contains varying amounts of gluten, and is not permitted to be used in "gluten-free foods" in Canada and the USA (2, 3). In a Canadian study on the tolerance of wheat starch by patients with celiac disease, the symptoms of the disease reappeared in the majority of the patients. The authors concluded that prolonged use of wheat starch by patients with celiac disease cannot be recommended. (4)

| USA (Code of Federal Regulations) | **Sec. 172.892 Food Starch – Modified** Regulations for how food starches may be modified. However, there is no requirement for the identification of the name of the plant source of the modified food starch. |
|---|---|
| CANADA (Food & Drug Regulations) | There is no requirement for the identification of the name of the plant source of the modified food starch. **NOTE:** At the time of printing this book, recommendations for identifying the plant source of all types of starches and modified starches and including them in the list of ingredients are being considered under the *Schedule of Amendments No. 1220 – Enhanced Labelling of Food Constituents*. |

**REFERENCES:**
1. Hekkens WThJM, Van Twist-de Graaf M. What is gluten-free – levels of tolerances in the gluten-free diet. *Die Nahrung* 1990; 34:483-487.
2. Zarkadas, M., Scott, F.W., Salminen, J. and Ham Pong, A. Common allergenic foods and their labelling in Canada – A Review. *Can J Aller & Clin Immunology* 1999; 4 (3): 118-141.
3. Thompson, T. Wheat starch, gliadin, and the gluten-free diet. *J Am Diet Assoc.* 2001; 101: 1456-1459.
4. Chartrand, L.J., Russo, P.A., Duhaime, A.G., Seidman, E.G. Wheat starch intolerance in patients with celiac disease. *J Am Diet Assoc.* 1997; 97 (6): 612-618.

## DEXTRIN

❖ Dextrin is starch partially hydrolyzed by heat alone or by heating in the presence of suitable food-grade acids and buffers, from any of several grain or root-based unmodified native starches [e.g., corn, waxy maize, milo, waxy milo, potato, arrowroot, wheat, rice, tapioca, sago, etc.] (1).

❖ It is used as a thickener, colloidal stabilizer, binder or surface-finishing agent (1).

❖ Dextrin is usually made from corn or tapioca in North America. However, contact the manufacturer to confirm the source of the dextrin.

| | |
|---|---|
| **USA**<br>(Code of Federal Regulations) | **Sec. 184.1277 Dextrin**<br>Based on definition above and reference below. |
| **CANADA**<br>(Food & Drug Regulations) | **Division 18**<br>Although dextrin does not appear in the standards for Sweetening Agents of Division 18, it is considered a food ingredient of this category.<br><br>**Division 16**<br>Lists the food additives that may be used as food enzymes in various products and ingredients including dextrins. |

**REFERENCES:**
   (1) CAS Reg. No. 9004-53-9 from *Food Chemical Codex*, Fourth Edition, 1996, published by National Academy Press, Washington, DC, USA.

## MALTODEXTRIN

❖ Maltodextrin is a purified, concentrated, nonsweet nutritive mixture of saccharide polymers obtained by partial hydrolysis of edible starch (1).

❖ It is used as an anticaking and free-flowing agent; formulation aid; processing aid; bulking agent; stabilizer and thickener; or surface finishing agent in a variety of foods (1).

❖ A variety of starches such as corn, waxy maize, potato, rice or wheat can be used. Corn, waxy maize or potato are the most common sources in North America. However, wheat is often used in European products and in some North American products. Contact the manufacturer to confirm the source of maltodextrin.

| | |
|---|---|
| **USA**<br>(Code of Federal Regulations) | **Sec. 184.1444 Maltodextrin**<br>CAS Reg. No. 9050-36-6. It is a nonsweet nutritive saccharide polymer that consists of D-glucose units linked primarily by [alpha]-1-4 bonds and has a dextrose equivalent (DE) of less than 20. It is prepared as a white powder or concentrated solution by partial hydrolysis of cornstarch, potato starch or rice starch with safe and suitable acids and enzymes.<br>[Note: FDA also permits the use of other starches including wheat.] |
| **CANADA**<br>(Food & Drug Regulations) | There is no standard for maltodextrin. The Food Chemical Codex is often used as a guide, however, different starches can be used. Food companies are strongly encouraged to indicate the source if it is from the major food allergens such as wheat. |

**REFERENCES:**
   (1) CAS Reg. No. 9050-36-6 from *Food Chemical Codex*, Fourth Edition, 1996, published by National Academy Press, Washington, DC, USA.

# Food Labeling in the USA and the Gluten-Free Diet

There is no specific regulation for the term "gluten-free", however, when manufacturers label a product as "gluten-free", FDA requests they adhere to the policy on "hypoallergenic foods".

## CFR 105.62 Hypoallergenic Foods

If a food purports to be or is represented for special dietary use by reason of the decrease or absence of any allergenic property or by reason of being offered as food suitable as a substitute for another food having an allergenic property, the label shall bear:

(a) The common or usual name and the quantity or proportion of each ingredient (including spices, flavoring and coloring) in case the food is fabricated from two or more ingredients.

(b) A qualification of the name of the food, or the name of each ingredient thereof in case the food is fabricated from two or more ingredients, to reveal clearly the specific plant or animal that is the source of such food or of such ingredient, if such food or such ingredient consists in whole or part of plant or animal matter and such name does not reveal clearly the specific plant or animal that is such a source.

(c) An informative statement of the nature and effect of any treatment or processing of the food or any ingredient thereof, if the changed allergenic property results from such treatment or processing.

## FDA Center for Food Safety and Applied Nutrition: Label Declaration of Allergenic Substances in Foods

In May 2001, Joseph Levitt, Director, Center for Food Safety and Applied Nutrition (CFSAN) issued a letter regarding the labeling of foods that contain allergenic substances. It provided information about the Food and Drug Administration's (FDA) new Compliance Policy Guide (CPG) on Allergens: Section 555.250 "Statement of Policy for Labeling and Preventing Cross Contact of Common Food Allergens" (1). This CPG reiterates the information in the 1996 Notice to Manufacturers by Dr. Fred Shank (Director, CFSAN) issued by the FDA to increase allergen awareness. While the FDA has not formally defined "allergens", it provided examples of foods that are most commonly known to cause serious allergic reactions (**peanuts**, **tree nuts**, **soybeans**, **milk**, **eggs**, **fish**, **crustacea** and **wheat**).

FDA is reviewing its labeling requirements for allergenic ingredients and considering whether rulemaking is necessary. While the agency does so, FDA asks manufacturers to examine their product formulations for ingredients and processing aids that contain known allergens that they may have considered to be exempt from declaration on the list of ingredients. Processing aids that contain allergenic ingredients **must always** be declared in accordance with CFR 101.4 (a)(1). However, spices, flavors and colors may be declared collectively without naming its sub-components. These sub-components may contain allergens, therefore, FDA strongly recommends that manufacturers **voluntarily** declare allergenic ingredients in a spice, flavor or color on the ingredient label.

(1) www.fda.gov/ora/compliance_ref/cpg/cpgfod/cpg555-250.htm

# FOOD LABELING IN CANADA AND THE GLUTEN-FREE DIET

## FOOD AND DRUG REGULATION B.24.018

No person shall label, package, sell or advertise a food in a manner likely to create an impression that it is gluten-free unless the food does not contain wheat, including spelt and kamut, or oats, barley, rye or triticale or any part thereof.

## FOOD AND DRUG REGULATION B.24.019

The label of a food that is labelled, packaged, sold or advertised as "gluten-free" shall carry the following information, per serving of stated size of the food:

(a) the energy value of the food, expressed in Calories (Calories or Cal) and kilojoules (kilojoules or kJ) and;

(b) the protein, fat and carbohydrate content of the food, expressed in grams.

NOTE: The Bureau of Food Safety and Consumer Protection of the Canadian Food Inspection Agency has a "Fair Labelling Practices Program" that monitors label claims. The "Gluten-Free" claim is being monitored, including random testing for gluten using the enzyme immunoassay.

## SCHEDULE OF AMENDMENTS NO. 1220 – ENHANCED LABELLING OF FOOD INGREDIENTS

The Canadian Food Inspection Agency (CFIA) and Health Canada (HC) have developed (after five years of extensive consultation) proposed labelling recommendations for manufacturers, distributors and importers. Although the "Schedule of Amendments No. 1220" is not yet official, CFIA/HC have strongly encouraged voluntary labelling of the major food ingredients known to cause allergies and sensitivities. As a result many Canadian manufacturers have made significant changes to the labelling of their ingredients. They are more frequently identifying the plant source of starches, modified starch and hydrolyzed proteins, as well as the components of flavors, seasonings, colors and other ingredients (1,2).

**Proposed Amendments**:

❖ Always list the following foods and their products when they are added to foods as ingredients or components.

- Peanuts
- Tree Nuts
- Sesame
- Milk
- Eggs
- Soy
- Sulphites (when present at a level of 10ppm in the food)
- Fish, Crustaceans and Shellfish
- **Cereal grains containing gluten**

❖ The plant source of all forms of hydrolyzed plant proteins, starches and modified starches should be included in the common name in the list of ingredients.

(1) Author's personal communication with CFIA, HC and many manufacturers.

(2) Author's observation of a variety of ingredient labels.

# GLUTEN-FREE ADDITIVES AND INGREDIENTS

This is not an all-inclusive list.

## Additives
- Acetic Acid
- Adipic Acid
- Benzoic Acid
- BHA
- BHT
- Carboxymethyl cellulose
- Calcium Disodium EDTA
- Fumaric Acid
- Lactic Acid
- Malic Acid
- Polysorbate 60; 80
- Propylene Glycol
- Sodium Benzoate
- Sodium Metabisulphite
- Sodium Nitrate
- Sodium Nitrite
- Sodium Sulphite
- Stearic Acid
- Tartaric Acid
- Tartrazine
- Titanium Dioxide

## Flavoring Agents
- Maltol
- Ethyl Maltol
- MSG
- Vanilla Extract
- Vanillan

## Sugars/Sweeteners
- Aspartame
- Brown Sugar
- Corn Syrup/Solids
- Dextrose
- Fructose
- Glucose
- Invert Sugar
- Lactose
- Mannitol
- Molasses
- Sorbitol
- Sucralose
- Sucrose
- White Sugar
- Xylitol

## Vegetable Gums
- Acacia Gum (Gum Arabic)
- Algin (Alginic Acid)
- Carageenan
- Carob Bean (Locust Bean)
- Cellulose
- Guar Gum
- Karaya Gum
- Methylcellulose
- Tragacanth
- Xanthan Gum

## Miscellaneous
- Annatto
- Baking Yeast
- Beta Carotene
- Brewers Yeast
- Caramel Color*
- Cream of Tartar
- Gelatin
- Lecithin
- Papain
- Pectin
- Psyllium

* Caramel color on page 21.

# GLUTEN-FREE ADDITIVES AND INGREDIENTS

## NOTES:

* **Caramel Color** is manufactured by heating carbohydrates, either alone, or in the presence of food-grade acids, alkalies and/or salts, and is produced from commercially available food-grade nutritive sweeteners consisting of fructose, dextrose (glucose), invert sugar, sucrose and/or starch hydrolysates and fractions thereof (1). Although gluten-containing ingredients [malt syrup (barley) and starch hydrolysates] can be used in the production of caramel color, they are not used according to food processors in North America (2, 3). Corn is used most often, as it produces a longer shelf life and a much better product (2, 3).

(1) Food Chemicals Codex, Fourth Edition, National Academy Press, Washington, DC, USA, 1996 CAS: [8028-89-5] is for caramel color.

(2) Mavis Molloy, RDN, Canadian Celiac Association Professional Advisory Board. *What is the difference between caramel colour and caramel flavour? Are they Gluten-Free?* Canadian Celiac Association Newsletter, Winter Edition 1997, p.4

(3) *Gluten Free-Living* magazine, November/December 2000

---

**WEB SITE REFERENCES FOR FOOD REGULATIONS AND LABELING:**

**A. Code of Federal Regulations: Title 21 Food & Drugs (USA)**
www.access.gpo.gov/cgi-bin/cfrassemble.cgi?title=200321

**B. Food & Drug Regulations (CANADA)**
www.hc-sc.gc.ca/food-aliment/e_index.html

**C. United States Department of Agriculture**
www.fsis.usda.gov/oa/faq/faq.htm

# GLUTEN-FREE DIET BY FOOD GROUPS (1)

| Food Products | Foods Allowed | Foods to Question (2) | Foods Not Allowed |
|---|---|---|---|
| **MILK PRODUCTS** | Milk, cream, most ice cream, buttermilk, plain yogurt, cheese, cream cheese, processed cheese, processed cheese foods, cottage cheese | Milk drinks, flavored yogurt, frozen yogurt, sour cream, cheese sauces, cheese spreads | Malted milk, ice cream made with ingredients not allowed |
| **GRAIN PRODUCTS** | **BREADS:** Bread and baked products containing amaranth, arrowroot, buckwheat, corn bran, corn flour, cornmeal, cornstarch, flax, legume flours (bean, garbanzo or chickpea, garfava, lentil, pea), millet, Montina™ Flour (Indian rice grass), potato flour, potato starch, quinoa, rice bran, rice flours (white, brown, sweet), sago, sorghum flour, soy flour, sweet potato flour, tapioca and teff | Buckwheat flour | Bread and baked products containing wheat, rye, triticale, barley, oats, wheat germ, wheat bran, graham flour, gluten flour, durum flour, wheat starch, oat bran, bulgur, farina, wheat based semolina, spelt, kamut, einkorn, emmer, farro, imported foods labeled "gluten-free" which may contain ingredients not allowed, e.g., wheat starch |
| | **CEREALS:**<br>**Hot:** Puffed Amaranth, cornmeal, cream of buckwheat, cream of rice (brown, white), hominy grits, rice flakes, quinoa flakes, soy flakes and soy grits<br>**Cold:** Puffed amaranth, puffed buckwheat, puffed corn, puffed millet, puffed rice, rice flakes and soy cereals | Rice and corn cereals, rice and soy pablum | Cereals made from wheat, rye, triticale, barley and oats; cereals with added malt extract or malt flavoring |
| | **Pastas:** Macaroni, spaghetti, and noodles from beans, corn, pea, potato, quinoa, rice, soy and wild rice | Buckwheat pasta | Pastas made from wheat, wheat starch and other ingredients not allowed |
| | **MISCELLANEOUS:**<br>Corn tacos, corn tortillas | Rice crackers, some rice cakes and popped corn cakes | Wheat flour tacos, wheat tortillas |

(1) Adapted and revised October 2000 by S. Case, M. Molloy and M. Zarkadas from Canadian Celiac Association *Celiac Disease Needs A Diet For Life* Handbook. Further revisions by S. Case, July 2003.

(2) See page 25.

# GLUTEN-FREE DIET BY FOOD GROUPS (1)

| Food Products | Foods Allowed | Foods to Question (2) | Foods Not Allowed |
|---|---|---|---|
| MEATS & ALTERNATIVES | MEAT, FISH, POULTRY: Fresh | Deli or processed meats such as luncheon meat, ham, bacon, meat and sandwich spreads, meat loaf, frozen meat patties, sausages, pâté, wieners, bologna, salami, imitation meat or fish products, meat product extenders | Fish canned in vegetable broth containing HVP/HPP*<br><br>Turkey basted or injected with HVP/HPP*<br><br>Frozen chicken containing chicken broth (made with ingredients not allowed) |
| | Eggs: Eggs | Egg substitutes, dried eggs | |
| | Others: Lentils, chickpeas (garbanzo beans), peas, beans, nuts, seeds, tofu | Baked beans, dry roasted nuts | |
| FRUITS & VEGETABLES | Fruits: Fresh, frozen and canned fruits and juices<br>Vegetables: Fresh, frozen and canned vegetables and juices | Fruit pie fillings, dried fruits, fruits or vegetables with sauces<br>French-fried potatoes (e.g., those in restaurants) | Scalloped potatoes (containing wheat flour)<br>Battered dipped vegetables |
| SOUPS | Homemade broth, gluten-free bouillon cubes, cream soups and stocks made from ingredients allowed | Canned soups, dried soup mixes, soup bases and bouillon cubes | Soups made with ingredients not allowed, bouillon and bouillon cubes containing HVP or HPP* or wheat |
| FATS | Butter, margarine, lard, vegetable oil, cream, shortening, homemade salad dressing with allowed ingredients | Salad dressings, some mayonnaise | Packaged suet |
| DESSERTS | Ice cream, sherbet, whipped toppings, egg custards, gelatin desserts; cakes, cookies, pastries made with allowed ingredients<br>Gluten-free ice cream cones, wafers and waffles | Milk puddings, custard powder, pudding mixes | Ice cream made with ingredients not allowed; cakes, cookies, muffins, pies and pastries made with ingredients not allowed; ice cream cones, wafers and waffles made with ingredients not allowed |

* If the plant source in HVP/HPP (hydrolyzed vegetable protein/hydrolyzed plant protein) is not identified or if the source is from wheat protein, HVP/HPP must be avoided.

# Gluten-Free Diet by Food Groups (1)

| Food Products | Foods Allowed | Foods to Question (2) | Foods Not Allowed |
|---|---|---|---|
| MISCELLANEOUS | **Beverages:** Tea, instant or ground coffee (regular or decaffeinated), cocoa, soft drinks, cider; distilled alcoholic beverages such as rum, gin, whiskey, vodka, wines and pure liqueurs; some soy, rice and nut beverages | Instant tea, flavored and herbal teas, flavored coffees, coffee substitutes, fruit-flavored drinks, chocolate drinks, chocolate mixes | Beer, ale and lager; cereal and malted beverages; soy, rice or nut beverages made with barley or oats |
| | **Sweets**: Honey, jam, jelly, marmalade, corn syrup, maple syrup, molasses, sugar (brown and white), icing sugar (confectioner's) | Spreads, candies, chocolate bars, chewing gum, Smarties®, marshmallows and lemon curd | Licorice and other candies made with ingredients not allowed |
| | **Snack foods:** Plain popcorn, nuts and soy nuts | Dry roasted nuts, flavored potato chips, tortilla or taco (corn) chips and soy nuts | Pizza, unless made with ingredients allowed |
| | **Condiments:** Plain pickles, relish, olives, ketchup, mustard, tomato paste, pure herbs and spices, pure black pepper, vinegars (apple or cider, distilled white, grape or wine, spirit), gluten-free soy sauce | Seasoning mixes, Worcestershire sauce | Soy sauce (made from wheat), mustard pickles (made from wheat flour), Malt vinegar |
| | **Other:** Sauces and gravies made with ingredients allowed, pure cocoa, pure baking chocolate, carob chips and powder, chocolate chips, monosodium glutamate (MSG), cream of tartar, baking soda, yeast, brewer's yeast, aspartame, coconut, vanilla, gluten-free communion wafers | Baking powder | Sauces and gravies made from ingredients not allowed, hydrolyzed vegetable/plant protein (HVP/HPP)*, communion wafers |

\* If the plant source in HVP/HPP is not identified or if the source is from wheat protein, HVP/HPP must be avoided.

# (2) NOTES ON "FOODS TO QUESTION"

| Category | Food Products | Notes |
|---|---|---|
| **MILK PRODUCTS** | Milk Drinks | ◆ Chocolate milk and other flavored drinks may contain wheat starch or barley malt. |
| | Cheese Spreads or Sauces (e.g., Nacho) | ◆ May be thickened/stabilized with wheat.<br>◆ Flavorings and seasonings may contain wheat. |
| | Flavored or Frozen Yogurt | ◆ May be thickened/stabilized with a gluten source<br>◆ May contain granola or cookie crumbs |
| | Sour Cream | ◆ Some low-fat/fat-free may contain modified food starch. |
| **GRAINS** | Buckwheat Flour | ◆ Pure buckwheat flour is gluten-free. Sometimes buckwheat flour may be mixed with wheat flour. |
| | Rice Cereals | ◆ May contain barley malt extract. |
| | Corn Cereals | ◆ May contain barley malt extract or oat syrup. |
| | Buckwheat Pasta | ◆ Some "soba" pastas contain pure buckwheat flour which is gluten-free but others may also contain wheat flour. |
| | Rice Cakes, Corn Cakes Rice Crackers | ◆ Multigrain often contains barley and/or oats.<br>◆ Some contain soy sauce (may be made from wheat). |
| **MEATS/ ALTERNATIVES** | Baked Beans | ◆ Some are thickened with wheat flour. |
| | Imitation Crab | ◆ May contain fillers made from wheat starch. |
| | Dry Roasted Nuts | ◆ May contain wheat. |
| | Processed Meat Products | ◆ May contain fillers made from wheat.<br>◆ May contain HPP or HVP made from wheat. |
| | Imitation Meats | ◆ Often contain wheat or oats. |
| **FRUITS & VEGETABLES** | Dried Fruits | ◆ Dates and other dried fruits may be dusted with wheat flour to prevent sticking. |
| | Fruits/Veg's with Sauces Fruit Pie Fillings | ◆ Some may be thickened with flour. |
| | French Fries | ◆ May contain wheat as an ingredient. Also, see page 85. |
| **SOUPS** | Canned Soups, Dried Soup Mixes, Soup Bases and Bouillon Cubes | ◆ May contain noodles or barley.<br>◆ Cream soups are often thickened with flour.<br>◆ May contain HPP or HVP (from wheat).<br>◆ Seasonings may contain wheat flour, wheat starch or hydrolyzed wheat protein. |
| **FATS** | Salad Dressings | ◆ Seasonings may contain wheat flour or wheat starch. |
| **DESSERTS** | Milk Puddings /Mixes | ◆ Starch source may be from wheat. |
| **MISCELLANEOUS** | Beverages | ◆ Some instant teas, herbal teas, coffee substitutes and other drinks may have grain additives.<br>◆ Non-dairy substitutes (e.g., rice, soy or nut beverages) may contain barley, barley malt extract or oats. |
| | Lemon Curd | ◆ Usually thickened with flour. |
| | Potato, Tortilla Chips and Soy Nuts | ◆ Some potato chips contain wheat.<br>◆ Seasoning mixes may contain wheat flour, wheat starch or hydrolyzed wheat protein. |
| | Baking Powder | ◆ Contains starch which may be from wheat. |
| | Seasoning Mixes | ◆ May contain wheat flour, wheat starch or hydrolyzed wheat protein. |
| | Worcestershire Sauce | ◆ May contain malt vinegar which is not gluten-free. |
| | Smarties® | ◆ Canadian product contains wheat flour. |

# CANADA'S FOOD GUIDE TO HEALTHY EATING
## (Adapted for Gluten-Free Diets)

| FOOD GROUP (servings per day) | 1 SERVING (examples) | HEALTHY TIPS |
|---|---|---|
| **GRAIN PRODUCTS** (Gluten-Free = GF) <br><br> 5-12 Servings | ◆ 1 slice GF bread <br> ◆ 1 GF muffin or bun <br> ◆ 30 g cold GF cereal <br> ◆ ¾ cup (175 mL) hot GF cereal (e.g., cream of buckwheat, cornmeal, cream of brown or white rice) <br> ◆ ½ cup (125 mL) GF pasta <br> ◆ ½ cup (125 mL) rice | Choose gluten-free whole grain and enriched products more often. <br><br> * NOTE: In Canada most GF breads and flours are low in fiber and not enriched with iron and B vitamins. |
| **VEGETABLES & FRUITS** <br><br> 5-10 Servings | ◆ 1 medium-sized vegetable or fruit <br> ◆ ½ cup (125 mL) fresh, frozen or canned vegetables or fruit <br> ◆ 1 cup salad <br> ◆ ½ cup (125 mL) juice | Choose dark green/orange vegetables and fruit more often (e.g., broccoli, carrot, spinach, squash, sweet potato, apricot, cantaloupe, orange). |
| **MILK PRODUCTS** <br><br> 2-3 servings (children 4-9 yrs) <br> 3-4 servings (youth 10-16 yrs) <br> 2-4 servings (adults) <br> 3-4 servings (pregnant and breast-feeding women) | ◆ 1 cup (250 mL) milk <br> ◆ 50 g cheese <br> ◆ 2 cheese slices <br> ◆ ¾ cup (175 g) yogurt | Choose lower-fat milk products more often. |
| **MEAT & ALTERNATIVES** <br><br> 2-3 Servings | ◆ 50-100 g meat, poultry, or fish <br> ◆ ⅓-⅔ can, 50-100 g of fish <br> ◆ 1-2 eggs <br> ◆ ½-1 cup (125-250 mL) legumes (beans, peas, lentils) <br> ◆ ⅓ cup (100 g) tofu <br> ◆ 2 tbsp. (30 mL) GF peanut butter | Choose leaner meats, poultry and fish as well as dried beans, peas and lentils more often. |

**\* Enjoy a variety of foods from each group every day \***

# THE FOOD GUIDE PYRAMID (USA)
## (Adapted for Gluten-Free Diets)

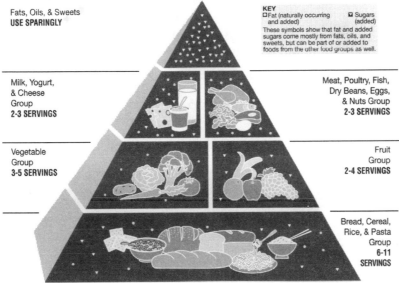

Source U.S. Department of Agriculture/U.S. Department of Health and Human Services

| FOOD GROUP | 1 SERVING (examples) |
|---|---|
| **BREAD, CEREAL, RICE & PASTA** (Gluten-Free = GF) <br><br> * NOTE: In the USA most GF breads and flours are low in fiber and not enriched with iron and B vitamins | ◆ 1 slice GF bread <br> ◆ 1 GF bun, roll or muffin <br> ◆ 1 oz. GF ready-to-eat cereal <br> ◆ ½ cup cooked GF cereal <br> ◆ ½ cup cooked GF pasta <br> ◆ ½ cup cooked rice |
| **VEGETABLE** | ◆ 1 cup raw leafy vegetable <br> ◆ ½ cup cooked or chopped raw vegetables <br> ◆ ¾ cup vegetable juice |
| **FRUIT** | ◆ 1 medium apple, banana, orange, pear <br> ◆ ½ grapefruit <br> ◆ ½ cup chopped fresh, cooked or canned fruit <br> ◆ ¼ cup dried fruit <br> ◆ ¾ cup fruit juice |
| **MILK, YOGURT & CHEESE** | ◆ 1 cup milk <br> ◆ 8 oz. yogurt <br> ◆ 1½ oz. natural cheese <br> ◆ 2 oz. processed cheese |
| **MEAT, POULTRY, FISH, DRY BEANS, EGGS & NUTS** | ◆ 2-3 oz. cooked lean meat, poultry or fish <br> ◆ ½ cup cooked dry beans or 1 egg counts as 1 oz. of lean meat <br> ◆ 2 tbsp. GF peanut butter or ⅓ cup nuts, counts as 1 oz. of lean meat |

# DIETARY FIBER

Dietary fiber is the part of whole grains, fruits, vegetables, legumes, nuts and seeds that cannot be broken down by the human digestive system. Although dietary fiber is not readily digested, it plays an important role in the body, particularly through its effect on the digestive system. Fiber helps maintain regular bowel movements. Also, a high-fiber diet can play a role in the prevention and treatment of certain chronic diseases such as colon cancer, coronary heart disease, diabetes mellitus and diverticular disease. Nutrition experts recommend consuming **25-35 grams** of dietary fiber per day.

Consuming adequate amounts of dietary fiber is important for people with celiac disease. Newly diagnosed individuals with celiac disease may have symptoms of diarrhea due to malabsorption caused by gluten damaging the absorptive surface of the intestinal tract. However, after following a strict gluten-free diet the malabsorption and diarrhea eventually subsides. Some people may then have problems with constipation as they are no longer able to consume high-fiber gluten-containing foods such as wheat bran and whole-wheat breads and cereals.

**Many gluten-free foods are low in dietary fiber,** so it is important to:

❖ Choose a variety of high-fiber gluten-free-foods on a regular basis (see pages 29-32).

❖ Increase dietary fiber into the diet gradually (i.e., start with a small amount at a time).

❖ Increase consumption of fluids, especially water, e.g., a minimum of 8-10 glasses per day.

# DIETARY FIBER CONTENT OF GLUTEN-FREE FOODS
# GRAINS, CEREALS & FLOURS

| Food Items (Raw) | 1 cup (250 mL) weight in grams | Dietary Fiber (grams) |
|---|---|---|
| Amaranth Seed | 195 | 29.6 |
| Amaranth Flour | 120 | 18.2 |
| Buckwheat Bran (Farinetta™) | 137 | 9.9 |
| Buckwheat Flour (Whole Groats) | 120 | 12 |
| Buckwheat Groats (roasted, dry) | 164 | 16.9 |
| Corn Bran (crude) | 76 | 65 |
| Cornmeal (degermed, enriched) | 138 | 10.2 |
| Flax Seed | 155 | 43.2 |
| Flax Seed Meal | 120 | 33.5 |
| Garbanzo Flour (Chickpea) | 120 | 20.9 |
| Garfava Flour (Garbanzo/Fava beans) | 157 | 12 |
| Bette's Gourmet Four Flour Blend* | 160 | 8 |
| Millet Seed | 200 | 17 |
| Montina™ Flour | 150 | 36 |
| Potato Flour | 160 | 9.4 |
| Potato Starch | 192 | 0 |
| Quinoa Seed | 170 | 10 |
| Quinoa Flour | 102 | 6 |
| Rice Bran (crude) | 118 | 24.8 |
| Rice Polish | 112 | 12.9 |
| Brown Rice | 185 | 6.5 |
| Brown Rice Flour | 158 | 7.3 |
| White Rice | 185 | 3.1 |
| White Rice Flour | 158 | 3.8 |
| Sorghum Flour | 146 | 8.2 |
| Soy Flour (defatted) | 100 | 17.5 |
| Soy Flour (full fat) | 84 | 8.1 |
| Wild Rice | 160 | 9.9 |
| **Gluten-Containing** | | |
| Wheat Bran | 58 | 24.8 |
| Whole-Wheat Flour | 120 | 14.6 |

* Bette's Gourmet Four Flour Blend (garfava flour, sorghum flour, cornstarch and tapioca flour)

**Nutrient values for Dietary Fiber For Foods pages 29 to 32, from:**
- USDA Nutrient Data Base for Standard Reference, Release #13
- Buckwheat Bran (Farinetta™) from Minn-Dak Growers, Grand Forks, ND, USA
- Garfava Flour and Bette's Gourmet Four Flour Blend from Authentic Foods Company, Gardena, CA, USA
- Garbanzo Flour and Potato starch from Bob's Red Mill
- Rice Polish from Ener-G Foods
- Montina Flour from Amazing Grains, Ronan, MT, USA

# DIETARY FIBER CONTENT OF GLUTEN-FREE FOODS
# BEANS, NUTS & SEEDS

| Food Items | 1 cup (250 mL) weight in grams | Dietary Fiber (grams) |
|---|---|---|
| **Cooked Beans** | | |
| Cranberry Beans (Romano) | 177 | 17.7 |
| Fava Beans (Broad Beans) | 170 | 9.2 |
| Garbanzo Beans (Chickpeas) | 164 | 12.5 |
| Kidney Beans | 177 | 13.1 |
| Lentils | 198 | 15.6 |
| Navy Beans | 182 | 11.7 |
| Pinto Beans | 171 | 14.7 |
| Soybeans | 172 | 10.3 |
| Split Peas | 196 | 16.3 |
| White Beans | 179 | 11.3 |
| **Nuts & Seeds** | | |
| Almonds (whole, blanched) | 145 | 15.1 |
| Brazil Nuts (dried, blanched) | 140 | 7.6 |
| Peanuts | 146 | 12.4 |
| Pecans (halves) | 108 | 10.4 |
| Walnuts (English, shelled halves) | 100 | 6.7 |
| Pumpkin Seeds (kernels, dried) | 138 | 5.4 |
| Sesame Seeds (kernels, dried, decorticated) | 150 | 17.4 |
| Sunflower Seeds (hulled kernels, dry/roasted) | 128 | 14.2 |

# DIETARY FIBER CONTENT OF GLUTEN-FREE FOODS
## FRUITS

| Food Items | Serving Size | Dietary Fiber (grams) |
|---|---|---|
| Apple | 1 medium | 3.7 |
| Applesauce (unsweetened) | 1 cup (250 mL) | 2.9 |
| Apricots (dried) | ½ cup (125 mL) | 5.9 |
| Apricots (fresh) | 2 | 1.7 |
| Banana | 1 medium | 2.8 |
| Blackberries | 1 cup (250 mL) | 7.6 |
| Blueberries | 1 cup (250 mL) | 3.9 |
| Boysenberries (frozen) | 1 cup (250 mL) | 5.1 |
| Cherries (sweet, raw) | 20 | 3.2 |
| Cranberries (whole) | 1 cup (250 mL) | 4.0 |
| Figs (dried) | 2 | 4.6 |
| Grapes (seedless) | 20 | 1.0 |
| Kiwi | 1 medium | 2.6 |
| Mango | 1 whole | 3.7 |
| Nectarine | 1 medium | 2.2 |
| Orange | 1 medium | 3.1 |
| Peach | 1 medium | 2 |
| Pear | 1 medium | 4 |
| Pineapple (diced, raw) | 1 cup (250 mL) | 1.9 |
| Plums | 2 small | 2 |
| Prunes (dried) | 2 | 1.2 |
| Raisins | 1 cup (250 mL) | 6.6 |
| Raspberries | 1 cup (250 mL) | 8.4 |
| Rhubarb (cooked) | 1 cup (250 mL) | 4.8 |
| Strawberries | 1 cup (250 mL) | 3.5 |

# DIETARY FIBER CONTENT OF GLUTEN-FREE FOODS
## VEGETABLES

| Food Items | Serving Size | Dietary Fiber (grams) |
|---|---|---|
| Asparagus (cooked) | 1 cup (250 mL) | 2.9 |
| Beans, Green (cooked) | 1 cup (250 mL) | 8 |
| Beets (cooked) | 1 cup (250 mL) | 3.4 |
| Broccoli (cooked) | 1 cup (250 mL) | 4.5 |
| Brussels Sprouts (cooked) | 1 cup (250 mL) | 4 |
| Cabbage (cooked) | 1 cup (250 mL) | 3.5 |
| Carrots (cooked) | 1 cup (250 mL) | 5.1 |
| Cauliflower (cooked) | 1 cup (250 mL) | 3.3 |
| Corn (cooked) | 1 cup (250 mL) | 4.6 |
| Celery | 11" (28 cm) stalk | 1.1 |
| Eggplant (cooked) | 1 cup (250 mL) | 2.5 |
| Lettuce, Iceberg (shredded) | 1 cup (250 mL) | 0.8 |
| Lettuce, Romaine (shredded) | 1 cup (250 mL) | 1 |
| Mushrooms (cooked) | 1 cup (250 mL) | 3.4 |
| Okra (cooked) | 1 cup (250 mL) | 4 |
| Onions (cooked) | 1 cup (250 mL) | 2.9 |
| Parsnips (cooked) | 1 cup (250 mL) | 6.2 |
| Peas, Green (cooked) | 1 cup (250 mL) | 8.8 |
| Peppers, Sweet, Green (chopped) | 1 cup (250 mL) | 2.7 |
| Potato (baked with skin) | 1 medium | 4.8 |
| Pumpkin (canned) | ½ cup (125 mL) | 3.5 |
| Radish (sliced) | 1 cup (250 mL) | 1.9 |
| Snow Peas (cooked) | 1 cup (250 mL) | 4.5 |
| Spinach (cooked) | 1 cup (250 mL) | 4.3 |
| Sweet Potato (baked with skin) | 1 medium | 3.4 |
| Squash, Acorn (cooked) | 1 cup (250 mL) | 9 |
| Turnips (cooked) | 1 cup (250 mL) | 3.1 |
| Tomatoes | 1 medium | 1.4 |
| Zucchini (cooked) | 1 cup (250 mL) | 2.5 |

# IRON

Iron, a mineral found in food, is needed to keep the body energized. Iron is an essential part of the hemoglobin in red blood cells which carry oxygen throughout the body. Oxygen is used to release energy from the food that is eaten.

Too little iron in your body can lead to iron deficiency anemia. If iron levels are low, less energy is produced in the cells. This results in symptoms such as profound fatigue, irritability, decreased appetite and increased susceptibility to infections. In children, low iron levels can also result in lower learning ability and depressed growth. It is not uncommon for people with newly diagnosed celiac disease to present with anemia. This is caused by malabsorption (inability of the body to absorb nutrients) due to gluten damaging the absorptive surface of the small intestine. It is critical to follow a strict gluten-free diet in order to allow the intestinal tract to heal. Eating iron-rich foods (see pages 34-36) is also important. If the anemia is severe, an iron supplement may be prescribed.

**There are two types of iron in foods, heme iron and non-heme iron:**

## Heme Iron

- ❖ Is more readily absorbed by the body (approximately 23% of the iron consumed is absorbed).
- ❖ Absorption is not changed by other foods in the diet.
- ❖ Is found only in red meat, fish and poultry.

## Non-Heme Iron

- ❖ Is not absorbed as well as heme iron (only 3-8% of the iron consumed is absorbed).
- ❖ Absorption can be increased or decreased by other foods in the diet.
- ❖ Is found in fruits, vegetables, grains and eggs.

## HOW TO MAXIMIZE IRON ABSORPTION

1. Choose foods with a higher iron content (see pages 35 and 36).
2. Eat a source of heme iron with non-heme iron at the same meal:
   e.g., ◆ Stir-fried beef, chicken, pork or fish with vegetables (e.g., broccoli) and rice and toasted almonds or sesame seeds.
   ◆ Chili with meat and beans.
3. Combine Vitamin C-rich foods with non-heme iron foods
   - ❖ Citrus fruits and juices, kiwi fruit, strawberries, cantaloupe, broccoli, tomatoes, potatoes, green and red peppers and cabbage are good sources of Vitamin C:
     e.g., ◆ Poached egg and glass of orange juice.
     ◆ Casserole with rice, beans, canned tomatoes or tomato sauce.
     ◆ Spinach salad with strawberries or orange segments.
4. Avoid coffee or tea with meals rich in iron as these beverages contain tannins which interfere with iron absorption. It is better to drink these beverages between meals.
5. Consume a Vitamin C-rich food with an iron supplement.

Adapted from *Iron Essential for Good Health* by Beef Information Centre, Canada.

# Dietary Reference Intake (DRI)* for Iron

| Age | Iron (mg/day) |
| --- | --- |
| 7-12 months | 11 |
| 1-3 years | 7 |
| 4-8 years | 10 |
| 9-13 years | 8 |
| 14-18 (female) | 15 |
| 14-18 (male) | 11 |
| 19-50 (female) | 18 |
| 19-50 (male) | 8 |
| 51-70 years | 8 |
| 70+ | 8 |
| Pregnant | 27 |

* For more than 50 years, nutrition experts have produced a set of nutrient and energy standards known as the Recommended Dietary Allowance (RDA). A major revision is currently underway to replace the RDA. These revised recommendations are called Dietary Reference Intake (DRI) and reflect collaborative efforts of American and Canadian scientists, through a review process overseen by the National Academy of Science's Food and Nutrition Board. The newly established levels for iron are listed above.

# IRON CONTENT OF GLUTEN-FREE FOODS

| Food | Serving Size | Iron (mg) |
|---|---|---|
| **Grains** | | |
| Amaranth, raw | 1 cup (250 mL) | 14.8 |
| Buckwheat Bran (Farinetta™) | 1 cup (250 mL) | 6.8 |
| Buckwheat Groats (roasted, dry) | 1 cup (250 mL) | 4.1 |
| Buckwheat Groats (roasted, cooked) | 1 cup (250 mL) | 1.3 |
| Buckwheat Flour, Whole Groat | 1 cup (250 mL) | 4.9 |
| Cornmeal (degermed, enriched) | 1 cup (250 mL) | 5.7 |
| Flax | 1 cup (250 mL) | 9.6 |
| Flax Seed Meal (ground flax seeds) | 1 cup (250 mL) | 7.5 |
| Garfava Flour (garbanzo & fava beans) | 1 cup (250 mL) | 7.9 |
| Millet (raw) | 1 cup (250 mL) | 6.0 |
| Montina™ Flour | 1 cup (250 mL) | 11.1 |
| Potato Flour | 1 cup (250 mL) | 2.2 |
| Potato Starch | 1 cup (250 mL) | 3.5 |
| Quinoa Flour | 1 cup (250 mL) | 9.4 |
| Quinoa (raw) | 1 cup (250 mL) | 15.7 |
| Rice Bran (crude) | 1 cup (250 mL) | 21.9 |
| Rice Flour, Brown | 1 cup (250 mL) | 3.1 |
| Rice Flour, White | 1 cup (250 mL) | 0.6 |
| Rice, White (parboiled, enriched, cooked) | 1 cup (250 mL) | 2 |
| Rice, Brown (cooked) | 1 cup (250 mL) | 0.8 |
| Sorghum Flour | 1 cup (250 mL) | 4.7 |
| Soy Flour (full fat) | 1 cup (250 mL) | 5.4 |
| Soy Flour (defatted) | 1 cup (250 mL) | 9.2 |
| **Nuts and Seeds** | | |
| Almonds (whole, blanched) | 1 cup (250 mL) | 5.4 |
| Brazil Nuts (dried, blanched) | 1 cup (250 mL) | 4.8 |
| Peanuts | 1 cup (250 mL) | 6.7 |
| Pecans (halves) | 1 cup (250 mL) | 2.7 |
| Walnuts, English (shelled, halved) | 1 cup (250 mL) | 2.9 |
| Pumpkin Seeds (kernels, dried) | 1 cup (250 mL) | 20.7 |
| Sesame Seeds (kernels, dried, decorticated) | 1 cup (250 mL) | 11.7 |
| Sunflower Seeds (hulled kernels, dry roasted) | 1 cup (250 mL) | 4.9 |
| **Beans, Peas, Lentils** | | |
| Cranberry Beans/Romano Beans (cooked) | 1 cup (250 mL) | 3.7 |
| Garbanzo Beans/Chickpeas (cooked) | 1 cup (250 mL) | 4.7 |
| Kidney Beans (cooked) | 1 cup (250 mL) | 5.2 |
| Lentils (cooked) | 1 cup (250 mL) | 6.6 |
| Navy Beans (cooked) | 1 cup (250 mL) | 4.5 |
| Pinto Beans (cooked) | 1 cup (250 mL) | 4.5 |
| Soybeans (cooked) | 1 cup (250 mL) | 8.8 |
| Split Peas (cooked) | 1 cup (250 mL) | 2.5 |
| White Beans (cooked) | 1 cup (250 mL) | 6.6 |

**Nutrient values from:** USDA Nutrient Data Base for Standard Reference, Release #13;
• Buckwheat Bran (Farinetta™) from Minn-Dak Growers, Grand Forks, ND, USA
• Garfava Flour from Authentic Foods Company, Gardena, CA, USA
• Sorghum Flour from Silliker Laboratories, Grand Prairie, TX, USA
• Montina™ Flour from Amazing Grains, Ronan, MT, USA

# IRON CONTENT OF GLUTEN-FREE FOODS

| Food | Serving Size | Iron (mg) |
|---|---|---|
| **Meat & Alternatives** | | |
| Beef Liver (cooked) | 3.5 oz. (100 g) | 5.8 |
| Ground Beef (cooked) | 3.5 oz. (100 g) | 2.1 |
| Roast Beef (cooked) | 3.5 oz. (100 g) | 1.9 |
| Beef Steak (cooked) | 3.5 oz. (100 g) | 3.1 |
| Chicken Breast (cooked) | 3.5 oz. (100 g) | 1 |
| Clams | 9 small or 4 large | 3.4 |
| Egg, Whole (cooked) | 1 large | 0.7 |
| Oysters (canned) | 3.5 oz. (100 g) | 6.7 |
| Pork Chop (cooked) | 3.5 oz. (100 g) | 1 |
| Pork Tenderloin (cooked) | 3.5 oz. (100 g) | 1.4 |
| Salmon (canned, drained, bones) | 3.5 oz. (100 g) | 1.1 |
| Sardines (canned in oil) | 8 medium (100 g) | 3.5 |
| Shrimp (canned, drained) | 3.5 oz. (100 g) | 2.7 |
| Shrimp (fresh, cooked) | 3.5 oz. (100 g) | 3.1 |
| Tuna (white, canned, drained) | 3.5 oz. (100 g) | 1 |
| Turkey (dark meat, cooked) | 3.5 oz. (100 g) | 2.3 |
| **Fruits** | | |
| Apricots (dried) | 1 cup (250 mL) | 6.1 |
| Prunes (dried) | 1 cup (250 mL) | 4.2 |
| Prune Juice | 1 cup (250 mL) | 3 |
| Raisins, seedless | 1 cup (250 mL) | 3.4 |
| **Vegetables** | | |
| Acorn Squash (cooked) | 1 cup (250 mL) | 1.9 |
| Asparagus (cooked) | 1 cup (250 mL) | 1.3 |
| Broccoli (cooked) | 1 cup (250 mL) | 1.3 |
| Brussels Sprouts (cooked) | 1 cup (250 mL) | 1.8 |
| Collards (frozen, cooked) | 1 cup (250 mL) | 1.9 |
| Green Peas (cooked) | 1 cup (250 mL) | 2.5 |
| Potato (white, baked with skin) | 1 medium | 2.7 |
| Spinach (cooked) | 1 cup (250 mL) | 6.4 |
| Spinach (raw) | 1 cup (250 mL) | 0.8 |
| **Miscellaneous** | | |
| Blackstrap Molasses | 1 tbsp. (15 mL) | 3.3 |

**Nutrient values from:** USDA Nutrient Data Base for Standard Reference, Release #13

# LACTOSE INTOLERANCE

## WHAT IS LACTOSE INTOLERANCE?

Milk and milk products contain a natural sugar called lactose. People who are lactose intolerant or, more precisely, who are lactose maldigesters, lack enough of the enzyme lactase needed to completely digest the lactose into its simple sugars, glucose and galactose. Symptoms of lactose intolerance may include some or all of the following: abdominal cramping, bloating, gas, nausea, headache and diarrhea. Symptoms may occur 15–30 minutes after digestion of lactose or as long as several hours later.

## CAUSES OF LACTOSE INTOLERANCE

**Primary lactase deficiency:** The level of lactase enzyme activity in some people may gradually fall with age to the point where they no longer tolerate as much as they used to. This type of intolerance affects as many as 70% of the world's population. It is more prevalent in Asians, Africans, Hispanics and North American aboriginals.

**Secondary lactase deficiency:** This is usually a temporary condition in which the level of lactase has fallen as a result of injury to the gastrointestinal tract in conditions such as celiac disease, inflammatory bowel disease, surgery, infections and with the use of certain drugs.

## DIETARY RECOMMENDATIONS FOR LACTOSE INTOLERANCE

Different people will tolerate various levels of lactose in their diet. Those people with secondary lactase deficiency such as celiac disease may need to eliminate lactose temporarily until the small intestine heals. Most people can digest small amounts of lactose. In addition, many people can become less lactose intolerant over time by **gradually** introducing milk products into their diet. Other factors can affect tolerance besides the total lactose content of foods.

**The following tips can help improve tolerance:**

### Milk

- ❖ Drink small amounts of milk throughout the day, ¼–½ cup (60-125 mL); avoid drinking large amounts at once.
- ❖ Enjoy milk with meals or snacks; avoid drinking it on an empty stomach.
- ❖ Try heating the milk; it may be easier to tolerate.
- ❖ The higher the fat content in the milk, the slower it is digested; since whole milk is higher in fat, you may tolerate it better than 2% and 2% better than 1% or skim milk.
- ❖ Cultured buttermilk and acidophilus milk are usually tolerated to the same degree as plain milk.

# LACTOSE INTOLERANCE CONT'D.

## Yogurt

❖ Yogurt is usually well tolerated. Although yogurt contains a lot of lactose, the lactase enzymes in the active cultures digest this lactose. Look for brands that contain "active" or "live" cultures as they are tolerated more easily.

## Cheese

❖ Aged, natural cheeses such as Cheddar, Edam, mozzarella contain very little lactose. Most of it is removed with the whey; the small amount remaining is broken down during the aging process.

❖ Fresh cheeses, such as creamed cottage cheese, ricotta and quark contain varying amounts of lactose.

❖ Dry-curd cottage cheese contains less lactose than creamed cottage cheese.

❖ Processed cheese has a lactose content similar to that of natural, aged cheese.

❖ Processed cheese food and processed cheese spread may have dairy products other than cheese added to them, therefore their lactose content may be higher.

❖ Light/lite cheese products may be very high in lactose.

## Special Products

Several products have been specially developed to help in the management of lactose maldigestion. For more product information see pages 129-133.

❖ **Lacteeze Milk** is a lactose-reduced milk available in skim, 1%, and 2% in the dairy case of grocery stores. The lactase enzyme has been added to the milk and 99% of the naturally occurring lactose has been converted to simple, easily digested sugars. Lacteeze milk is slightly sweeter than regular milk but it has the same nutritional value and can be used in cooking and baking.

❖ **Lactaid Milk** is another brand of lactose-reduced milk available in skim and 2% (in Canada) and fat-free, low fat (1%), reduced fat (2%), whole and calcium-fortified (in USA) in the dairy case of grocery stores. It also comes in a 2% 1 litre Ultra High Temperature (UHT) shelf stable package (in Canada).

❖ **Lactaid Drops\*** contain enzymes that can be added to liquid dairy products making them more easily digestible. Approximately 70-99% of the lactose is broken down based on the number of drops used (5-10 drops). They are available in most drug stores.

❖ **Lacteeze Enzyme Drops\*** also contain enzymes that break down the lactose in dairy products and are available in drug stores.

\* The nutritional value of the dairy product is not changed when you use enzyme drops or tablets.

# LACTOSE INTOLERANCE CONT'D.

- ❖ **Lacteeze 4000 Tablets*** contain extra-strength natural enzymes that are taken just before meals or snacks that contain lactose. The tablets are available from most drug stores.

- ❖ **Lacteeze Children's Tablets*** are available in strawberry flavor.

- ❖ **Lactaid Tablets*** is another brand of lactase enzymes available in Regular (Original) and Extra-Strength tablets and Ultra-Strength Caplets or Chewable Tablets (vanilla flavor).

- ❖ **Lacteeze Ice Cream** is available in 1-quart (1 L) containers and comes in four flavors. A ½ cup (125 mL) serving contains 6.7 g fat.

- ❖ **Soy Beverages** are available in various flavors and many are gluten-free (see pages 130 and 131). However, not all are enriched/fortified with calcium and Vitamin D.

* The nutritional value of the dairy product is not changed when you use enzyme drops or tablets.

# LACTOSE CONTENT OF SELECTED DAIRY FOODS

| Food | Serving Size | Lactose (grams per serving) |
|---|---|---|
| Buttermilk | 1 cup (250 mL) | 10 |
| Evaporated Milk | 1 cup (250 mL) | 24 |
| Lacteeze Milk | 1 cup (250 mL) | 0.1* |
| Milk (1% or skim) | 1 cup (250 mL) | 11 |
| Milk (2%) | 1 cup (250 mL) | 11 |
| Milk (whole) | 1 cup (250 mL) | 11 |
| Sweetened Condensed Milk | 1 cup (250 mL) | 30 |
| Butter | 1 tsp. (5 mL) | trace |
| Cheddar Cheese | 1 oz (30 g) | 1 |
| Cottage Cheese (creamed) | 1 cup (250 mL) | 6 |
| Cream Cheese | 1 oz (30 g) | 1 |
| Parmesan Cheese (grated) | 1 oz (30 g) | 1 |
| Swiss Cheese | 1 oz (30 g) | 1 |
| Ice Cream | 1 cup (250 mL) | 12 |
| Ice Milk | 1 cup (250 mL) | 18 |
| Lacteeze Ice Cream | 1 cup (250 mL) | 0.1* |
| Sherbet | 1 cup (250 mL) | 4 |
| Lacteeze Yogurt | ½ cup (125 mL) | 0.5* |
| Yogurt (low fat) | ½ cup (125 mL) | 2.5** |
| Whipping Cream | ½ cup (125 mL) | 3 |
| Half & Half Cream | 1 tbsp. (15 mL) | 0.6 |
| Light Cream | 1 tbsp. (15 mL) | 0.4 |
| Sour Cream | ½ cup (125 mL) | 4 |

\* Manufacturer information

\*\* The lactose in yogurt is digested by the lactase enzymes in the active cultures. However, lactase activity in yogurt may vary from brand to brand. Yogurts that have cultures added after pasteurization have more lactase activity. Look for brands that contain "live or active" cultures.

ADAPTED FROM: *Adverse Reactions to Foods*, ©1991, American Dietetic Association. Used with permission.

## Nutritional Requirements

Milk and milk products are important sources of calcium, phosphorous, magnesium, riboflavin, vitamins A, D, B12 and protein. Milk products supply more than 75% of the calcium in the Canadian and American diet. Other foods contain some calcium but most contain smaller amounts of calcium or the calcium is in a form that the human body absorbs poorly. If an individual is unable to consume the recommended number of servings of milk and milk products, a nutritional supplement may be necessary. Contact a dietitian for more information.

# DIETARY REFERENCE INTAKE (DRI)* FOR CALCIUM

| Age | Calcium (mg/day) |
|---|---|
| **INFANTS** | |
| 0-6 months | 210 |
| 7-12 months | 270 |
| **CHILDREN** | |
| 1-3 years | 500 |
| 4-8 years | 800 |
| **FEMALES/MALES** | |
| 9-13 | 1300 |
| 14-18 | 1300 |
| 19-30 | 1000 |
| 31-50 | 1000 |
| 51-70 | 1200 |
| 71+ | 1200 |

* For more than 50 years, nutrition experts have produced a set of nutrient and energy standards known as the Recommended Dietary Allowance (RDA). A major revision is currently underway to replace the RDA. These revised recommendations are called Dietary Reference Intake (DRI) and reflect collaborative efforts of American and Canadian scientists, through a review process overseen by the national Academy of Science's Food and Nutrition Board. The newly established levels for calcium are listed above.

# CALCIUM CONTENT OF GLUTEN-FREE FOODS DAIRY PRODUCTS

| Food | Serving | Calcium (mg) | Rating |
|------|---------|--------------|--------|
| Brie cheese | 2 oz. (50 g) | 92 | ★ |
| Buttermilk | 1 cup (250 mL) | 303 | ★★★ |
| Camembert cheese | 2 oz. (50 g) | 194 | ★★ |
| Cheese, firm, such as Brick, Cheddar, Colby, Edam and Gouda | 2 oz. (50 g) 1" x 1" x 3" (2.5 x 2.5 x 8 cm) | 350 | ★★★ |
| Cottage cheese, creamed, 2%, 1% | ½ cup (125 mL) | 76 | ★ |
| Feta cheese | 2 oz. (50 g) | 255 | ★★ |
| Ice Cream | ½ cup (125 mL) | 90 | ★ |
| Ice Milk | ½ cup (125 mL) | 138 | ★ |
| Milk (whole, 2%, 1%, skim)* | 1 cup (250 mL) | 315 | ★★★ |
| Milk, chocolate | 1 cup (250 mL) | 301 | ★★★ |
| Milk, powder, dry | 3 tbsp. (45 mL) | 308 | ★★★ |
| Mozzarella cheese | 2 oz. (50 g) | 287 | ★★★ |
| Mozzarella cheese, partly skimmed | 2 oz. (50 g) | 366 | ★★★ |
| Parmesan cheese, grated | 3 tbsp. (45 mL) | 261 | ★★ |
| Processed cheese slices | 2 thin (42 g) | 256 | ★★ |
| Processed cheese slices | 2 regular (62 g) | 384 | ★★★ |
| Processed cheese spread | 3 tbsp. (45 mL) | 270 | ★★ |
| Ricotta cheese | ¼ cup (60 mL) | 135 | ★ |
| Ricotta cheese, partly skimmed | ¼ cup (60 mL) | 177 | ★★ |
| Swiss cheese | 2 oz. (50 g) | 480 | ★★★ |
| Yogurt drink | 1 cup (250 mL) | 274 | ★★★ |
| Yogurt, frozen | ½ cup (125 mL) | 147 | ★ |
| Yogurt, fruit-flavored | ¾ cup (175 g) | 240 | ★★ |
| Yogurt, plain | ¾ cup (175 g) | 296 | ★★★ |

* Add about 100 mg of calcium for calcium-enriched milk

**Code:** ★    – Source of Calcium
★★    – Good source of calcium
★★★    – Excellent source of calcium

This rating is established according to federal Food and Drugs Regulations. It is based on the content of calcium in foods and is not based on the amount of calcium actually absorbed by the body.

**Source:** Calcium values come from Health Canada, Canadian Nutrient File, 1997.

**From:** *Calcium For Life: Are You on the Right Track*, Dairy Farmers of Canada

# CALCIUM CONTENT OF GLUTEN-FREE FOODS
# OTHER FOODS

| Food | Serving | Calcium (mg) | Rating |
|---|---|---|---|
| Almonds | ½ cup (125 mL) | (200) | ★★ |
| Baked Beans | 1 cup (250 mL) | (163) | ★★ |
| Bok Choy, cooked | ½ cup (125 mL) | 84 | ★ |
| Brazil Nuts | ½ cup (125 mL) | 130 | ★ |
| Broccoli, cooked | ½ cup (125 mL) | 38 | |
| Chickpeas, cooked | 1 cup (250 mL) | 85 | ★ |
| Chili Con Carne | 1 cup (250 mL) | (72) | ★ |
| Collards, cooked | ½ cup (125 mL) | 81 | ★ |
| Dates | ¼ cup (60 mL) | 14 | |
| Figs, dried | 3 | 81 | ★ |
| Kale, cooked | ½ cup (125 mL) | 49 | |
| Lentils, cooked | 1 cup (250 mL) | 49 | |
| Nuts, mixed | ½ cup (125 mL) | 51 | |
| Orange | 1 medium | 56 | ★ |
| Orange Juice, calcium fortified | 1 cup (250 mL) | 300-350 | ★★★ |
| Prunes, dried, uncooked | 3 medium | 12 | |
| Raisins | ¼ cup (60 mL) | 21 | |
| Red Kidney Beans, cooked | 1 cup (250 mL) | (52) | |
| Rice, white or brown, cooked | ½ cup (125 mL) | 10 | |
| Salmon, pink, canned, with bones | half a 7.5 oz. (213 g) can | 225 | ★★ |
| Salmon, sockeye, canned, with bones | half a 7.5 oz. (213 g) can | 243 | ★★ |
| Sardines, canned, with bones | 6 medium (72 g) | 275 | ★★★ |
| Sesame Seeds | ½ cup (125 mL) | (89) | ★ |
| Soybeans, cooked | ½ cup (125 mL) | 93 | ★ |
| Soy Beverage | 1 cup (250 mL) | 10 | |
| Soy Beverage, fortified | 1 cup (250 mL) | 312 | ★★★ |
| Tofu, regular, processed with calcium sulfate* check label | ⅓ cup (100 g) | 150 | ★ |
| White Beans, cooked | 1 cup (250 mL) | (170) | ★★ |

The numbers between parentheses () indicate the calcium from these sources is known to be absorbed less efficiently by the body.

* The Calcium content for tofu is an approximation based on products available on the market. Calcium content varies greatly from one brand to the other and can be quite low. Tofu processed with magnesium chloride also contains less calcium.

**Code:** ★ Source of Calcium; ★★ Good source of calcium; ★★★ Excellent source of calcium

This rating is established according to federal Food and Drugs Regulations. It is based on the content of calcium in foods and is not based on the amount of calcium actually absorbed by the body.

**SOURCE:** Calcium values come from Health Canada, Canadian Nutrient File, 1997.

# GLUTEN-FREE (GF) MEAL-PLANNING IDEAS

## BREAKFAST

❖ GF cold cereal (see pages 22, 87-89), sliced fresh fruit, milk*.

❖ GF Granola (see recipes on pages 69 and 70) and milk*.

❖ Cooked cereal (cornmeal, cream of white or brown rice, cream of buckwheat) with chopped dates, apricots or raisins, cinnamon, brown sugar and milk*.

❖ Gluten-free toast and yogurt with fruit**, chopped nuts and coconut.

❖ GF toasted bread, bun, bagel or English muffin with cream cheese/fruit** or GF peanut butter and jam or honey, milk* or juice.

❖ GF muffin, fresh fruit** and yogurt.

❖ GF French toast (warm bread in microwave first to improve absorption of the egg mixture), fruit** and syrup.

❖ GF freezer waffles, fruit** and syrup and a glass of milk*.

❖ GF pancakes (use a GF mix or make your own from GF flours), with fruit** and syrup.

❖ GF toasted bread, egg and/or leftover fried potatoes.

❖ Fruit smoothie (skim milk powder*, fresh or frozen fruit**, honey or sugar, ground flax, water, crushed ice).

\*   Non-dairy, gluten-free substitutes (e.g., soy, rice or almond beverages) can also be used.

\*\* Fruits: canned crushed pineapple or peach slices, fresh or frozen strawberries or blueberries, applesauce and a sprinkle of cinnamon, sliced bananas or kiwis.

## SANDWICH TIPS

Gluten-Free breads can become dry and crumbly so here are a few tips:

❖ When you buy rice bread, slice (if not sliced) and freeze immediately, placing waxed paper between slices so you can remove one at a time. Seal entire amount in a plastic bag.

❖ Toasting bread improves flavor and keeps it from crumbling.

❖ Make a sandwich on lightly toasted bread and freeze it for lunch the next day.

❖ Consider buying a bread machine, as homemade gluten-free breads are much fresher and economical than ready made breads.

❖ Try open-face sandwiches and put them under a broiler. (e.g., tuna or pure crab meat with shredded cheese)

# LUNCH

- ❖ Homemade soups (vegetable, chicken, corn chowder, cream of potato, lentil, pea, etc.) and a GF muffin or bagel with melted cheese.
- ❖ Canned GF soup (see pages 125-127) and GF bread sticks (see page 95), brushed with melted butter and garlic powder and heat in the oven.
- ❖ Toasted GF cheese bread or GF grilled cheese sandwich with canned or homemade GF soup.
- ❖ GF bagel with cheese and GF ham, fresh fruit and yogurt.
- ❖ GF bagel with turkey, lettuce, tomato, cucumbers, sprouts and avocado; baby carrots and fresh fruit.
- ❖ Fettuccini Alfredo (GF pasta, butter or margarine, garlic powder, Parmesan cheese, milk) with a salad.
- ❖ GF pasta with homemade cheese sauce or GF Tomato Pasta Sauce (in jars or homemade) and salad.
- ❖ GF crackers, hummus (garbanzo beans, sesame seed oil, garlic), raw vegetables and fresh fruit.
- ❖ Wild Rice with Vegetable Casserole (see page 78).
- ❖ Pastato Mac and Cheese or Pastariso Pasta & Cheese Dinner, raw vegetables and dip (GF salad dressing).
- ❖ Quinoa salad (see page 76) and milk.
- ❖ Canned GF baked beans, coleslaw and homemade corn bread.
- ❖ Green salad with added meat, chicken and/or canned shrimp, tuna, salmon and GF bun.
- ❖ GF pasta salad with chicken, GF ham or canned shrimp, tuna or crab and fresh fruit.
- ❖ Spinach salad with sunflower seeds, chickpeas, feta cheese, strawberries and GF rice crackers.
- ❖ Stuffed baked potato (cheese and GF ham or broccoli and cheese) – make ahead, freeze and heat in microwave.
- ❖ Homemade chili served over a baked potato or toasted GF bun, top with grated cheese.
- ❖ Pizza (use GF crust mix or GF prebaked frozen crust, GF pizza sauce, grated cheese, chopped green peppers, mushrooms, onions, GF ham or salami).
- ❖ GF hot dog bun and GF wiener or sausage, raw vegetables.
- ❖ Rice cakes with peanut butter and banana, melted cheese, egg, salmon or tuna salad.
- ❖ Eggs scrambled in microwave or omelet with GF toast.
- ❖ GF pancakes, waffles or French toast (see breakfast ideas) and GF sausage.
- ❖ Leftovers (casseroles, chili, stew, meat and potatoes, chicken and rice).
- ❖ Precooked rice, stored and frozen to heat later with shredded cheese and leftover meat or chicken and vegetables.
- ❖ Soft corn tortillas made into "wraps", stuffed with: (A) cooked mung bean noodles or rice noodles, meat or shrimp with vegetables (e.g., sprouts, tomatoes, cucumber, green pepper) drizzled with a mixture of GF soy sauce, honey, ginger and garlic powder **OR** (B) kernel corn with cooked rice and pesto sauce, add cooked ground beef, fresh vegetables, and top with salsa and yogurt or shredded cheese.

## SUPPER/DINNER

- ❖ Rice, hamburger and tomato casserole with grated cheese.
- ❖ GF lasagna and salad.
- ❖ Shish Kebobs served over rice.
- ❖ GF pasta (see pages 117-119) with homemade cheese sauce or GF pasta sauce (in jars or homemade) and salad.
- ❖ Creamed salmon or tuna with green peas served on GF toast.
- ❖ Cabbage rolls or Lentil Leaf Rolls (see page 79).
- ❖ Homemade beef stew (thickened with GF starch) and GF bread.
- ❖ Chili con carne, GF cornbread or corn chips and raw vegetables.
- ❖ Steak, baked potato and vegetables.
- ❖ Baked chicken* or fish*, rice or GF pasta, cooked vegetables and/or salad.
  *Crunchy Coating: crushed potato or tortilla chips, crushed GF cereal, nuts, rice bread crumbs or cornmeal.
- ❖ Lentil stew and GF toasted cheese bread.
- ❖ GF tacos or tortillas – ground beef, GF taco seasoning, grated cheese, chopped lettuce and tomatoes, GF salsa and sour cream in corn tortilla or served over tortilla chips.
- ❖ Stir-fry beef, pork, chicken or seafood and vegetables, (GF soy sauce, arrowroot or tapioca starch, garlic and ginger powder, mixed with water to make a sauce) served over rice with toasted almonds and/or sesame seeds.
- ❖ Barbecue chicken, pork chops or fish (GF barbecue sauce) with rice pilaf (white, brown or wild) or Quinoa and Wild Rice Pilaf (see page 77) and vegetables.
- ❖ Lentil Pizza Squares (see page 80).
- ❖ GF pizza (see lunch) and salad.
- ❖ Roast chicken or turkey with dressing (GF bread crumbs), mashed potatoes, gravy (thickened with GF starch) and vegetables.
- ❖ Sweet and sour meatballs served over rice with stir-fried vegetables.
- ❖ Oven-Fried Chicken (see page 74), baked potato, cooked vegetables or salad.
- ❖ Turkey meatballs with Lemon Sauce (see page 75), rice or kasha and cooked vegetables.
- ❖ Roast pork, applesauce, mashed potatoes, gravy (thickened with GF starch) and vegetables.
- ❖ Meatloaf (GF rice cereal, GF instant mashed potatoes, GF bread crumbs or crushed corn chips or potato chips and egg, herbs or spices), GF pasta with GF tomato sauce and tossed salad.
- ❖ Beef or chicken kabobs, millet, quinoa or buckwheat or buckwheat pilaf with nuts and dried fruits, and steamed vegetables.
- ❖ Poached or broiled salmon, brown and/or wild rice and green beans.
- ❖ Hamburger patty or grilled chicken breast, corn on the cob, coleslaw and watermelon.

# SNACKS

- ❖ Fruit juice.
- ❖ Fresh fruit.
- ❖ Dried fruit (e.g., raisins, apricots).
- ❖ Most canned fruits.
- ❖ Pumpkin or sunflower seeds (plain or GF flavored), (see page 123).
- ❖ Nuts (plain).
- ❖ Dried fruit and nut mixtures.
- ❖ Soy nuts (plain or GF flavored), (see pages 122, 123).
- ❖ Corn nuts (plain).
- ❖ GF Crunchy Granola (see page 70).
- ❖ Celery sticks with peanut butter and/or raisins.
- ❖ Celery sticks with flavored GF cream cheese.
- ❖ Raw vegetables and dip (GF salad dressings/yogurt).
- ❖ Popcorn.
- ❖ GF pretzels (see page 122).
- ❖ Plain corn tortilla chips, salsa, grated cheese and sour cream.
- ❖ GF flavored mini or large rice cakes (see pages 101-103).
- ❖ GF rice crackers with hummus.
- ❖ GF rice cakes or GF bagel with cream cheese and apple slices.
- ❖ GF rice cakes with peanut butter and jelly, honey or banana.
- ❖ GF granola or snack bars (see pages 69, 70, 88, 123, 124).
- ❖ GF muffins (see pages 65-68 and 93-95) and cheese cubes.
- ❖ GF pudding.
- ❖ Yogurt.
- ❖ String cheese or cheese slices.
- ❖ GF soup and/or GF crackers.
- ❖ GF crackers and cheese or cheese spread.

NOTE: See pages 122-124 for GF snack products.

Thanks to Jacquelin Gates, Dietitian, Medical Advisory Committee, Calgary CCA Chapter, for many of the meal and snack ideas.

# GLUTEN-FREE COOKING

## TIPS FOR TASTY GLUTEN-FREE BAKING

Yes, you can make tasty and satisfying baked goods without gluten. Gluten in wheat flour provides the structure for the baked goods. Gluten-Free (GF) products tend to be more compact and drier than wheat products. Baking with different GF flours can give you a wide variety of tastes and textures. Generally, it is best to use a combination of gluten-free flours. For the beginner, muffins, pancakes and cookies are the easiest to prepare. There are many excellent cookbooks that provide detailed information about gluten-free baking (see pages 164 and 165). Here are some tips to get you started.

## CHOOSING AN ADAPTABLE RECIPE

Look for recipes that use a small amount of wheat flour (less than 2 cups) or a combination of wheat with other flours, when you plan to substitute GF flours. Recipes that call for cake flour are more easily adapted for GF flour.

### Using Gluten-Free Flours

**Amaranth Flour** is ground from the tiny, grain-like amaranth seed which is high in fiber, protein, calcium, iron and other nutrients. It has a nutty, robust flavor and is best combined with other flours in baked products.

**Arrowroot Starch** is ground from the root of a West Indian plant. It is an excellent thickener, especially for creams and glazes. Arrowroot can be exchanged for cornstarch.

**Buckwheat Flour** is ground, unroasted buckwheat groats (dehulled buckwheat kernels). The dark flour has a strong, distinctive flavor as it contains a higher percentage of finely milled particles of buckwheat hulls and is higher in fiber and nutrients. The light flour has a mild, mellow flavor as it contains fewer or no buckwheat hulls. Buckwheat flour is best used in small amounts for flavor with more bland flours.

**Corn Flour,** milled from corn (maize), is very light in texture. It can be blended with cornmeal for cornbread or corn muffins. It is best used in combination with other flours.

**Garfava Flour** is blended from a combination of garbanzo beans (chickpeas) and fava (broad) beans. This flour developed by Authentic Foods creates baked goods with excellent volume and good moisture content. It is high in protein and fiber.

**Garbanzo Flour** is ground garbanzo beans (chickpeas) and can be used with other flours. It is high in protein and fiber.

**Montina™ Flour** is ground from the seeds of Indian rice grass. It is very high in fiber, iron and protein, and adds texture and a sweet, nutty flavor to baked products. Due to its high fiber content, replace 20% of the flour portion in a recipe with Monina™.

**Nut Flours** are made from ground almonds, chestnuts, hazelnuts or pecans which are high in protein, fiber and other nutrients. Due to their high fat content, keep refrigerated or frozen in air-tight containers.

**Potato Flour** is more coarse than potato starch. It is creamy and heavy in texture. It absorbs much more liquid than potato starch. Potato flour is best combined in small quantities with other flours (e.g., rice, tapioca and cornstarch).

**Potato Starch** is a fine, white starch excellent for baking if sifted several times and used in baked products containing eggs. It can also be used as a thickener.

**Quinoa Flour** is ground from the quinoa seed which is high in protein, iron and other vitamins and minerals. It is best combined with other flours as it has a strong flavor.

**Rice Flour** is available in various forms such as sweet, brown or white rice flour. Sweet rice flour, also known as glutinous rice flour is a sticky flour which helps bind ingredients together when baking. Brown rice flour is higher in fiber, however, store it in the refrigerator because oils in the bran can become rancid rapidly. White rice flour is very bland. Rice flours have a slightly gritty texture and are best used in combination with other flour such as potato or corn.

**Sorghum Flour** is ground from new food sorghum varieties. It can be substituted for rice flour or used in gluten-free flour mixes (e.g., Bette's Gourmet Four Flour Blend from Authentic Foods using Garfava flour, sorghum flour, cornstarch and tapioca starch flour).

**Soy Flour,** either regular or defatted, is a smooth, nutty-tasting flour milled from soybeans. The defatted flour makes a better product; since it is lower in fat, it will store longer. Store regular soy flour in the refrigerator. Soy flour is best used in combination with other flours in baking as it has a strong flavor. It is very high in protein and a good source of B vitamins, calcium, iron and magnesium.

**Tapioca Starch Flour** is derived from the cassava root. It is colorless when cooked, tasteless and excellent for thickening soups, fruit pies, puddings, creams and glazes. Tapioca starch and potato starch can be interchanged quite successfully.

**Whole Bean Flour,** from romano (cranberry) beans, provides more calcium, iron, potassium, thiamin, riboflavin, folate and dietary fiber than other flours. It is also high in protein. Products baked from this are denser than those made from wheat flour so you require less for best results.

**For more information about flours see pages 53-58, 110-115.**

### NOTE ABOUT BEAN FLOURS:

❖ Bean flours contain more nutrients than the traditional gluten-free flours such as rice, tapioca and potato. Also, baked products made with bean flours have a better texture that more closely resembles wheat products but the flavor will be different.

❖ Many companies mill bean flours. In order to reduce as much of the flatulent effects of the beans, some companies "treat" the beans before grinding. These treatments are usually the company's trade secret and call the process by names such as "toasted", "micronized", "precooked" or "processed". People with celiac disease should introduce bean flours gradually into their diet and usually tolerate the flours that have been "treated" better than flours without treatment before milling.

REFERENCE:
Bette Hagman. *Alas! Not All Bean Flours Are The Same*. Gluten Intolerance Group (GIG) Newsletter, April 2001.

# SUBSTITUTIONS

## Substitutions for 1 tablespoon (15 mL) Wheat Flour

| ½ tbsp. | Cornstarch | 7 mL |
|---|---|---|
| ½ tbsp. | Potato Starch | 7 mL |
| ½ tbsp. | White Rice Flour | 7 mL |
| ½ tbsp. | Arrowroot Starch | 7 mL |
| 2 tsp. | Quick-Cooking Tapioca | 10 mL |
| 2 tsp. | Tapioca Starch | 10 mL |
| 2 tbsp. | Uncooked Rice | 30 mL |

## Substitutions for 1 cup (250 mL) Wheat Flour*

Store in an airtight container and use ⅞ cup (215 mL) of Mix A
or 1 cup (250 mL) of Mix B for 1 cup (250 mL) wheat flour

| MIX A: | 2 cups | Brown Rice Flour | 500 mL |
|---|---|---|---|
| | 2 cups | Sweet Rice Flour | 500 mL |
| | 2 cups | Rice Polish | 500 mL |
| MIX B: | 4 cups | White Rice Flour | 1 L |
| | 1⅓ cups | Potato Starch | 325 mL |
| | 1 cup | Tapioca Starch | 250 mL |

## Other Substitutions for 1 cup (250 mL) Wheat Flour*

| ⅝ cup | Potato Starch | 150 mL |
|---|---|---|
| ⅞ cup | White or Brown Rice Flour | 215 mL |
| 1 cup | Cornmeal | 250 mL |
| 1 cup | Fine Cornmeal | 250 mL |
| ¾ cup | Coarse Cornmeal | 175 mL |
| ⅝ cup | White or Brown Rice Flour | 150 mL |
| | PLUS | |
| ⅓ cup | Potato Starch | 75 mL |
| 1 cup | Soy Flour | 250 mL |
| | PLUS | |
| ¼ cup | Potato Starch | 50 mL |
| ¾ cup | Rice Flour | 175 mL |
| | PLUS | |
| ¼ cup | Cornstarch | 50 mL |
| ⅞ cup | Whole Bean Flour | 215 mL |

\* A combination of flours/starches give a better gluten-free product. For specific flour mixes see recipes in gluten-free cookbooks (pages 158-160, 164, 165), using a variety of gluten-free flours.

# GENERAL BAKING HINTS

## BAKING TIPS

- ❖ Measure carefully using level measurement.
- ❖ Remember to "flour" pan with cocoa when making chocolate cake.
- ❖ Put a pan of water in the oven during baking. This will help keep the moisture in your baked goods.
- ❖ When using glass baking pans reduce oven temperature by 25°F (10°C).

## FLAVOR TIPS

- ❖ Adding chocolate chips, nuts, fruits (e.g., bananas, applesauce), dried fruits (e.g., raisins, apricots), yogurt or honey improves the flavor of baked goods.
- ❖ Most GF breads taste better toasted or warmed.

## TEXTURE TIPS

- ❖ Remember to sift flours, starches and mixes before measuring and then sift together again. Generally, sifting improves the texture of the product.
- ❖ Coarse flours require more leavening than white flour. For each cup of coarse flour, use 2½ tsp. (12 mL) gluten-free baking powder. Coarse flours can also require more sifting, especially in products where texture is important.
- ❖ Unflavored powdered gelatin works well as a binder in rice flour recipes. Soften the gelatin in half the water called for in the recipe before adding. Use 1 tsp. (5 mL) Certo®, or ½ tsp.(2 mL) xanthan gum or guar gum can also be used as a binding agent in baked recipes.
- ❖ GF breads can be crumbly. Substituting buttermilk for the milk or water results in a lighter, more finely textured product.
- ❖ Using carbonated beverages in place of water or milk results in a lighter textured product (e.g., pancakes, cakes).
- ❖ Let gluten-free dough sit at least ½ hour or overnight in the refrigerator to soften. This results in a better textured product.
- ❖ GF muffins and biscuits are less crumbly and better textured when made in small sizes, thus they are more successful than loaves of bread made from the same recipe.
- ❖ Baking is affected by temperature and altitude. On a hot day or in a hot kitchen, baking with a lot of margarine, butter or shortening will give the dough or batter a more liquid consistency. Pastry is most affected. Cold ingredients are necessary.
- ❖ Cornstarch and tapioca starch are best for thickening sauces and gravies.
- ❖ To bind meat loaf, use gluten-free instant mashed potatoes, gluten-free bread crumbs or crackers, gluten-free rice cereal, crushed corn or potato chips, rice flour and/or egg.

# GENERAL BAKING HINTS CONT'D.

## STORAGE TIPS

❖ GF flours have no preservatives and are quite perishable. Wrap them tightly and store in the freezer in an airtight container. A three- to four-week supply can be kept in the refrigerator without spoilage.

❖ Store baked products in plastic bags when still warm to preserve moisture. Refrigerate baked products to decrease crumbliness.

❖ Bread becomes stale quickly. If the baked product will not be eaten within two days, slice, wrap and freeze to ensure minimum loss of moisture and flavor. Breads can be frozen for one to two months and cookies for three to four months.

# GLUTEN-FREE ALTERNATIVES

## AMARANTH

Amaranth is a broad-leafed plant which produces flowerets containing tiny grain-like tan seeds. Although it is used as a grain, it is not an actual grain and is a member of the Amaranthaceae family. Amaranth seeds are sold in several forms:

### Whole-Grain Amaranth

- ❖ It has a pleasant, nut-like flavor.
- ❖ Boil 1 cup (250 mL) of the whole grain in 2½ cups (625 mL) liquid (e.g., water, GF soup broth or fruit juice) until seeds are tender (about 20 minutes). For a hot cereal, cook in fruit juice or water and add chopped dried fruits and nuts.
- ❖ Can be mixed with beans for a main dish, added to rice and cooked together for a unique flavor or used to thicken soup or stew.
- ❖ The grain is mixed with tapioca flour to make cereal products and snack foods.

### Amaranth Flour*

- ❖ Best combined with other gluten-free flours to make pancakes, flat breads and other baked goods. To enhance the nutritional quality of recipes, replace ¼ to ⅓ of gluten-free flours with amaranth flour.

### Toasted Amaranth Bran Flour

- ❖ It has a mild, toasty nutty flavor and is very good in quick breads and cookies.
- ❖ Replacement quantities similar to amaranth flour (see above).

### Amaranth Pre-Gel Powder

- ❖ Can be used as a thickener for puddings, sauces and soups or as a protein supplement in cooking and beverages (e.g., smoothies).

### Puffed Amaranth

- ❖ Can be used as a cold or hot cereal; as a topping on salads and fruits; in baked goods (e.g., granola bars, cookies); as a breading for fish, chicken or meat; or combined with spices for a stuffing or side dish.

* For recipe see page 69.

### Nutritional Information

- ◆ Amaranth is high in protein, dietary fiber, iron, magnesium, phosphorus, potassium and zinc. It is also a source of calcium and B vitamins.

See page 166 for nutrient composition.

Excerpts taken from Nu-World Amaranth, Nu-World Foods publications.

# BUCKWHEAT

Buckwheat is botanically classified as a fruit (not a cereal grain) of the dicotyledonous plants, a member of the Polygonaceae family, which is closely related to rhubarb. It is triangular in shape and has a black shell. The kernel inside the shell is known as a groat. Groats (dehulled buckwheat kernels) are sold in several forms:

## Roasted Groats

❖ Roasting gives the buckwheat kernels a distinctive, nutty flavor.

❖ Groats are called "kasha" and are packaged in four granulations (whole, coarse, medium and fine).

❖ Can be steamed, boiled or baked and served "as is" with seasoning, or added to soups and stews for thickening and flavor, and used as a stuffing.

## Unroasted Groats*

**Whole** – cooked and used as a side dish

**Ground** – into grits and often labeled "cream of buckwheat" hot cereal

**Ground** – into flour

❖ Dark flour has a stronger, distinctive flavor as it contains a higher percentage of finely milled particles of buckwheat hulls and is higher in fiber and nutrients.

❖ Light flour has a mild, mellow flavor as it contains fewer buckwheat hulls.

  ◆ Use nuts and spices to enhance buckwheat flavor.

  ◆ Both flours are 100% buckwheat and can be added to pancakes and breads.

NOTE: Be aware that some companies mix buckwheat flour with wheat flour, so look for pure 100% buckwheat flour.

## Buckwheat Bran (Farinetta™)

❖ Is from the outer aleurone layer of the buckwheat groat and is high in protein, iron, riboflavin, niacin and numerous beneficial phytochemicals. Farinetta™ is licensed and trademarked by Minn-Dak Growers Ltd.

  ◆ Can be used in pancake and muffin recipes or added to chili or casseroles.

* For recipes see pages 75 and 82.

## Nutritional Information

❖ Buckwheat provides a very good source of high-quality protein in the plant kingdom. It is high in magnesium, phosphorus, potassium, pyridoxine (B6) and is also a source of dietary fiber, iron, niacin, thiamin and zinc.

See page 166 for nutrient composition.

Excerpts taken from The Birkett Mills and Minn-Dak Growers Ltd. publications

# FLAX

Flax seed is widely grown across the Canadian prairies and Northern USA and is harvested for a variety of purposes. Flax is a dicot in the Linaceae family.

## Storage and Handling

❖ Use flax seed whole, or grind it at home in a coffee grinder, food processor, or blender, to the consistency of finely-ground coffee. Grinding ensures that all seeds are broken up, thus providing the most nutritional benefit.

❖ Store whole flax seed at room temperature for up to a year.

❖ Store ground (milled) flax seed in a sealed opaque container in the refrigerator or freezer for up to 90 days. For optimum freshness, it is best to grind flax seed as you need it. (The natural fats in flax seed will go rancid quickly if left exposed to heat and air.)

## Using Flax Seed*

❖ Ground (milled) flax seed has a light nutty flavor and is good on cereal, in salads, as a dessert topping, in yogurt or added to muffins, cookies, breads, pancakes or waffles.

❖ Add ¼ cup (60 mL) ground (milled) flax seed to recipes containing rice bran. It will give a better texture and counters the heaviness of the bran.

❖ Baked goods with ground flax seed will brown more rapidly.

❖ Flax can be used as an egg replacer.

* For recipes see pages 65, 70, 74.

## Nutritional Information

Flax has been consumed throughout history for its nutritional and health benefits. Flax is rich in alpha-linolenic acid (an essential omega-3 fatty acid), dietary fiber (soluble and insoluble) and plant lignans. These components play a role in the maintenance and improvement of our general health. In fact, research indicates beneficial effects from including flax seed in the diet. Flax seed may help protect against coronary heart disease as well as breast and colon cancer. Flax seed may have a positive influence on a host of other concerns, including blood cholesterol levels and auto-immune diseases such as arthritis and lupus. It can promote bowel regularity. Flax is also high in Vitamin B6, folate, calcium, iron, magnesium, phosphorus, potassium, zinc, protein and dietary fiber.

See page 166 for nutrient composition.

Adapted from *Flax: Family Favorites* by the Flax Council of Canada and Saskatchewan Flax Development Commission.

# QUINOA

Quinoa ("keen-wa") is not a grain but is a broad leaf plant of the Chenopodiaceae family which is a close relative of the weed, lamb's quarters. It has been consumed for thousands of years in South America and now many varieties are grown in North America. The seed looks like a cross between sesame seed and millet. Quinoa seeds are naturally covered with saponin, an extremely bitter resin-like substance which protects it from birds and insects. To be edible the saponin must be removed. Northern Quinoa Corporation has developed a special process to remove this coating, making it pan-ready and fast cooking. Quinoa is sold in several forms:

## Quinoa Seed*

- ❖ Can be used in salads, casseroles, desserts, as well as a thickener for soups, chili and stews.
- ❖ Cooks very quickly (10-15 minutes).

## Quinoa Flakes

- ❖ Can be eaten as a hot breakfast cereal.

## Quinoa Flour*

- ❖ Can be used in baked products.
- ❖ Strong flavor so best combined with other GF flours.

## Quinoa Pasta

- ❖ Is combined with corn or rice and is available in a variety of shapes.
- ❖ Cooks in 5-9 minutes.

* For recipes see pages 72, 76, 77.

## Nutritional Information

Quinoa contains more high-quality protein than other grains and cereals. The quality of this protein compares very closely to that of dried skimmed milk. Quinoa is high in iron, magnesium, phosphorus, potassium and zinc. It is also a source of thiamin, riboflavin, niacin, calcium and dietary fiber.

See page 166 for nutrient composition.

Excerpts taken from Northern Quinoa Corporation publications.

# SORGHUM

Sorghum is a major cereal grain that grows in hot, semi-arid tropical and dry temperate areas of the world (e.g., USA, Mexico, Africa, India and China). It is similar in composition and processing properties to corn. New sorghum varieties have been developed in the USA. These sorghums have a hard white grain free of any bitter flavors or dark colors often associated with other sorghums. These characteristics make sorghum a good choice for the manufacture of a large range of food products such as cereals, snack foods, baked products and beer. Sorghum can be milled to produce flour, meal and grits.

## Flour*

- ❖ It can be substituted for rice flour or other gluten-free flour mixes in baked products.
- ❖ A combination of sorghum flour and other GF flours works well as sorghum's bland flavor and light color does not alter the taste of finished products.
- ❖ It is similar to other "non-gluten" containing cereals (i.e., tends to be dry and needs help to make baked products rise) therefore follow these helpful hints:
  - ◆ Add ½-1 tbsp. (7-15 mL) of cornstarch to every 1 cup (250 mL) of flour to improve smoothness and moisture retention.
  - ◆ Use xanthan gum as a binder and moisture retention agent (½ tsp. [2 mL] per 1 cup [250 mL] of flour for cookies and 1 tsp. [5 mL] per 1 cup [250 mL] of flour for breads.)
  - ◆ Add a little extra oil or shortening if recipes are too dry.
  - ◆ Add an extra egg or egg white for improved smoothness and crumb structure.
  - ◆ Add a little extra baking powder and/or soda to give an extra rising capability.

## Whole Grain

- ❖ Is used as an alternative for rice or barley in puddings, soups, etc.

* For recipes see pages 61, 66, 71, 73.

## Nutritional Information

Sorghum is high in phosphorus and potassium. It is also a source of dietary fiber, protein, thiamin, niacin, Vitamin B6 and iron.

See page 167 for nutrient composition.

Adapted from Twin Valley Mills (Ruskin, Nebraska) publications.

# TEFF

Teff or Tef, a grass native to Ethiopia, is a member of the Eragrostoideae family. It is the smallest of all grains in the world (about 100 teff grains are the size of 1 wheat kernel). This major cereal crop in Ethiopia is used to make "injera", a flat, thin porous bread. Teff is now grown in the USA and is available in brown or ivory seed varieties. It has a unique, mild molasses-like flavor and is sold as the whole grain and as teff flour.

## Whole-Grain

❖ Add ½ tsp.-1 tbsp. (7-15 mL) to 1 serving of a gluten-free hot cereal while cooking.

❖ Bring 2 cups (500 mL) of lightly salted water to a boil and then add ½ cup (125 mL) teff grain. Cover and simmer 15-20 minutes, or until water is absorbed, stirring occasionally. For a breakfast cereal, add honey, raisins, nuts, fruits and/or cinnamon to the cooked teff grain for flavor.

❖ Use as a thickener for soups, stews or gravies.

## Flour*

❖ Use in baked goods, pancakes and puddings.

* For recipe see page 62.

## Nutritional Information

Teff seeds are more nutritious than the major grains (e.g., wheat, barley, corn) for several reasons: the small seed size means:

❖ The germ and bran (the outer portions where nutrients are concentrated) account for a much larger volume of the seed compared to other grains.

❖ Teff is almost always produced as a whole-grain flour.

Teff is high in protein, calcium, magnesium and iron. It is also a source of thiamin, riboflavin, niacin and zinc.

See page 167 for nutrient composition.

# WILD RICE

Wild rice, an aquatic grass indigenous to North America, grows extensively in shallow lakes and streams. Despite its name, it is not a member of the rice family but from the Zizania family. Most wild rice grown in Northern Saskatchewan and Manitoba is "OCIA" certified organic. Wild rice has a distinct, nut-like, roasted flavor that is enjoyable by itself or combined with other ingredients. It is sold plain, mixed with other rices, as a flour and made into pasta.

## Handling and Preparation

❖ Wash wild rice in a wire strainer and run cold water over it.

❖ Use 4 cups (1 L) of water for every 1 cup (250 mL) of rice and cook approximately 40-60 minutes, until the rice kernels have burst their shells and fluffed out.

❖ The volume of rice increases up to 4 times, i.e., 1 cup (250 mL) raw rice = 4 cups (1 L) cooked rice.

❖ Cooked rice can be kept in the refrigerator for 1 week or frozen (it remains in excellent condition upon thawing). Cool rice before freezing. The precooked rice can be used in casseroles, salads or side dishes.

* For recipes see pages 77, 78, 81.

## Nutritional Information

Wild rice is a source of dietary fiber, protein, phosphorus, potassium and zinc.

See page 167 for nutrient composition.

Excerpts taken from Riese's Canadian Lake Wild Rice publication.

# GLUTEN-FREE RECIPES

# BANANA SEED BREAD

*The combination of sorghum and bean flour really enhances the banana flavor of this loaf. Serve it for dessert or with a slice of old Cheddar for lunch.*

| | |
|---|---|
| 1 cup | whole bean flour |
| 1 cup | sorghum flour |
| ¼ cup | tapioca starch |
| ¼ cup | packed brown sugar |
| 2½ tsp. | xanthan gum |
| 1 tbsp. | bread machine yeast OR instant yeast |
| 1¼ tsp. | salt |
| ½ cup | sunflower seeds* |
| ¾ cup | water |
| 1 cup | mashed banana |
| 1 tsp. | vinegar |
| ¼ cup | vegetable oil |
| 2 | eggs |

❖ In a large bowl or plastic bag, combine whole bean flour, sorghum flour, tapioca starch, brown sugar, xanthan gum, yeast, salt and sunflower seeds Mix well and set aside.

❖ Pour water, banana, vinegar and oil into the bread machine baking pan. Add eggs

❖ Select the Rapid 2-Hour Basic Cycle. Allow the liquids to mix until combined. Gradually add the dry ingredients as the bread machine is mixing. Scrape with a rubber spatula while adding the dry ingredients. Try to incorporate all the dry ingredients within 1 to 2 minutes. When mixing and kneading are complete, leaving the bread pan in the bread machine, remove the kneading blade. Allow the bread machine to complete the cycle.

\* Use raw, unroasted, unsalted sunflower seeds. For a nuttier flavor, toast the sunflower seeds.

**Variation:** Pumpkin seeds or chopped pecans can replace the sunflower seeds.

Recipe reprinted with permission from: ***125 Best Gluten-Free Recipes*** by **Donna Washburn** and **Heather Butt**, Robert Rose Inc. Publisher, 2003; www.bestbreadrecipes.com

# SORGHUM BREAD

*Bette Hagman, a.k.a. the "Gluten-Free Gourmet" is an expert in the area of gluten-free baking. She has been developing recipes combining the new food Sorghum varieties with other gluten-free flours.*

| | |
|---|---|
| 1 cup | sorghum flour |
| ⅔ cup | tapioca flour |
| ⅔ cup | cornstarch |
| 1½ tsp. | xanthan gum |
| ⅓ cup | dry milk powder OR nondairy substitute* |
| ½ tsp. | salt |
| 1 tsp. | unflavored gelatin |
| 1 tsp. | GF baking powder |
| 3 tbsp. | sugar |
| 2¼ tsp. | dry yeast granules |
| 2 | eggs |
| ½ tsp. | dough enhancer OR vinegar |
| 3 tbsp. | vegetable oil |
| 1 cup | lukewarm water (more or less) |

❖ Grease a 4½ x 8½" loaf pan and dust with rice flour.

❖ Combine the dry ingredients in a medium bowl.

❖ In the mixing bowl of a heavy-duty mixer, whisk together the eggs, dough enhancer and oil. Add most of the water, holding back about 3 tbsp. to add as needed. Turn the mixer to low and add the flour mixture a little at a time. The batter should be the consistency of cake batter. Add the remaining water a little at a time to achieve this texture. Turn the mixer to high and beat for 3½ minutes. Spoon the batter into the prepared pan, cover and let rise in a warm place; about 35 minutes for rapid rising yeast; 60 or so minutes for regular yeast, or until dough reaches the top of the pan.

❖ Bake for 50 to 55 minutes in a 400°F oven, covering after 10 minutes with aluminum foil.

❖ Turn out immediately to cool. For a softer crust rub immediately with butter or margarine. Cool before slicing.

* Bette wrote, "I used the adult drink powder Ensure as my nondairy substitute and it turned out very well. The extra flavor and vanilla in the powder made the best tasting bread."

This recipe was developed by **Bette Hagman** for **Twin Valley Mills,** and is used here with their permission. Twin Valley Mills, LLC., RR #1, Box 45, Ruskin, NE, USA 68974; Phone: 402-279-3965; www.twinvalleymills.com

# INJERA (ETHIOPIAN FLAT BREAD)

*This flat, thin porous bread is a traditional Ethiopian finger food. Injera is served with beef or chicken in a sauce or with vegetarian spicy lentils in a sauce.*

| | |
|---|---|
| 2 tbsp. | yeast (2 packages) |
| 6½ cups | warm water |
| 1½ lbs. | Teff flour |

- Dissolve yeast in ¼ cup water.
- Combine the teff flour, yeast and 6¼ cups water in a large bowl. Mix well. Ensure that no clumps are left at the bottom or side of the bowl.
- Cover the dough with plastic wrap and let it ferment for 2 to 3 days at room temperature. (Those with sensitive stomachs, consider making the Injera the same day rather than waiting for 2 to 3 days. It will have a slightly "sweet" taste but that is considered normal.)
- Drain off the water that has risen to the top of the dough.
- Gradually add fresh warm water to the dough, just enough to make a thin smooth batter (like pancake batter); mix well. Cover the batter and let it stand until it rises, approximately 10 to 25 minutes.
- Heat a 10" skillet or frying pan until a drop of water bounces on the pan's surface.
- Scoop about ⅓ cup of the batter and pour it into the pan quickly. Swirl the pan so that the entire bottom is evenly coated. Cover the pan quickly and let the injera cook for 1 to 2 minutes. (Injera does not easily stick or burn). Remove the cover and wait for a few seconds. It is cooked through when bubbles or "eyes" appear all over the top. If your first try is undercooked, cook the next one a little longer or use a smaller amount (¼ cup) of batter. Do not turn the injera over in the pan. Use a spatula to remove the cooked injera and place it on a clean towel.
- Let the injera cool and then stack them on a serving tray. Do not stack hot as they will stick together.
- Continue making the injera until the batter is finished.
- Injera should be soft and pliable so that it can be rolled or folded like a crêpe or tortilla. Properly cooked, injera will be thinner than a pancake but thicker than a crêpe.

Recipe courtesy of **Girma and Ethiopia Sahlu**, Regina, SK, Canada

# PIZZA CRUST

*This unique flour mixture produces a super pizza crust. Top the crust with a zesty tomato sauce, grated mozzarella and your favorite toppings for a great lunch, dinner or snack.*

| | |
|---|---|
| 1 tbsp. | dry yeast |
| 2/3 cup | Garfava flour* |
| 1/2 cup | tapioca flour |
| 2 tbsp. | dry milk or nondairy milk powder |
| 2 tsp. | xanthan gum |
| 1/2 tsp. | salt |
| 1/2 tsp. | sugar |
| 1 tsp. | gelatin powder |
| 1 tsp. | GF Italian seasoning |
| 2/3 cup | warm water |
| 1 tsp. | olive oil |
| 1 tsp. | cider vinegar** |

❖ Preheat oven to 425°F.

❖ Using an electric mixer on high, beat all the ingredients together in a bowl for 3 minutes.

❖ Turn dough onto a 12" non-stick pan lightly greased with olive oil. Dust dough liberally with rice flour and pat with hands to edges of pan.

❖ Bake for 10 to 15 minutes.

❖ Remove pizza crust from oven; top with toppings and bake another 15–20 minutes, or until browned.

*Garfava flour is a combination of garbanzo beans and fava beans. It was developed by Authentic Foods.

**AUTHOR NOTE: Distilled white vinegar is also gluten-free and can be substituted for cider vinegar.

Reprinted with permission from:

*Special Diet Solutions* by **Carol Fenster, Savory Palate, Inc.**, www.savorypalate.com

and

**Authentic Foods**, 1850 W. 169th St., Suite B, Gardena, CA, USA 90247; Phone 310-366-7612; www.authenticfoods.com

# COTTAGE CHEESE BREAD

*Cottage cheese enhances the texture of this versatile and easy quick bread.*

| | |
|---|---|
| ⅓ cup | **butter OR margarine** |
| ¼ cup | **brown sugar** |
| 3 | **eggs** |
| 1 cup | **cottage cheese OR ⅔ cup buttermilk** |
| 2 cups | **brown rice flour OR 1⅔ cups white rice flour and ⅓ cup rice bran** |
| 1 tsp. | **baking soda** |
| 2 tsp. | **GF baking powder** |

- ❖ Preheat the oven to 350°F.
- ❖ Line the bottoms of 3, 3½ x 5¾" bread pans with waxed paper and grease the sides.
- ❖ With a mixer, beat together, butter and sugar.
- ❖ Add eggs one at a time, beating after each addition.
- ❖ Beat in cottage cheese or buttermilk.
- ❖ Mix flour, baking powder and soda, then add to the egg mixture.
- ❖ BEAT WELL. Add extra milk or water if the batter is too stiff.
- ❖ Pour the batter into the pans.
- ❖ Bake for 40-45 minutes, until the bread tests dry with a toothpick.

Yield: 3 loaves

Recipe printed with permission of **Beryl Forgay**, Regina, SK, Canada from ***Baking Without Gluten***, Second Edition

# RAISIN OR BLUEBERRY CORNMEAL MUFFINS

*The tang of buttermilk and the texture of cornmeal add interest to these versatile muffins. Check out the variation options and create your own favorites.*

| | |
|---|---|
| 2 cups | gluten-free flour mix (your favorite or see page 60) |
| 1⅓ cups | cornmeal |
| ¾ cup | sugar |
| 1 tbsp. | GF baking powder |
| ¾ tsp. | baking soda |
| ½ tsp. | salt |
| 2 | eggs |
| ⅔ cup | canola oil |
| 1 tsp. | vanilla |
| 1 tbsp. | milled flaxseed (optional) |
| 1⅓ cups | buttermilk |
| 1 cup | raisins OR frozen blueberries (see variations below)* |

- ❖ Preheat oven to 350°F.
- ❖ Combine dry ingredients in a deep bowl.
- ❖ In a separate bowl, beat eggs; add oil, buttermilk and vanilla.
- ❖ Make a well in the dry mixture, stir in the egg mixture and beat well. Fold in the fruit.
- ❖ This will be a very thin batter, unlike gluten-containing muffin batter.
- ❖ Line muffin cups with paper liners and fill cups ⅔ full with batter.
- ❖ Bake for 15-20 minutes.

Makes about 18 medium muffins.

**Variations:** Instead of raisins or blueberries, substitute GF chocolate chips, sunflower seeds, sliced hazelnuts, dried cranberries, sesame seeds, coconut (1 cup) or a combination of any or all these.

Recipe courtesy of **Enid Young**, Regina, SK, Canada

# BLUEBERRY SORGHUM MUFFINS

*Sorghum flour, cornstarch and soy flour make an interesting gluten-free combination for these muffins ...*

| | |
|---|---|
| 1½ cups | sorghum/cornstarch mix (3 cups sorghum flour to 1 cup cornstarch) |
| ¼ cup | soy flour |
| ¼ cup | sugar |
| 2½ tsp. | GF baking powder |
| ¾ tsp. | salt |
| 1 tsp. | xanthan gum |
| 2 | eggs |
| 1 cup | milk OR soy milk |
| ⅓ cup | vegetable oil |
| 1 tsp. | vanilla extract |
| 1 cup | blueberries (rinsed and drained) |

❖ Preheat oven to 350°F.

❖ Put the dry ingredients in a bowl and whisk together.

❖ Beat eggs lightly, add milk, oil and vanilla; beat until well mixed.

❖ Add wet ingredients to dry ingredients and beat until smooth. You can beat as long as needed, dough will not get "tough" like muffins made with wheat flour.

❖ Add blueberries and fold in gently.

❖ Fill muffin cups (use paper liners) ⅔ full.

❖ Bake for 19 minutes, or until a toothpick comes out clean.

Makes about 12 medium muffins.

Recipe courtesy of **Amy Perry** and **Meredith Wiking** of **Nebraska Grain Sorghum Board,** 301 Centennial Mall South, P.O. Box 94982, Lincoln, NE, USA 68509; Phone: 402-471-4276; Fax: 402-471-3040; E-mail: sorghum@nrcdec.nrc.state.ne.us

# MIGHTY TASTY MUFFINS

*The special flours and cereals used in these muffins complement
the brown sugar and spice mixtures.*

| | |
|---|---|
| 2 tbsp. | Bob's Red Mill™ Mighty Tasty GF Hot Cereal (brown rice, corn, "sweet" white sorghum, buckwheat) |
| ⅔ cup | milk |
| 1 tbsp. | apple cider vinegar* |
| 1 | large egg |
| ⅓ cup | molasses |
| 1 tsp. | vanilla |
| ¾ cup | Bob's Red Mill™ GF Garbanzo and Fava flour |
| ½ cup | potato starch |
| ¼ cup | tapioca flour |
| ⅓ cup | brown sugar, packed |
| 1 tsp. | GF baking powder |
| ½ tsp. | baking soda |
| 1 tsp. | xanthan gum |
| ¼ tsp. | nutmeg |
| ½ tsp. | cinnamon |
| ¼ tsp. | ground ginger |
| ¼ tsp. | allspice |
| ½ tsp. | salt |

❖ Preheat oven to 350°F.
❖ In a large bowl, combine the first 6 ingredients. Let sit for 15 minutes, while the cereal softens.
❖ In a separate bowl, combine the remaining ingredients.
❖ Add the dry ingredients to the liquid ingredients and stir until just moistened.
❖ Spoon the batter into greased muffin tins. Fill tins ⅔ full.
❖ Bake for approximately 20 minutes, or until the tops of the muffins are firm.

Yields: 12 muffins.

* **AUTHOR NOTE:** Distilled white vinegar is also gluten-free and can be substituted for apple cider vinegar.

Recipe used with permission from **Bob's Red Mill Natural Foods, Inc.**, 5209 S.E. International Way, Milwaukie, OR, USA 97222; www.bobsredmill.com

Recipe adapted from *Special Diet Solutions* by **Carol Fenster, PhD, Savory Palate, Inc.** www.savorypalate.com

# CARROT PUMPKIN MUFFINS

*This recipe is moist and delicious. Using applesauce, pineapple and pumpkin reduces the fat and sugar content as compared to traditional carrot muffins or cake.*

| | |
|---|---|
| 1¾ cups | sugar |
| 3 | egg whites |
| 1 | whole egg |
| ½ cup | vegetable oil |
| 1 cup | unsweetened applesauce |
| 1 cup | puréed pumpkin |
| 1 tbsp. | vanilla |
| 1⅓ cups | cooked puréed carrots OR ¾ cup crushed pineapple |
| 3 cups | flour mix (rice – 3 parts, potato starch – 1½ parts, tapioca starch – 1 part) |
| 1 tsp. | salt |
| 1 tbsp. | baking soda |
| 2 tsp. | GF baking powder |
| 2 tsp. | xanthan gum |
| 1 tbsp. | ground cinnamon |

❖ Combine sugar, eggs and oil, cream until light and fluffy. Add applesauce, pumpkin, vanilla, carrots and pineapple.

❖ Sift dry ingredients together and slowly fold into batter. Spoon batter into paper-lined muffin pans, fill ⅔ full, or into cake pans. Bake at 350°F for 15-20 minutes (muffins) or 25-40 minutes for cake, depending on the size of the cake pans.

❖ Cool for 10 minutes. Remove cake from the pan and peel off the paper.

Makes 24-30 muffins or one, 9 x 13" or two, 9" round cakes.

NOTE: Use muffin liners instead of greasing pans (also helps maintain moisture for storing muffins). Use parchment paper (available from kitchen stores and some grocery stores) as the lining on the bottom of cake pans to avoid greasing pans (remove as much fat as possible).

NOTE: Ideally, make muffins and freeze them, that way you never feel you have to eat the whole cake or it will go bad!

VARIATION: To make just carrot cake, eliminate the pumpkin and use all applesauce (total of 2 cups applesauce).

Recipe courtesy of **Laurel Hutton, Laurel's Sweet Treats, Inc.,** 16004 SW Tualatin – Sherwood Road, #123, Sherwood, OR, USA 97140; www.glutenfreemixes.com

# AMARANTH GRAIN-FREE GRANOLA

*Eat this chunky granola out of hand as a snack, top it with fruit juice or milk for a quick healthy breakfast or sprinkle it over yogurt or ice cream for dessert.*

| | |
|---|---|
| 1½ cups | amaranth flour |
| 1 cup | chopped walnuts OR other nuts |
| ½ cup | potato starch |
| ½ cup | peanuts |
| ½ cup | sunflower OR sesame seeds |
| ½ cup | unsweetened coconut |
| 1½ tsp. | cinnamon |
| ¾ cup | mashed bananas or puréed fruit |
| ¼ cup | maple syrup or honey |
| 1 tbsp. | lemon juice |
| ¼ cup | vegetable oil |
| 1½ tsp. | pure vanilla extract |
| ⅔ cup | raisins |

❖ Preheat oven to 300°F.

❖ Combine the flour, walnuts or other nuts, potato starch, peanuts, sunflower seeds or sesame seeds, coconut and cinnamon in a large bowl.

❖ Mix the bananas or fruit purée, maple syrup or honey, lemon juice, oil and vanilla in a small bowl. If honey is very thick, heat mixture briefly to liquefy.

❖ Pour the liquid mixture over the dry mixture. Stir well to coat dry ingredients. If mixture seems too dry, add a few tablespoons of water.

❖ Spread the granola on a lightly oiled jelly-roll pan. Bake for 45 to 60 minutes, stirring every 15 minutes. Remove the granola from the oven and let it cool. Add raisins.

Makes about 7–8 cups.

Recipe courtesy **Nu-World Amaranth, Nu-World Foods**, PO Box 2202, Naperville IL, USA 60567; Phone: 630-369-6819; www.nuworldfoods.com

# CRUNCHY GRANOLA

*This delicious, high-fiber granola is loaded with nutrients. Great for breakfast, as a
snack, or it can be used to make granola bars or as a topping for yogurt,
ice cream or frozen yogurt or a fruit crisp (apple, blueberry, peach).
Various substitutions can be used for nuts and dried fruits.*

| | |
|---|---|
| ½ cup | shredded coconut |
| ½ cup | sunflower seeds |
| ¼ cup | sesame seeds |
| 1 cup | chopped nuts |
| ½ cup | chopped dates |
| ½ cup | chopped dried apricots |
| ½ cup | raisins |
| | hot water |
| 4 cups | GF corn flakes |
| 3 cups | GF crisp rice cereal |
| 3 tbsp. | flax seed meal |
| ¼ cup | oil |
| ½ cup | honey |
| 1 tbsp. | apple juice |
| 1 tsp. | vanilla |
| ½ tsp. | nutmeg |
| ½ tsp. | cinnamon |

❖ Preheat oven to 300°F.

❖ Toast coconut, sunflower and sesame seeds and nuts in a shallow pan under the broiler for a few minutes (watch carefully to prevent burning). Remove from the oven, stir and return to the oven to finish toasting. Remove from oven and cool.

❖ Soak dried fruit in hot water to clean and soften for 10 minutes. Drain. Chop the fruit into bite-sized pieces.

❖ Mix cereals, flax, coconut, nuts and seeds.

❖ Mix oil, honey, juice, vanilla, nutmeg and cinnamon together.

❖ Place the cereal/nut mixture in a large roasting or broiler pan; pour the liquid ingredients over and mix well.

❖ Bake for 1 hour, stirring every 10-15 minutes. Add the dried fruits and return to the oven for last 15 minutes.

❖ Remove the granola from the oven and let it cool. Stir a few times as it cools.

❖ Store in an air-tight container in a cool place (refrigerator or freezer).

Recipe courtesy of **Laurel Hutton, Laurel's Sweet Treats, Inc.**, 16004 SW Tualatin – Sherwood Road, #123, Sherwood, OR, USA 97140; www.glutenfreemixes.com

# SORGHUM PEANUT BUTTER COOKIES

*Peanut butter and brown sugar are a dynamite flavor combo and sorghum and garbanzo flours add interesting texture to a favorite cookie recipe.*

| | |
|---|---|
| 1½ cups | creamy peanut butter |
| 1 cup | shortening OR margarine |
| 2⅓ cups | firmly packed brown sugar |
| 6 tbsp. | milk |
| 2 tsp. | vanilla |
| 2 | eggs |
| 3 cups | sorghum flour |
| ½ cup | garbanzo (chickpea) flour |
| ½ cup | sweet rice flour |
| 4 tsp. | xanthan gum |
| 1 tsp. | salt |
| 1½ tsp. | baking soda |

❖ Preheat oven to 375°F.

❖ Combine peanut butter, shortening, brown sugar, milk and vanilla in a large bowl. With an electric mixer, beat on medium speed until well blended.

❖ Add eggs. Beat just until blended.

❖ Combine flours, salt and baking soda. Add to creamed mixture at low speed. Mix just until blended.

❖ Using a mini ice cream scoop, drop dough portions 2" apart on baking sheets lined with parchment paper. Flatten slightly in a crisscross pattern with the tines of a fork.

❖ Bake for 8-10 minutes, or until set and just beginning to brown. Cool for 2 minutes on the baking sheets. Remove cookies from pan and cool completely.

Makes about 6 dozen cookies.

Recipe courtesy of **Barbara Klimet, Executive Director** of **Nebraska Grain Sorghum Board,** 301 Centennial Mall South, P.O. Box 94982, Lincoln, NE, USA 68509; Phone: 402-471-4276; Fax: 402-471-3040; E-mail: sorghum@nrcdec.nrc.state.ne.us

# Rum and Quinoa Crunch Cookies

*Quinoa has more high-quality protein than any other grain.*
*These crisp cookies can be flavored to suit your taste.*

| | |
|---|---|
| ¾ cup | **butter or margarine** |
| 1 cup | **sugar** |
| 2 | **eggs, beaten** |
| 2 tsp. | **rum extract** |
| 2 cups | **NorQuin quinoa flour** |
| ¼ cup | **white rice flour** |
| 1½ tsp. | **baking powder** |
| ⅓ cup | **toasted quinoa grain** |

- ❖ Preheat oven to 350°F.
- ❖ Cream butter; add sugar and cream together thoroughly.
- ❖ Add beaten eggs and rum extract.
- ❖ Mix dry ingredients together and add to wet ingredients.
- ❖ Chill the dough.
- ❖ Roll out a small amount of dough at a time on a lightly floured surface (use rice flour). Cut dough into desired shapes and place on greased cookie sheets OR shape into balls or drop by teaspoonfuls onto cookie sheet. Flatten with floured glass to ¼" thickness.
- ❖ Bake for 10-15 minutes.

Makes about 50 cookies (using 1 tsp. dough/cookie).

**Variation:** 2 tsp. lemon extract or 2 tsp. almond extract may be substituted for the rum extract.

This cookie recipe is courtesy of:

**El Peto**, El Peto Products Ltd., 41 Shoemaker St, Kitchener, ON, Canada N2E 3G9; Phone 519-748-5211; www.elpeto.com

and

**Northern Quinoa Corporation**, Box 519, Kamsack, SK, Canada S0A 1S0; Phone 866-368-9304 or 306-542-3949; www.quinoa.com

# BREADING MIX

*Use this well-seasoned coating for panfrying or baking chicken pieces,*
*pork chops or fish.*

| | |
|---|---|
| 2 cups | sorghum flour |
| 6 tbsp. | cornstarch |
| 1 tsp. | garlic powder |
| 1 tsp. | onion powder |
| 1 tsp. | black pepper |
| 4 tsp. | GF seasoning salt |
| ½ tsp. | GF celery salt |

❖ Mix all the ingredients together.

❖ To use, spoon out the amount needed to coat meat for frying.

❖ Meat or fish may be dipped in a mixture of milk and beaten egg before dredging for a thicker, crispier coating.

❖ Store any unused mix in an airtight container in a cool, dry place. It may also be frozen.

Makes about 2⅓ cups of mix.

This recipe courtesy of **Barbara Klimet**, Executive Director, **Nebraska Grain Sorghum Board,** 301 Centennial Mall South, P.O. Box 94982, Lincoln, NE, USA 68509; Phone: 402-471-4276; Fax: 402-471-3040; E-mail: sorghum@nrcdec.nrc.state.ne.us

# OVEN-FRIED CHICKEN

*Ground flax seed and GF crackers or corn flakes are used to add crunch to this crispy chicken dish.*

| | |
|---|---|
| 1 | egg, beaten |
| 3 tbsp. | skim milk |
| ½ cup | ground flax seed (flax seed meal) |
| ½ cup | GF crackers or GF corn flakes (finely crushed) |
| ¼ tsp. | pure black pepper |
| 1 tbsp. | dried parsley flakes |
| 1 tsp. | chili powder |
| 1 tsp. | garlic powder |
| 1 tsp. | salt |
| 2-3 lbs. | chicken pieces |
| 2 tbsp. | melted butter* |

❖ Preheat oven to 350°F.

❖ In a small bowl, combine egg and milk.

❖ In a shallow container, combine ground flax, GF cracker or corn flake crumbs, pepper, parsley, chili, garlic and salt.

❖ Skin the chicken and rinse with warm water. Pat dry.

❖ Dip chicken pieces into egg mixture; coat with the crumb mixture.

❖ Place chicken on a greased ¾ x 10 x 15" baking pan so pieces do not touch.

❖ Drizzle chicken pieces with melted butter.

❖ Bake for 45 minutes, or until chicken is tender and no longer pink. Do not turn chicken pieces while baking.

Makes 6 servings.

* For a lower-fat version, omit the butter.

Adapted from:

*Flax: Family Favorites – Recipes and Healthful Tips* by **The Flax Council of Canada**, 465 – 167 Lombard Ave., Winnipeg, MB, Canada  R3B 0T6; Phone 204-982-2115;  www.flaxcouncil.ca

and

**Saskatchewan Flax Development Commission**, A5A - 116 - 103rd St. E., Saskatoon, SK, Canada  S7N 1Y7; Phone: 306-664-1901; E-mail: saskflax@saskflax.com

# TURKEY MEATBALLS
# WITH LEMON SAUCE

*Kasha, roasted buckwheat groats, adds a distinctive
nutty flavor to these tasty meatballs.*

| | |
|---|---|
| 1 cup | cooked kasha (any granulation) |
| 1 | egg, beaten |
| 1 tsp. | grated lemon peel |
| 1½ lbs. | ground raw turkey |
| 2 tbsp. | cooking oil |
| 1 cup | GF chicken or turkey broth |
| ¼ cup | plain yogurt |
| 1 tbsp. | cornstarch |
| 1 tbsp. | lemon juice |
| 1 | small carrot, finely shredded |
| 1 | green onion, diced |

❖ Prepare kasha according to package directions, using chicken broth (gluten-free).

❖ Combine the kasha and the next 3 ingredients in mixing bowl; blend well.

❖ Shape the mixture into 12 balls.

❖ In a large skillet, heat the oil and brown the turkey balls on all sides. Add the broth, cover and simmer for 20 minutes. Use a slotted spoon to transfer the turkey to a serving dish.

❖ In a small bowl, combine the yogurt, cornstarch and lemon juice.

❖ In the skillet, combine the yogurt mixture with the pan juices and cook until the sauce is thickened and bubbly. Add the carrot and onion. Cook for a few minutes and pour the sauce over the turkey.

Serves 4 to 5 as an hors d'oeuvre or 2 to 3 as a main course.

**AUTHOR NOTE:** Original recipe had 1 tsp. Worcestershire sauce, however, many brands of Worcestershire sauce contain malt vinegar (gluten) and/or soy sauce (often contains wheat).

Recipe adapted with permission from **"The Birkett Mills"**, P.O. Box 440 A, Penn Yan, NY, USA 14527; www.thebirkettmills.com

# QUINOA SALAD

*The delicate flavor of quinoa is similar to couscous.*
*It can be used as a pasta substitute in cold pasta salads.*

**Lemon Garlic Dressing:**

| | |
|---|---|
| 4 | garlic cloves, minced |
| ¼ cup | red wine vinegar |
| ¼ cup | canola oil |
| ¼ cup | water |
| 1 | lemon, juiced |
| | salt and pepper to taste |

| | |
|---|---|
| 4 cups | NorQuin quinoa, cooked |
| 1 cup | grated carrots |
| ½ cup | sliced green onions |
| ½ cup | chopped celery |
| ¼ cup | sunflower seeds |
| ¼ cup | slivered almonds |
| 3 tbsp. | sesame seeds |
| ½ cup | sliced mushrooms |

❖ Combine dressing ingredients and let stand for at least 10 minutes.

❖ Prepare salad ingredients and combine.

❖ Toss salad with dressing and serve.

Makes 6 servings (1 cup each).

Recipe courtesy of **Northern Quinoa Corporation**, Box 519, Kamsack, SK, Canada S0A 1S0; Phone 866-368-9304 or 306-542-3949; www.quinoa.com

# QUINOA AND WILD RICE PILAF

*This rich combination of flavors is very satisfying.*

| 1 cup | wild rice |
|---|---|
| 1 cup | quinoa seed |
| ⅓ cup | chopped GF bacon |
| 1 tbsp. | margarine or oil |
| ½ cup | celery |
| 1 | onion, chopped |
| 1 cup | sliced mushrooms |

❖ Wash wild rice in a wire strainer and run cold water over it.

❖ In a large heavy saucepan, cook wild rice in 4 cups of boiling water, covered. Bring to a boil, cover and simmer over low heat for about 1 hour, until all the water has been absorbed.

❖ During the last 15 minutes, add Quinoa and, if rice is almost dry, 1 additional cup of boiling water.

❖ While the rice is cooking, fry the bacon in a pan. When crisp, remove and drain.

❖ Melt margarine in a skillet and add celery, onion and mushrooms; sauté for about 5 minutes.

❖ Combine vegetables and bacon with the rice and Quinoa mixture in a casserole.

❖ Microwave on high for 10 minutes or bake at 350°F for ½ hour.

Makes 6 ½ cups of pilaf.

Recipe courtesy of **Northern Quinoa Corporation**, Box 519, Kamsack, SK, Canada S0A 1S0; Phone 866-368-9304 or 306-542-3949; www.quinoa.com

# WILD RICE & VEGETABLE CASSEROLE

*Creamy wild rice has a nutty flavor that is wonderful with the robust flavor of broccoli and also with the more delicate flavors of cauliflower and asparagus.*

| | |
|---|---|
| ½ cup | **wild rice (2 cups cooked)** |
| | **pepper and sage to taste** |
| 10 oz. | **can cream soup (gluten-free)** |
| 1 bunch | **broccoli, cauliflower OR asparagus** |
| 1 cup | **grated Cheddar cheese** |

- ❖ Wash wild rice in a wire strainer and run cold water over it.
- ❖ Combine 2 cups of water and ½ cup of wild rice in a heavy saucepan. Bring to a boil, cover and simmer over low heat for approximately 45 minutes, until the rice kernels have burst their shells and fluffed out. Drain off excess water. Stir the rice with fork; cover and let stand for 15 minutes.
- ❖ Preheat oven to at 350°F.
- ❖ Put cooked rice, seasoned with a little pepper and sage, into a greased casserole.
- ❖ Cover with undiluted cream soup.
- ❖ Steam vegetables for 5 minutes then place over soup.
- ❖ Sprinkle with cheese.
- ❖ Bake for about 20 minutes.

Makes 8 servings.

Recipe courtesy of **Riese's Canadian Lake Wild Rice**, La Ronge, SK, Canada S0J 1L0; Phone: 306-425-2314

# LENTIL LEAF ROLLS

*These rice and lentil-filled "cabbage rolls" are beautifully flavored with dill.*

| | |
|---|---|
| ¾ cup | short-grain rice |
| ¾ cup | water |
| ½ tsp. | salt |
| 1 tbsp. | canola oil |
| ½ cup | finely chopped onion |
| 2 tbsp. | chopped fresh dill |
| 1 tsp. | salt |
| ⅛ tsp. | pepper |
| 1½ cups | lentils, cooked |
| 30 | lettuce, Swiss chard, beet, spinach or cabbage leaves |
| 1 | gluten-free vegetable bouillon cube |
| ½ cup | boiling water |
| ½ cup | cream milk, 10% mf |

❖ Preheat oven to 325°F.

❖ Combine rice, water and salt in a small saucepan. Bring to boil, stir once, and reduce heat to simmer. Cover, cook 12 minutes until water is absorbed.

❖ In a small skillet, over medium heat, heat oil and sauté onions for 4 minutes, until they start to turn brown.

❖ Combine onions with dill, salt, pepper, lentils and rice.

❖ Prepare leaves by washing them and cutting larger leaves into smaller pieces (approximately 3 to 4" squares).

❖ Blanch leaves by putting them into a large bowl; pour boiling water over leaves;blanch for 30 seconds*.

❖ Drain leaves, rinse in cold water and drain again.

❖ At the base of each leaf, put 1½ tbsp. rice and lentil filling.

❖ Roll up leaves while tucking in sides.

❖ Place the rolls, seam down, in a lightly oiled 2-quart casserole.

❖ Dissolve bouillon cube in boiling water. Pour over rolls.

❖ Pour cream milk over rolls.

❖ Cover with a few remaining leaves.

❖ Cover with a lid or foil. Bake for 1½ hours.

❖ Check rolls after 1 hour. If they need more liquid, add a little cream milk.

Makes 10 servings.

* Cabbage leaves may need to be steamed longer to make them more pliable.

Adapted from *Wraps & Rolls*, May 1998, **Saskatchewan Pulse Growers**, www.saskpulse.com

# LENTIL PIZZA SQUARES

*Serve these Pizza Squares with a green salad for a casual main course or as a substantial snack.*

| | |
|---|---|
| ¼ cup | canola oil |
| ¾ cup | chopped onion |
| 1 cup | sliced mushrooms |
| 1 | garlic clove, minced |
| 4 | eggs |
| 1½ cups | lentil purée*, cooled |
| 1½ cups | low-fat sour cream** |
| 7½ oz. | can tomato sauce** |
| ¾ cup | cornmeal |
| 1 tsp. | crumbled dried basil |
| 1 tsp. | crumbled dried oregano |
| ½ tsp. | salt |
| 1½ cups | grated low-fat Cheddar cheese |
| 1½ cups | grated low-fat mozzarella cheese |
| ½ cup | sliced pepperoni or salami** |
| ½ cup | diced sweet green pepper |

❖ Preheat oven to 350°F.

❖ In a skillet, heat oil and add onion, mushrooms and garlic. Sauté until onion is translucent. Remove from heat and let cool.

❖ In a large mixing bowl, beat eggs. Blend in lentil purée, sour cream, tomato sauce, cornmeal, basil, oregano, salt and the mushroom mixture. Stir in cheeses.

❖ Turn into a 9 x 13" baking dish sprayed with non-stick vegetable spray.

❖ Garnish with pepperoni or salami and green peppers.

❖ Bake for 40-45 minutes, or until firm to touch. Let stand 10 minutes before cutting.

Cut into 12 squares. Makes 8 to 12 servings.

### *Lentil Purée:

| | |
|---|---|
| ¾ cup | lentils |
| 2 cups | water |

❖ To prepare Lentil Purée, rinse lentils and drain.

❖ Cover with water and bring to a boil. Reduce heat and simmer for 45 to 50 minutes.

❖ Drain off any excess liquid and mash with a potato masher.

** Gluten-free brand required.

Adapted from:
   ***Discover the Pulse Potential*** (1994), **Saskatchewan Pulse Growers**
Available from:
   **Food Focus**, A5A – 116 – 103rd St. E., Saskatoon, SK, Canada  S7N 1Y7;
   Phone 306-652-2691;  www.saskpulse.com

# WILD RICE FRUIT DESSERT

*This version of the ever popular "Ambrosia" has the added texture of wild rice.*
*The whole family will love this one.*

| | |
|---|---|
| 1 cup | **wild rice (4 cups cooked)** |
| 14 oz. | **can pineapple chunks, drained** |
| 10 oz. | **can mandarin oranges, drained** |
| 14 oz. | **can fruit cocktail, drained** |
| ½ cup | **chopped walnuts** |
| 3 cups | **miniature marshmallows** |
| 3 oz. | **cherry jelly powder** |
| 1 cup | **whipping cream** |

❖ Wash wild rice in a wire strainer and run cold water over it.

❖ Combine 4 cups of water and 1 cup of wild rice in a large heavy saucepan. Bring to a boil; cover and simmer over low heat for approximately 45 minutes, until the rice kernels have burst their shells and fluffed out. Drain off any excess water. Stir with a fork; cover and let stand for 15 minutes.

❖ Put wild rice in a large bowl and cool

❖ Drain juice from canned fruits.

❖ Add fruit, rice, nuts and marshmallows to cooled, wild rice.

❖ Mix in dry jelly powder.

❖ Whip cream until stiff and fold into fruit mixture.

❖ Refrigerate at least 1 hour.

❖ Decorate with fresh fruit.

Makes about 10 to 12 servings.

Recipe courtesy of **Riese's Canadian Lake Wild Rice**, La Ronge, SK, Canada  S0J 1L0; Phone: 306-425-2314

# CREAMY "I CAN'T BELIEVE IT'S NOT RICE!" PUDDING

*A traditional dessert favorite, this "rice pudding" version uses buckwheat groats instead of rice. Serve warm or cold, garnished with whipped cream and chopped nuts and/or fresh fruit. A splash of maple syrup is also a delicious option.*

| | |
|---|---|
| 4 cups | water |
| ¼ tsp. | salt |
| 2 tbsp. | butter OR margarine (optional) |
| 2 cups | whole white buckwheat groats (Wolff's or Pocono) |
| 2 | eggs |
| 1 cup | milk |
| ⅓ cup | honey (preferably clover or other mild honey) |
| 1 tsp. | vanilla extract |
| ½ tsp. | ground cinnamon |
| ½ tsp. | grated lemon peel |
| dash | fresh nutmeg |
| 1 tbsp. | dark rum (optional) |
| 1 cup | grated apple, cored but not peeled |
| ¼ cup | raisins |
| ½ cup | sour cream |
| | whipped cream and chopped nuts or fresh fruit, for garnish |

- ❖ In a medium saucepan heat water, salt and butter. Quickly stir in buckwheat groats. Reduce heat to low and cover pan tightly. Simmer for 15 minutes, until groats are tender and the liquid is absorbed.
- ❖ Beat together the eggs, milk and honey until well-blended. Add the vanilla, cinnamon, lemon peel, nutmeg and rum.
- ❖ In a large bowl, combine groats, apple, raisins and milk/egg mixture.
- ❖ Spread the pudding evenly in a buttered 8" square pan.
- ❖ Bake at 350°F for 25-30 minutes, stirring every 5 minutes.
- ❖ Remove the pudding from the oven. Let it cool for 15 minutes, then stir in the sour cream.

Yield: 4-6 servings

Recipe used with permission for **"The Birkett Mills"**, Box 440A, Penn Yan, NY, USA 14527; www.thebirkettmills.com

# GLUTEN-FREE SHOPPING

In the beginning be prepared to spend a lot more time in the stores shopping for gluten-free foods. You need to read every label and begin to learn which ingredients are gluten-free and which contain gluten. Excellent resources to take with you are:

*Canadian Celiac Association (CCA) Pocket Dictionary: Acceptability of Foods and Ingredients for the Gluten-Free Diet*

This pocket-sized book provides a brief description of each item along with an assessment of its acceptability for the gluten-free diet.

*CCA Eat Well Be Well: A Guide to Gluten-Free Manufacturer's Products*

This pocket-sized book includes many regular commercial products in Canada which are gluten-free.

*Clan Thompson Pocket Guide to Gluten-Free Foods*

This pocket-sized book includes many foods from major brands found in the USA that are gluten-free.

**To order these resources see pages 157, 158, 163.**

To order these resources see pages 157, 158, 163.

## CAUTION

Manufacturers often change ingredients in their products. Always check ingredient labels for changes and the inclusion of suspect ingredients. If in doubt, phone the manufacturers. Be very explicit in your request for information:

❖ Is there any wheat, rye, triticale, spelt, kamut, barley or oats or their derivatives in the product?

❖ Are the components of a particular ingredient also free of the offending grains?
  e.g., baking powder (may contain wheat starch)
  e.g., seasonings and flavorings (may contain wheat or barley malt extract)
  e.g., starches, modified starches, hydrolyzed plant or vegetable protein (HPP or HVP) made from wheat or wheat starch.

## HELPFUL HINTS

Set up files in a 3-ring binder to organize all the product information you collect. Divide it into two sections:

- Regular Supermarket Foods
- Foods from Gluten-Free Companies

Take notes, including the date, when you call the manufacturers. Keep product lists from gluten-free companies and indicate whether or not you liked the product.

# GLUTEN-FREE SHOPPING LIST
The following is a sample list to get you started on your gluten-free diet.

**BREAD PRODUCTS**
- ☑ GF bread, bagels, buns, pizza crusts
- ☐ GF freezer waffles
- ☐ GF muffins

**CEREALS**
- ☐ Amaranth, buckwheat, corn, millet, quinoa, rice
- ☐ GF corn flakes, GF crisp rice
- ☐ Cream of buckwheat or rice (brown or white)

**PASTA**
- ☑ Corn; legume; potato; quinoa; rice

**CRACKERS/RICE CAKES**
- ☑ GF rice crisp/crunch crackers
- ☐ GF mini flavored rice cakes
- ☐ GF large plain or flavored rice cakes

**RICE**
- ☐ White; brown; wild

**GLUTEN-FREE FLOURS**
- ☐ Amaranth flour
- ☐ Arrowroot or tapioca starch
- ☐ Cornstarch
- ☐ Cornmeal
- ☑ Garbanzo/Fava Bean flour
- ☐ Potato starch
- ☐ Quinoa flour
- ☐ Rice flour (white, brown)
- ☐ Sorghum flour
- ☐ Soy flour

**GLUTEN-FREE INGREDIENTS & BAKING MIXES**
- ☐ GF bread mix
- ☑ GF pancake/waffle mix
- ☐ GF muffin mix
- ☐ GF baking powder
- ☐ Baking soda
- ☐ Xanthan gum or Guar gum
- ☑ Vanilla

**LEGUMES (DRY OR READY TO EAT)**
- ☐ Lentils
- ☐ Split Peas
- ☐ Beans (e.g., kidney, garbanzo, white)
- ☐ GF canned baked beans

**GRAINS, OTHER**
- ☐ Amaranth
- ☐ Buckwheat groats
- ☐ Flax seed or flax seed meal
- ☐ Quinoa

**SPICES**
- ☐ Pure black pepper
- ☐ Onion powder
- ☑ Garlic powder
- ☐ GF Italian seasoning
- ☐ GF lemon pepper seasoning

**MISCELLANEOUS**
- ☐ Honey, sugar, brown sugar, molasses
- ☑ Jam, jelly
- ☐ GF puddings
- ☑ Gelatin (flavored)
- ☐ Vinegar

**SAUCES**
- ☐ GF barbecue sauce
- ☐ GF pizza sauce
- ☐ GF pasta sauce
- ☐ GF salsa
- ☐ GF soy sauce

**GF SOUPS**, (see pages 125-127)

**NUTS & SEEDS**
- ☐ Almonds, peanuts, pecans, walnuts
- ☐ Pumpkin seeds
- ☐ Sesame and sunflower seeds
- ☐ Peanut butter

**MEAT, FISH AND POULTRY**
- ☐ Fresh or frozen (plain)
- ☐ GF deli meats

**DAIRY**
- ☐ Milk (whole, 2%, 1%, or skim)
- ☐ Milk powder
- ☐ Yogurt
- ☐ Cheese
- ☐ Cream cheese
- ☐ Eggs

**FRUITS**
- ☐ Fresh, canned or frozen (plain)
- ☑ Dried fruits

**VEGETABLES**
- ☐ Fresh, canned or frozen (plain)
- ☐ Tomato paste
- ☑ Tomatoes, canned

**FATS AND OILS**
- ☑ Butter or margarine
- ☑ Vegetable oil (e.g., canola, olive)
- ☐ GF salad dressings

# CROSS CONTAMINATION

In addition to always checking about ingredients in gluten-free foods, you must also be aware of the possibility of cross contamination (a process by which a gluten-free product comes into contact with something that is not gluten-free).

## AVOIDING CROSS CONTAMINATION AT HOME

- ❖ Store all **gluten-free** products in separate labeled containers. Some families buy bright stickers and put them on everything that is and/or should remain gluten-free. In addition, you may want to keep all **gluten-free** foods in a separate place in the cupboard and refrigerator.
- ❖ Buy separate containers of items like peanut butter, jam or mayonnaise that are used by other family members and therefore could become contaminated.
- ❖ Buy squeeze bottles of condiments such as ketchup, mustard and relish.
- ❖ Have a separate butter dish and cutting board that are used for **gluten-free** foods only.
- ❖ Have your own toaster. If not, use a toaster oven, where the rack can be removed and washed if others have used it.
- ❖ Always make sure that the counter space you are using to prepare **gluten-free** foods is freshly washed to ensure it is free from crumbs or flour dust.
- ❖ Make sure pots, utensils, etc., that are also used for other foods are thoroughly scrubbed before using with **gluten-free** foods.
- ❖ Have your own set of utensils and other items for gluten-free baking, e.g., wooden spoons, sifter.

## CROSS CONTAMINATION OUTSIDE OF THE HOME

- ❖ Avoid buying products from bulk bins as the products can become contaminated by scoops that have been used in another bin.
- ❖ Be aware that French fries may have been cooked in the same oil where battered gluten-containing foods (e.g., fish, chicken fingers) have been fried.
- ❖ Request that the cook clean the grill before preparing your foods, and keep your meal away from meals that may contain gluten.
- ❖ Be careful at buffets as spoons may have been used for more than one dish.
- ❖ Check with airline to see if a gluten-free meal can be ordered. However, always put "extra" snacks such as dried fruits, nuts and seeds, fresh fruit and/or mini rice cakes in your carry-on bag as the meal may not be appropriate or suitable. Also, you may encounter flight delays and need gluten-free snacks.

# GLUTEN-FREE PRODUCTS

Gluten-free products listed on pages 87-133 were exhaustively researched from sources believed to be reliable at the time of printing and recorded April 2002 to June 2003. However, the author assumes no liability for any errors, omissions or inaccuracies in the product information section. Many of the products are made by companies who manufacture gluten-free products exclusively. There are other companies who produce gluten-free as well as gluten-containing products. Most manufacturers have quality control procedures and take extra precautions to prevent cross contamination. However, manufacturers of gluten-containing and gluten-free products cannot guarantee that the product is 100% gluten-free, due to the possibility of cross contamination or human error. It should also be noted that manufacturers of regular commercial food products often change ingredients used in their products. Carefully reading the labels on a regular basis, and contacting the company (if in doubt), is of utmost importance to confirm that the products have remained gluten-free.

The following gluten-free product lists are not all-inclusive and the availability of some products will vary depending on where you live in Canada or the USA. Also, companies discontinue products, therefore some items may no longer be available. The tables on pages 87-133 were designed to assist you in purchasing gluten-free products. The package sizes of these products are listed in ounces with the equivalent size in grams. Gluten-free products can be purchased from several sources:

## GLUTEN-FREE COMPANIES AND DISTRIBUTORS

❖ A very large selection of products can be purchased directly (see pages 134-156).

## HEALTH FOOD STORES

❖ Often carry a good variety of products.

❖ Be aware of cross contamination, especially for items in bulk bins or those bulk bagged in the store. Ask what procedures they use to reduce the risk of cross contamination, e.g., cleaning the area and equipment used to portion and package bulk items; keeping gluten-free foods separate from gluten-containing foods.

## GROCERY STORES

❖ Most large chains carry some gluten-free products throughout the store.
Examples include:
    Baking mixes – Celimix, Gluten-Free Pantry, Kingsmill, Kinnikinnick
    Cereals – cornmeal, hominy grits, puffed corn, millet or rice
    Cookies – Frookie, Kingsmill, Pamela's
    Rice cakes and crackers
    Flours/starches – corn, potato, rice, tapioca
    Pasta – corn, legume, rice

## COMMERCIAL BAKERIES

❖ Some bakeries make gluten-free products in addition to regular gluten-containing bakery items.

❖ Be aware of the possibility of cross contamination. Ask the bakery what procedures they use to reduce the risk of cross contamination: e.g., cleaning of area and equipment, baking gluten-free products in a separate area and in separate pans and/or on specific days when no gluten-containing items are produced.

# CEREALS

❖ Most regular cereals (rice, corn) are **NOT** gluten-free as they usually contain barley malt extract or flavoring, e.g., **Kellogg's Corn Flakes, Rice Krispies**.

❖ Some cereals labeled "**wheat free**" are **NOT** gluten-free:

e.g., **Erewhon Crispy Brown Rice Cereal (Original and No Salt Added)**
    –contains organic barley malt

**Perky's Nutty Corn** – contains oat syrup

**Arrowhead Mills Kamut Flakes** – kamut contains gluten

**Nature's Path Enviro Kidz – Orangutan O's** – barley malt extract, oats

❖ Products containing spelt or kamut are **NOT** gluten-free

# GLUTEN-FREE CEREALS

| Company | Product | Grams | Ounces |
|---|---|---|---|
| ANCIENT HARVEST | Organic Quinoa Flakes | 340 g, 4.54 kg | 12 oz., 10 lbs. |
| ARROWHEAD MILLS | Corn Flakes | 312 | 11 |
| | Corn Grits (white or yellow) | 680 | 24 |
| | Maple Buckwheat Flakes | 341 | 12 |
| | Puffed Corn | 170 | 6 |
| | Puffed Millet | 170 | 6 |
| | Puffed Rice | 170 | 6 |
| | Rice and Shine Hot Cereal | 680 | 24 |
| | Sweetened Rice Flakes | 341 | 12 |
| BARBARA'S BAKERY | Brown Rice Crisps | 312 | 11 |
| | Fruit Juice Sweetened Corn Flakes | 255 | 9 |
| | Puffins, Honey Rice | 340 | 12 |
| BARKAT | Organic Porridge Flakes (rice and millet) | 500 | 17.6 |
| BOB'S RED MILL | Brown Rice Farina Hot Cereal | 737 | 26 |
| | Creamy Buckwheat Hot Cereal | 510 | 18 |
| | Mighty Tasty GF Hot Cereal | 680 | 24 |
| | Millet Grits/Meal | 454 | 16 |
| | Polenta (Organic Corn Grits) | 680 | 24 |

# GLUTEN-FREE CEREALS CONT'D.

| Company | Product | Grams | Ounces |
|---|---|---|---|
| **BREADSHOP** | Puff's 'n Honey | 284 | 10 |
| **CANASOY** * Also available in bulk. | Organic Brown Rice Flakes* | 454 | 16 |
| | Organic Soy Flakes* | 454 | 16 |
| | Toasted Soy Grits* | 454 | 16 |
| **CREAM OF THE CROP** | Organic Buckwheat Hot Cereal | 400 | 14.1 |
| **DR. SCHAR** | Muesli | 375 | 13.2 |
| **EL PETO** | Cream of Rice – Apple Cinnamon | 500 g, 1 kg, 2.5 kg | 17.5 oz., 2.2 lbs., 5.5 lbs. |
| | Cream of Rice – Brown | | |
| | Cream of Rice – White | | |
| **ENER-G FOODS** | Crisp Rice Cereal | 235 | 8 |
| | Toasted Granola and Trail Mix | 454 | 16 |
| | Rice Nuts | 227 | 8 |
| **ENJOY LIFE FOODS** | Cinnamon Crunch Granola* | 400 | 14 |
| | Very Berry Granola* | 400 | 14 |
| *Enriched with thiamin, riboflavin, niacin, Vit. A, B6, B12, E, folate, calcium and zinc. | | | |
| **EREWHON** | Aztec Crunch Corn & Amaranth | 284 | 10 |
| | Brown Rice Cream (organic) | 454 | 16 |
| | Corn Flakes (organic) | 312 | 11 |
| | Crispy Brown Rice (gluten-free label) | 284 | 10 |
| | Rice Twice | 284 | 10 |
| **GLUTANO** | Breakfast Pops (organic) | 250 | 8.8 |
| | Corn Flakes (organic) | 250 | 8.8 |
| | Muesli (organic) | 250 | 8.8 |
| **GLUTINO** | Buckwheat Flakes | 750 | 26.5 |
| | Puffed Buckwheat | 300 | 10.6 |
| **HEALTH VALLEY** | Blue Corn Flakes (organic) | 312 | 11 |
| | Corn Crunch Ems | 357 | 12.6 |
| | Rice Crunch Ems | 357 | 12.6 |
| **HAMMERMÜHLE** | Corn Flakes | 250 | 8.8 |
| | Fruit Muslix | 400 | 14.1 |
| | Honey Cinnamon | 200 | 7 |
| **KINNIKINNICK** * Alta Products: Gluten-Free/Casein-Free | Bucky Hot Buckwheat Cereal* | 450 | 16 |
| | Gudrun's Corn Flakes* | 450 | 16 |
| | Gudrun's Crispy Rice* | 450 | 16 |
| | Gudrun's Granola* | 450 | 16 |
| | Gudrun's Muesli* | 450 | 16 |
| **LIV-N-WELL** | Buckwheat Flakes (hot cereal) | 454 g, 2.27 kg, 20 kg | 16 oz., 5 lbs., 44 lbs. |
| | Cream of Rice – Brown | | |
| | Cream of Rice – White | | |
| | Puffed Buckwheat | 300 g, 10 kg | 10.6 oz., 22 lbs. |

# GLUTEN-FREE CEREALS CONT'D.

| Company | Product | | Grams | Ounces |
|---|---|---|---|---|
| LUNDBERG | Hot Rice Cereal | Cinnamon Raisin, | 280 | 10 |
| | | Purely Organic | 280 | 10 |
| | | Sweet Almond | 280 | 10 |
| NATURE'S PATH | Organic Crispy Rice | | 284 | 10 |
| | EnviroKidz Organic Amazon Frosted Flakes | | 400 | 14 |
| | EnviroKidz Organic Gorilla Munch | | 284 | 10 |
| | EnviroKidz Organic Koala Crisp | | 324 | 11.5 |
| | EnviroKidz Organic Peanut Butter Panda Puffs | | 300 | 10.6 |
| | Organic Fruit Juice Sweetened Corn Flakes | | 300, 750 | 10.6, 26.4 |
| | Organic Honey'd Corn Flakes | | 300, 750 | 10.6, 26.4 |
| | Organic Mesa Sunrise Multigrain (Corn, Flax, Amaranth) | | 300, 750 | 10.6, 26.4 |
| NEW MORNING | Cocoa Crispy Rice Cereal | | 284 | 10 |
| NU-WORLD AMARANTH | **Nu-World Foods** | | | |
| | Amaranth Cereal Snaps (plain) | | 340 | 12 |
| | Amaranth Cereal Snaps (cocoa, cinnamon) | | 284 | 10 |
| | Puffed Amaranth Cereal | | 227 | 8 |
| | Amaranth Berry Delicious Hot Cereal | | 227 | 8 |
| PANNE RIZO | Honey Fruit and Nut Granola | | 255 | 9 |
| PRESIDENT'S CHOICE | Ancient Grains Golden Maize Multigrain Corn Flakes | | 325 | 11.5 |
| HEALTH FOOD STORE BRANDS | Flaked Corn | | bulk | bulk |
| | Brown Rice Cream | | bulk | bulk |
| | Brown Rice Flakes | | bulk | bulk |
| | Brown Rice Flakes (organic) | | bulk | bulk |
| | Soy Flakes | | bulk | bulk |
| | Soy Grits | | bulk | bulk |
| SHILOH FARMS | Polenta (organic) | | 425 | 15 |
| | Soy Flakes | | 454 | 16 |
| | Soy Grits | | 340 | 12 |
| THE BIRKETT MILLS | Pocono Cream of Buckwheat Hot Cereal | | 369 | 13 |
| WHOLE FOODS MARKET | 365 Everyday Value Honey Frosted Flakes | | 283 | 10 |
| WILD OATS MARKETS | Puffed Corn | | 170 | 6 |
| | Puffed Millet | | 170 | 6 |
| | Puffed Rice | | 170 | 6 |

# BAKED PRODUCTS

❖ Most gluten-free bread products are found in supermarket freezer sections or at some local bakeries.

❖ Some breads are vacuum-packed for a shelf life of 4 months to 1 year from the date of manufacture, e.g., **Ener-G Foods, Kingsmill**.

❖ Ready to eat gluten-free bread products are convenient but are expensive. More economical options include:
- ◆ Use gluten-free mixes and bake your own, see pages 103-111.
- ◆ Make your own using various gluten-free flours, see pages 110-115.
- ◆ There are many gluten-free cookbooks available (see pages 164 and 165), and several recipes are found on pages 60-82.

## GLUTEN-FREE BREADS

| Company | Product | Grams | Ounces |
|---|---|---|---|
| **BARKAT** | Brown Rice Bread | 450 | 15.9 |
| | White Rice Bread | 450 | 15.9 |
| **CYBROS** | Mock Rye Bread | 680 | 24 |
| | 100% Rice Bread | 454 | 16 |
| | Rice n' Raisin Bread | 454 | 16 |
| | Tapioca Almond Bread | 680 | 24 |
| **DR. SCHAR** | Ertha Brown Bread | 250 | 8.8 |
| | Pan Carré Sliced Bread | 400 | 14.1 |
| | Rustico Multigrain Bread | 400 | 14.1 |
| | Sweet Bread (Bon Matín) | 200 | 7 |
| **EL PETO**<br><br>Breads are vacuum packed for orders shipped outside of Ontario. Not shelf stable.<br><br>* Also available with fibre (ground flax). | Cheese Bread | 670 | 23.5 |
| | Flax Seed Loaf | 650 | 22.5 |
| | Gourmet Bread | 650 | 22.5 |
| | Italian Style Bread* | 650 | 22.5 |
| | Hi-Fibre Brown Rice Bread | various sizes | various sizes |
| | Millet Bread | 650 | 22.5 |
| | Multi Grain Bread | 650 | 22.5 |
| | Onion Bread | 670 | 23.5 |
| | Potato Bread | 650 | 22.5 |
| | Raisin Bread | 650 | 22.5 |
| | Tapioca Bread | 650 | 22.5 |
| | White Rice Bread | various sizes | various sizes |
| **ENER-G FOODS**<br><br>Breads are in shelf stable, vacuum packages.<br><br>SEE NOTE ON PAGE 91<br><br>* Also available in 2-slice travel packages. | Brown Rice Bread* | 492 | 17 |
| | Fruit Bread (seasonal item) | 794 | 28 |
| | Harvest Bread | 600 | 21.2 |
| | Hi-Fiber Rice Bread* | 396 | 14 |
| | Papa's Bread | 504 | 17.8 |
| | Raisin Bread* | 720 | 25.4 |
| | Raisin Bread (no egg)* | 504 | 18 |
| | Rice Starch Bread (low protein)* | 564 | 19.8 |
| | Seattle Brown Bread | 600 | 21.2 |
| | Six Flour Bread | 576 | 20.3 |

# GLUTEN-FREE BREADS CONT'D.

| Company | Product | Grams | Ounces |
|---|---|---|---|
| **ENER-G FOODS** cont'd. | Tapioca Bread* | 492 | 17.4 |
| | White Rice Bread* | 492 | 17.4 |

IN USA: labeled as "bread" and enriched with thiamin, riboflavin, niacin, iron and folic acid, (all breads enriched except Seattle and Six Flour).
IN CANADA: labeled as "loaf" and not enriched.

| Company | Product | Grams | Ounces |
|---|---|---|---|
| **FOOD FOR LIFE BAKING COMPANY** * Made with brown rice flour and rice bran. | Bhutanese Red Rice Bread*, Brown Rice Bread*, China Black Rice Bread*, Raisin Pecan Bread*, Rice Almond Bread*, Rice Pecan Bread*, White Rice Bread | 680 | 24 |
| **GLUTAFIN** *Enriched with iron, niacin and thiamin. | GFWF Fiber Loaf (sliced or unsliced)* | 400 | 14.1 |
| | GFWF White Loaf (sliced or unsliced)* | 400 | 14.1 |
| **GLUTANO** | Buckwheat Bread | 500 | 17.6 |
| | Multi Grain Bread | 500 | 17.6 |
| | Par Baked White Sliced Bread | 300 | 10.6 |
| | Sesame Bread | 500 | 17.6 |
| | Wholemeal Sliced Bread | 500 | 17.6 |
| **GLUTEN-FREE COOKIE JAR** | Cinnamon Raisin Bread* | 695 | 24.4 |
| | Crusty French Bread* | 525 | 18.6 |
| | Crusty Herb Bread | 525 | 18.6 |
| | Marble Rye Bread* | 525 | 18.6 |
| | Primo White Bread* | 635 | 22.4 |
| * Dairy-Free | Pita Bread* (4) | 340 | 12.0 |
| | Pumpernickel Bread* | 525 | 18.6 |
| **GLUTEN-FREE PANTRY** | Cinnamon Raisin Bread (frozen) | 737 | 26 |
| | Favorite Sandwich Bread (frozen) | 680 | 24 |

| Company | Product | | Grams | Ounces |
|---|---|---|---|---|
| **GLUTINO** | **Corn Breads** | Corn Bread | 580 | 20.5 |
| | | Corn Cheese Bread | 600 | 21.2 |
| | | Corn Fibre Bread | 600 | 21.2 |
| | | Corn Raisin Bread | 600 | 21.2 |
| * Gluten-Free/Casein-Free, no hydrogenated oil or refined sugar. | | Californian Bread | 600 | 21.2 |
| | | Premium Corn Bread* | 600 | 21.2 |
| | | Premium Fiber Bread* | 600 | 21.2 |
| | | Premium Flax Seed Bread* | 600 | 21.2 |
| ** Gluten-Free/Casein-Free | | Premium Raisin Bread* | 648 | 22.9 |
| | Egg Bread** | | 700 | 24.7 |
| All corn and premium breads enriched with thiamin, riboflavin, niacin, iron, calcium and B6. | **Rice Breads** | White Rice Bread** | 700 | 24.7 |
| | | White Rice Bread with Fibre** | 750 | 26.5 |
| | Tapioca Bread** | | 650 | 22.9 |
| **HAMMERMÜHLE** | Chestnut Bread | | 500 | 17.6 |
| | Sesame Seed Bread, Sunflower Seed Bread | | 250 | 8.8 |
| **KINGSMILL** | Brown Rice Bread (vacuum packed or frozen) | | 550 | 19.4 |
| | Country White Bread (USA)* | | 400 | 14 |
| * Breads are in shelf stable, vacuum packages. | Multigrain Bread (USA)* | | 400 | 14 |
| | Multigrain Bread (vacuum packed) | | 450 | 15.9 |
| | White Rice Bread (vacuum packed or frozen) | | 550 | 19.4 |

# GLUTEN-FREE BREADS CONT'D.

| Company | Product | Grams | Ounces |
|---|---|---|---|
| **KINNIKINNICK** | Brown Rice Bread* | 600 | 21.5 |
| | Brown Sandwich Bread* | 585 | 21 |
| *Alta Products: | Cheese Tapioca Rice Bread | 650 | 23 |
| Gluten-Free/Casein-Free | Corn Bread* | 600 | 21.5 |
| | Festive Bread (seasonal)* | 600 | 21.5 |
| | Italian White Tapioca Rice Bread* | 600 | 21.5 |
| | Many Wonder Multigrain Rice Bread* | 660 | 23 |
| | Raisin Sandwich Bread* | 615 | 22 |
| Breads are enriched with | Robin's Honey Brown Rice Bread* | 650 | 23 |
| thiamin, riboflavin, niacin, | Raisin Tapioca Rice Bread* | 650 | 23 |
| folic acid and iron. | Starlight White Grain-Free Bread* | 450 | 16 |
| | Sunflower Flax Rice Bread* | 650 | 23 |
| | Tapioca Rice Bread* | 600 | 21.5 |
| | True Fibre Multigrain Rice Bread* | 560 | 20 |
| | White Rice Bread* | 600 | 21.5 |
| | White Sandwich Bread* | 565 | 20 |
| **PANNE RIZO** | Cinnamon Raisin Bread | 710 | 25 |
| *Also available | Country Brown* | 625 | 22 |
| as Dairy-Free. | Sesame Butter Crust | 625 | 22 |
| **VALPIFORM** | Sliced Country French Bread (par-baked) | 400 | 14.1 |
| | Sliced Fibre Bread (par-baked) | 400 | 14.1 |

# GLUTEN-FREE/YEAST-FREE BREADS

| Company | Product | Grams | Ounces |
|---|---|---|---|
| **EL PETO** | YF Cheese Bread | 670 | 23.5 |
| | YF Flax Seed Loaf | 650 | 22.5 |
| | YF Hi-Fibre Brown Rice Bread | 650 | 22.5 |
| | YF Millet Bread | 650 | 22.5 |
| | YF Multi Grain Bread | 650 | 22.5 |
| | YF Onion Bread | 670 | 23.5 |
| | YF Potato Bread | 650 | 22.5 |
| | YF Tapioca Bread | 650 | 22.5 |
| | YF White Rice Bread | 650 | 22.5 |
| **ENER-G FOODS** | YF Brown Rice Bread | 624 | 22 |
| *Available in 2-slice travel | YF White Rice Bread* | 636 | 22.4 |
| packages | YF Sweet Bread* | 564 | 19.9 |
| **KINNIKINNICK** | YF Brown Rice Bread* | 600 | 21.5 |
| *Alta Products: | YF Raisin Rice Bread* | 650 | 23 |
| Gluten-Free/Casein-Free | YF White Tapioca Bread* | 600 | 21.5 |
| | Candadi Yeast Free Multigrain Rice Bread* | 650 | 23 |
| **PANNE RIZO** | Soda Bread | 540 | 19 |

# BAGELS, BAGUETTES, BUNS, MUFFINS, PIZZA CRUSTS, ROLLS

| Company | Product | | Grams | Ozs. | Number |
|---|---|---|---|---|---|
| **BARKAT** | Brown Rice Pizza Crust | | 150 | 5.3 | 1 |
| | White Rice Pizza Crust | | 150 | 5.3 | 1 |
| **CHEBE** <br><br> *Yeast-Free | **Frozen Dough** | Bread Sticks* | 340 | 12 | 12 |
| | | Sandwich Buns* | 340 | 12 | 4 |
| | | Large Pizza* (11") | 312 | 11 | 1 |
| | | Pizza "On the Go"* | 284 | 10 | 2 |
| | 100% Rice Nuggets | | 340 | 12 | 24-26 |
| | 100% Rice Rolls | | 340 | 12 | 9-11 |
| **CYBRO'S** | Mock Rye Rolls | | 340 | 12 | 10-12 |
| | 100% Rice Nuggets | | 340 | 12 | 24-26 |
| | 100% Rice Rolls | | 340 | 12 | 9-11 |
| **DIETARY SPECIALTIES** <br> *Casein-Free | **English Muffins** | Plain, Cinnamon, Raisin | 400 | 14.1 | 4 |
| | Hamburger Buns* | | 340 | 12 | 4 |
| | Homestyle Rolls* | | 340 | 12 | 4 |
| | Snack Size Cheese Breads | | 340 | 12 | 12 |
| **DR. SCHAR** | Baguette | | 400 | 14.1 | 2 |
| | Duo Lunch Rolls | | 150 | 5.3 | 2 |
| | Focaccia Rolls | | 150 | 5.3 | 4 |
| | Panini White Bread Buns | | 200 | 7 | 2 |
| | Pizza Base | | 300 | 10.6 | 2 |
| | Sunna Wholemeal Bread Rolls | | 200 | 7 | 2 |
| **EL PETO** <br><br><br><br><br><br><br> *Also make Sugar-Free muffins sweetened with fruit juice. | **Hamburger Buns** | Brown, Brown (no corn), Italian with Sesame, Millet, Multi Grain, Potato, Tapioca, White | 500 | 17.5 | 8 |
| | **Hot Dog Buns** | Brown, Italian with Sesame, Millet, Potato, White | 500 | 17.5 | 8 |
| | **Dinner Rolls** | Brown, Italian, Gourmet, Multi Grain, White | 500 | 17.5 | 8 |
| | **Rolls** | Cheese, Onion, Raisin | 500 | 17.5 | 8 |
| | **Pizza Crust** | Basil, Millet, Plain (pre-baked) | 500 | 17.5 | 2 |
| | **Muffins*** | Apple Spice, Banana, Blueberry, Carob Chip, Carrot, Chocolate Chip, Cranberry, Raisin Rice Bran, Tropical Delight | 500 | 17.5 | 6 |
| | Waffles | Belgian | 300 | 10.5 | 2 |
| **ENER-G FOODS** <br><br> Products are in shelf stable, vacuum packages. <br><br> *USA: products enriched with thiamin, riboflavin, niacin, iron and folic acid. | **Dinner Rolls** | Tapioca Dinner Rolls* | 290 | 10.2 | 5 |
| | **Hamburger Buns** | Brown Rice*, Tapioca* | 340 | 12 | 4 |
| | | White Rice* | 400 | 14.1 | 4 |
| | | Seattle Brown* | 476 | 16.8 | 4 |
| | **Hot Dog Buns** | Tapioca* | 340 | 12 | 4 |
| | | Seattle Brown* | 476 | 16.8 | 4 |
| | **English Muffins** | Brown (with sweet potato flour)* | 488 | 17.2 | 4 |
| | | Plain (with tofu) | 472 | 16.7 | 4 |
| | Rice Pizza Shells (6")* (low protein) | | 372 | 13.1 | 3 |
| | Rice Pizza Shells (10")* (low protein) | | 960 | 33.8 | 3 |
| | Scones | | 280 | 9.9 | 4 |

# BAGELS, BAGUETTES, BUNS, MUFFINS, PIZZA CRUSTS, ROLLS

| Company | Product | | Grams | Ozs. | Number |
|---|---|---|---|---|---|
| ENJOY LIFE FOODS | Bagels* | Cinnamon Raisin, Onion, Original, Sesame | 500 | 17.6 | 5 |
| | * Enriched with thiamin, riboflavin, niacin, B12, iron, folate, calcium, magnesium and zinc | | | | |
| FOOD FOR LIFE BAKING CO. | Muffins | Banana | 342 | 12 | 6 |
| | | Carrot | 342 | 12 | 6 |
| FOODS BY GEORGE | Muffins | Blueberry, Corn | 482 | 17 | 6 |
| | English Muffins | Cinnamon Currant, Plain, No-Rye Rye | 397 | 14 | 4 |
| | Pizza Crusts (6") | | 255 | 9 | 3 |
| GILLIAN'S FOODS | French Rolls | Plain, Caramelized Onion, Cinnamon Raisin, Poppy Seed, Sesame Seed, Sundried Tomato | 312 | 11 | 12 |
| GLUTAFIN *Enriched with iron, niacin and thiamin. | GFWF Pizza Base | | 220 | 7.8 | 2 |
| | Rolls | GFWF Fibre* | 280 | 10 | 4 |
| | | GFWF White* | 280 | 10 | 4 |
| GLUTANO | Par-Baked Baguette | | 200 | 7 | 1 |
| | Par-Baked French Rolls | | 200 | 7 | 2 |
| GLUTEN FREE COOKIE JAR | Bagels | Cinnamon Raisin*, Plain*, Poppy-seed*, Pumpernickel*, Sesame* | 560 | 19.6 | 6 |
| | Rolls | Cinnamon Raisin* | 270 | 9.4 | 3 |
| * Dairy-Free | | Dinner* | 390 | 13.6 | 6 |
| | | French* | 665 | 23.4 | 4 |
| | | Portuguese Cheese | 220 | 7.8 | 3 |
| | | Portuguese Cheese (mini) | 280 | 9.8 | 12 |
| | Scones | Blueberry, Irish Soda Bread | 170 | 6.0 | 3 |
| GLUTEN-FREE DELIGHTS | Dinner Rolls | | 468 | 16.5 | 5 |
| | Hamburger Buns | | 468 | 16.5 | 5 |
| | English Muffins | | 312 | 11 | 5 |
| * Dairy-Free | Muffins | Blueberry*, Chocolate Chip*, Cinnamon Raisin* | 340 | 12 | 6 |
| | Pizza Crust (8") | | 227 | 8 | 1 |
| GLUTINO | Baguettes | Corn, Premium Corn* | 430 | 15.2 | 2 |
| *Gluten-Free/ | Bagels | Plain, Poppyseed, Sesame | 300 | 10.6 | 4 |
| Casein-Free, | | Cinnamon & Raisin | 350 | 12.4 | 4 |
| no hydrogenated | English Muffins (corn) | | 325 | 11.5 | 4 |
| oil or refined sugars | Hamburger Buns | Corn | 520 | 18.3 | 6 |
| | | Premium Corn* | 560 | 19.8 | 6 |
| All corn and | Hot Dog Buns | Corn | 500 | 17.6 | 6 |
| premium corn | | Premium Corn* | 560 | 19.8 | 6 |
| products are | Muffins | Banana, Blueberry, Carrot, Chocolate Chip, Date, Raisin | 600 | 21.2 | 6 |
| enriched with | Pizza Crusts (pre-baked) | Corn | 375 | 13.2 | 4 |
| thiamin, riboflavin, | Pizza Crusts (pre-baked) | Premium Corn* | 374 | 13.2 | 4 |
| niacin, iron, | Tortillas (corn) | | 400 | 14.1 | 20 |
| calcium and B6 | Waffles | Belgian or Blueberry | 200 | 7.1 | 2 |
| KINGSMILL | Pizza Crusts (pre-baked) (8") (vacuum packed and frozen) | | 150 | 5.3 | 1 |

# BAGELS, BAGUETTES, BUNS, MUFFINS, PIZZA CRUSTS, ROLLS

| Company | Product | | Grams | Ozs. | Number |
|---|---|---|---|---|---|
| **KINNIKINNICK** | English Muffins* | | 375 | 13.5 | 4 |
| | Hamburger Buns* | | 400 | 14.5 | 4 |
| | Hot Dog Buns* | | 350 | 12.5 | 4 |
| *Alta Products: Gluten-Free/ Casein-Free | **Muffins** | Banana*, Blueberry*, Carrot*, Chocolate Chip*, Cranberry*, Raisin Bran* | 350 | 12.5 | 6 |
| | Pizza Crust (7")* | | 540 | 19.5 | 3 |
| | Pizza Crust (10")* | | 660 | 23.5 | 3 |
| All baked products enriched with thiamin, riboflavin, niacin, folic acid and iron. | **Tapioca Rice Bagels** | Plain*, Cinnamon Raisin*, Multigrain*, New York*, Sesame* | 400 | 14.5 | 4 |
| | Tapioca Rice Cheese Bread Sticks | | 400 | 14.5 | 6 |
| | Tapioca Rice Multigrain Seed & Fibre Bun* | | 400 | 14.5 | 4 |
| | Tapioca Rice Tray Buns* | | 350 | 12.5 | 6 |
| | Waffles (Regular)* | | 500 | 18 | 8 |
| **LIFESTREAM** | Buckwheat Wild Berry Toaster Waffles | | 312 | 11 | 8 |
| | Mesa Sunrise Toaster Waffles | | 312 | 11 | 8 |
| **NATURE'S HILIGHTS** | **Pizza Crust** (frozen) – made from whole grain brown rice | | 284 | 10 | 2 |
| **NU-WORLD AMARANTH** | **Nu-World Foods Flatbread/Pizza Crust** (pre-baked) – 6" | | | | |
| | Amaranth Buckwheat | | 113 | 4 | 2 |
| | Amaranth Garbanzo | | 113 | 4 | 2 |
| | Amaranth Sorghum | | 113 | 4 | 2 |
| **PANNE RIZO** | Fruity Tea Buns | | 600 | 21 | 4 |
| | **Hamburger Buns** | White, Brown* | 355 | 12.5 | 4 |
| | **Hot Dog Buns** | White, Brown* | 355 | 12.5 | 4 |
| *Gluten-Free/ Casein-Free | **Muffins** | Banana*, Banana Pecan*, Carrot Walnut, Banana Chocolate Chip*, Chocolate Zucchini Nut, Cranberry Orange*, Fruit & Fibre*, Maple Pumpkin*, Rice Bran* | 850 | 30 | 6 |
| | Pizza Shells | | 213 | 7.5 | 2 |
| | Quejos Cheese Buns | | 285 | 10 | 4 |
| **VALPIFORM** | Crusty French Dinner Rolls (par-baked) | | 280 | 10 | 3 |
| | French Baguettes (par-baked) | | 320 | 11.3 | 2 |
| **VAN'S** *Wheat-Free products are Gluten-Free | **Toaster Waffles** (wheat-free)* | Apple Cinnamon, Blueberry, Flax and Original | 255 | 9 | 6 |
| | Toaster Mini Waffles (wheat-free) | | 212 | 7.5 | 32 |

## Gluten-Free/YEAST-FREE – BUNS AND ROLLS

| Company | Product | | Grams | Ozs. | Number |
|---|---|---|---|---|---|
| **EL PETO** | **YF Hamburger Buns** | Brown, Millet, Multi-Grain, Potato, Tapioca, White | 500 | 17.5 | 8 |
| | **YF Hot Dog Buns** | Brown, Millet, Potato, White | 500 | 17.5 | 8 |
| | **YF Dinner Rolls** | Brown, Multi Grain, White | 500 | 17.5 | 8 |
| | **YF Pizza Crust** | Plain, Millet | 500 | 17.5 | 2 |
| **ENER-G FOODS** | YF Rice Pizza Shells (6" and 10") | | 360 | 12.7 | 3 |

# GLUTEN-FREE CAKES, LOAVES, PIES, MISCELLANEOUS

| Company | Product | | Grams | Ozs. | Number |
|---|---|---|---|---|---|
| **DIETARY SPECIALTIES** | Cheesecake | | 454 | 16 | |
| | Classic Pound Cake | | 369 | 13 | |
| | Pie Shells | | 200 | 7 | 2 |
| **DR. SCHAR** | Magdalenas (apricot-filled cupcakes) | | 150 | 5.3 | |
| | Brioches (cupcakes) | | 150 | 5.3 | |
| | Fantasia (sponge cake) | | 500 | 17.6 | |
| | Meranetti (chocolate fudge cupcakes) | | 175 | 6.2 | |
| | Tea Cakes | | 150 | 5.3 | 4 |
| **EL PETO** <br> * Can't be shipped. | **Pies** (8") | Apple, Blueberry, Cherry, Peach, Pumpkin*, Raspberry, Walnut | 500 | 17.5 | |
| | **Pie Dough** | | 400 | 14 | |
| | **Tarts** | Buttertart, Lemon, Pecan, Raspberry | NA | NA | 6 |
| | **Tart Shells** | Unsweetened <br> Sweetened | NA | NA | 12 |
| **ENER-G FOODS** <br> * USA: products enriched with thiamin, riboflavin, niacin, iron and folic acid. | Brownies* | | 560 | 19.7 | |
| | Chocolate Cinnamon Rolls | | 736 | 25.9 | 8 |
| | Cinnamon Rolls | | 672 | 23.7 | 8 |
| | Donut Holes | | 30 | 1.1 | 20 |
| | Plain Donuts* | | 210 | 7.4 | 6 |
| | Fruit Cake (seasonal item) * | | 567 | 20 | |
| | Pound Cake* | | 279 | 9.8 | |
| **FOODS BY GEORGE** | Brownies | | 397 | 14 | 6x8" tray |
| | Crumb Cake | | 567 | 20 | 6x8" tray |
| | Pecan Tart | | 113 | 4 | 1 |
| | Pound Cake | | 454 | 16 | 7" loaf |
| **GLUTEN-FREE DELIGHTS** <br><br><br> * Seasonal item | Caramel Rolls | | 312 | 11 | 5 |
| | Cinnamon Rolls | | 312 | 11 | 5 |
| | **Donut Holes** | Cinnamon Sugar, Cinnamon Sugar (dairy free), Chocolate | 227 | 8 | 24 |
| | **Donuts** | Chocolate Iced, Cinnamon Sugar, Double Chocolate, Plain, Vanilla Frosted | 200 | 7 | 6 |
| | Lemon "Loves" | | 340 | 12 | 5x8" tray |
| | **Muffins** | Blueberry, Chocolate Chip, Cinnamon Raisin | 340 | 12 | 6 |
| | Mini Cherry Pies (4.5")* | | 680 | 24 | 3 |
| | Mini Pecan Pies (4.5") | | 680 | 24 | 2 |
| **GLUTEN-FREE COOKIE JAR** <br><br> *Dairy-Free | Brownies* | | 340 | 12 | 4 |
| | **Bundt Cakes** | Iced Chocolate* | 515 | 18.4 | 3 small |
| | | Iced Chocolate* | 700 | 24.7 | 1 large |
| | | Orange Chiffon* | 275 | 9.8 | 3 small |
| | | Orange Chiffon* | 445 | 15.8 | 1 large |

# GLUTEN-FREE CAKES, LOAVES, PIES, MISCELLANEOUS CONT'D.

| Company | Product | | Grams | Ozs. | Number |
|---|---|---|---|---|---|
| **GLUTAFIN** | **Cakes** | Banana | 300 | 10.6 | |
| | | Date & Walnut | 300 | 10.6 | |
| | | Lemon Madeira | 300 | 10.6 | |
| **GLUTINO**<br><br><br><br><br>* Seasonal items | Banana Cake | | 300 | 10.6 | 1 |
| | Brownies | | 300 | 10.6 | 1 |
| | Brown Sugar Rolls* | | 300 | 10.6 | |
| | Carrot Cake | | 325 | 11.5 | 1 tray |
| | **Cup Cakes** | Chocolate, Marble, Vanilla | 200 | 7.1 | 6 |
| | Date Squares | | 300 | 10.6 | 1 tray |
| | Queen Elizabeth Date Cake* | | 325 | 11.5 | |
| | Upside Down Pineapple Cake* | | 350 | 12.3 | |
| | Pie Crusts | | 175 | 6.2 | 3 |
| **KINNIKINNICK**<br>* Alta Products:<br>Gluten-Free/<br>Casein-Free<br><br>Baked products<br>enriched with<br>thiamin,<br>riboflavin, niacin,<br>folic acid and<br>iron.<br><br>NA = weights not<br>available | Apple Pie* | | NA | NA | 1 |
| | Banana Loaf* | | NA | NA | 1 |
| | Carrot Cake* | | NA | NA | 1 |
| | Chocolate Cupcakes* | | NA | NA | 6 |
| | Chocolate Walnut Fritellas* | | 480 | 16.9 | 6 |
| | Iced Fudge Chocolate Cake | | NA | NA | NA |
| | **Donuts** | Chocolate Dipped*, Cinnamon Sugar*, Glazed Chocolate*, Maple Dipped*, Plain*, Sugar*, Vanilla Dipped* | 600 | 21.5 | 6 |
| | Fruit Cake (seasonal item) | | 500 | 18 | 1 |
| | Mixed Berry Pie* | | NA | NA | 1 |
| | Tapioca Rice Cinnamon Buns* | | 500 | 18 | 6 |
| | White Cake* | | NA | NA | 1 |
| **NATURE'S HILIGHTS** | Deluxe Double Chocolate Brownies (frozen, ready to serve) | | 454 | 16 | 10 |
| **PANNE RIZO**<br><br><br><br><br><br>* Gluten-Free/<br>Casein-Free | Applesauce Spice Bars | | 400 | 14.1 | 6 |
| | Apple Danish | | 600 | 21.2 | 4 |
| | Belgian Berry Gallettes | | 200 | 7 | 1 |
| | Brownie (Chocolate Macadamia Nut) | | 295 | 10.4 | 6 |
| | Buttertarts | | 240 | 8.5 | 6 |
| | **Cakes** | Angel Food, Carrot, Chocolate Fudge Classic White | various sizes | | |
| | Cinnamon Bun Swirls | | 150 | 5.3 | 4 |
| | Date Squares, | | 300 | 10.5 | 6 |
| | Pecan Squares | | 365 | 12.9 | 4 |
| | **Pies*** | Apple Cinnamon, Blackberry, Cherry, Peach, Pumpkin | 425 | 15 | 6" |
| | Rocky Road Bar* | | 85 | 3 | 1 |
| **RED MILL FARMS** | Banana Nut Cake | | 340 | 12 | |
| | Dutch Chocolate Cake | | 340 | 12 | |
| **VALPIFORM** | Mini Marble Cakes (Sponge Cake) | | 180 | 6.3 | 6 |

# COOKIES

❖ Not all "wheat-free" cookies are gluten-free; e.g., **Mrs. Denson's** (barley), **Barbara's Wheat-free Fig Bars** (barley/oats), **Country Choice** (oats).

## GLUTEN-FREE COOKIES

| Company | Product | Grams | Ounces |
|---|---|---|---|
| **Banducci & Daughters** | **Angel Kisses**   Original, Chocolate, Raspberry | 60, 140, 308 | 2.25, 5, 11 |
| **Bi-Aglut** | Biscotti, Chocolate Wafers | 175 | 6.2 |
| | Chocolate Chip, Frolle Biscuits | 180 | 6.3 |
| | Lady Fingers (Savoiardi) | 150 | 5.3 |
| **Cybro's** | Lemon Almond, Peanut Butter, Sugar | 255 | 9 |
| **Dietary Specialties** | Chocolate Chip, Cinnamon, Coconut, Orange | 125 | 4.4 |
| **Dr. Schar** | Biscottini | 200 | 7 |
| | Biscotti | 175 | 6.2 |
| | Biscotti with Chocolate | 150 | 5.3 |
| | Biscuits with Cocoa Crème Filling (Cioccolini) | 150 | 5.3 |
| | Chocolate Chip Biscuits (Pepitas), Frollini Biscuits Gingerbread-Lebkuchen | 200 | 7 |
| | Hazelnut Biscuits (Noccioli) | 150 | 5.3 |
| | Lady Fingers (Savoiardi) | 200 | 7 |
| | **Wafers**              Cocoa, Hazelnut, Vanilla | 100 | 3.5 |
| | Waffle Bread (Cialde Wafer) | 75 | 2.6 |
| **El Peto**  *180 g/6.3 oz. | Almond Shortbread*, Carob Chip, Chocolate Chip, Chocolate Coconut Macaroons, Coconut Macaroons Chocolate Hazelnut, Cinnamon Hazelnut, Gingersnaps, Orange Delight, Raspberry Hazelnut | 200 | 7 |
| **Ener-G Foods**  * Also available in bulk. | Almond Butter and Biscotti (Chocolate Chip) | 208 | 7.3 |
| | Biscotti (Plain) | 280 | 9.9 |
| | Chocolate Chip Potato* | 272 | 9.6 |
| | Chocolate Hazelnut | 304 | 10.7 |
| | Chocolate Sandwich | 420 | 14.8 |
| | Coconut Macaroons* | 256 | 9 |
| | French Almond | bulk only | bulk only |
| | Ginger* | 272 | 9.6 |
| | Lemon Sandwich | 264 | 9.3 |
| | Vanilla Chocolate Sandwich | 320 | 11.2 |
| | Vanilla Lemon Cream | 304 | 10.7 |
| | Vanilla | 288 | 10.2 |
| | White Chocolate Chip Macadamia Nut | 288 | 10.2 |
| **Foods by George** | Chocolate Chip, Cinnamon Currant, Pecan | 184 | 6.5 |
| **Frookies** | Chocolate Chip, Double Chocolate Chip, Peanut Butter Chunk | 184 | 6.5 |
| **Enjoy Life Foods** | Chocolate Chip, Double Chocolate, Ginger, No Oats Oatmeal | 70   (1 cookie)  170  (12 cookies) | 2.5  6 |

# GLUTEN-FREE COOKIES CONT'D.

| Company | Product | Grams | Ounces |
|---|---|---|---|
| **GLUTAFIN** | Biscuits | 200 | 7 |
| | Bourbon Chocolate Cream Biscuits | 125 | 4.4 |
| | Chocolate Chip & Peanut Cookies | 100 | 3.5 |
| | Custard Creams | 125 | 4.4 |
| | Digestive Biscuits | 150 | 5.3 |
| | Gingernut Cookies | 125 | 4.4 |
| | Milk Chocolate Biscuits | 150 | 5.3 |
| | Milk Chocolate Digestives | 150 | 5.3 |
| | Shortcake Biscuits | 125 | 4.4 |
| | Sweet Biscuits | 150 | 5.3 |
| | Tea Biscuits | 150 | 5.3 |
| **GLUTANO** | Apricot Biscuits | 150 | 5.3 |
| | Biscuits | 125 | 4.4 |
| | Chocolate Chip Biscuits | 150 | 5.3 |
| | Chocolate O's Sandwich Cookies | 175 | 6.2 |
| | Co Co Cookies | 125 | 4.4 |
| | Custard Cream Biscuits | 150 | 5.3 |
| | Digestive Maize Biscuits | 200 | 7 |
| | Ginger Cookies | 100 | 3.5 |
| | Half Covered Chocolate Cookies | 125 | 4.4 |
| | Half Covered Chocolate Digestive Biscuits | 280 | 10 |
| | Hazelnut Cookies | 125 | 4.4 |
| | Short Cake Ring Biscuits | 100 | 3.5 |
| | Tarteletts | 125 | 4.4 |
| | Wafers          Chocolate, Lemon | 125 | 4.4 |
| **GLUTEN-FREE COOKIE JAR** <br><br> * Dairy-Free | Brown Sugar Wafers* | 340 | 12 |
| | Chocolate Chips* | 340 | 12 |
| | Chocolate Chip Walnut* | 340 | 12 |
| | Chocolate Swirls* | 340 | 12 |
| | Cookie Jar Cut-outs* | 340 | 12 |
| | Decorated Cut-outs* | 340 | 12 |
| | Italian Ricotta Cheese | 340 | 12 |
| | Orange* | 340 | 12 |
| | Peanut Butter* | 340 | 12 |
| | Pumpkin* | 340 | 12 |
| **GLUTEN-FREE DELIGHTS** <br><br> * Dairy-Free | Chocolate Chip* | 284 | 10 |
| | Frosted Cut-outs | 284 | 10 |
| | Mock Oatmeal | 284 | 10 |
| | Mock Oatmeal Raisin | 200 | 7 |
| | Molasses Crispy-Chewy* | 284 | 10 |
| | Peanut Butter* | 284 | 10 |
| | Raspberry Swirls | 200 | 7 |
| | Snickerdoodle (seasonal) | 255 | 9 |
| | Sugar | 255 | 9 |
| | Triple Chip | 284 | 10 |
| **GLUTINO** | Chocolate Chip | 225 | 7.9 |
| | Cherry Bites | 200 | 7.1 |

# GLUTEN-FREE COOKIES CONT'D.

| Company | Product | Grams | Ounces |
|---|---|---|---|
| **JENNIES** | Coconut Macaroons | 227 | 8 |
| | **Coconut Macaroons** Carob Chip, Chocolate Chip, Coconut, Dutch Chocolate, Fruit Filled, Rum | 57 | 2 |
| **KINNIKINNICK**<br><br>*Alta Products:<br>Gluten-Free/Casein-Free<br><br>Products enriched with<br>thiamin, riboflavin,<br>niacin, folic acid and iron<br><br>**Sugar-Free cookies<br>do not contain<br>hydrogenated oils. | Almond Biscotti* | 100 | 4 |
| | Ben's Peanut Butter Chocolate Chip* | 220 | 8 |
| | Black Forest* | 220 | 8 |
| | Chocolate Covered Almond Biscotti | 100 | 4 |
| | Ginger Snap* | 190 | 7 |
| | Graham Style* | 235 | 8.5 |
| | Holiday Pinwheel* | 220 | 8 |
| | Lemon Poppyseed* | 220 | 8 |
| | Macaroon* | 230 | 8.5 |
| | Montana's Chocolate Chip* | 220 | 8 |
| | Rocky Road* | 215 | 8 |
| | **Wolfesbrand*** Almond, Double Chocolate Almond, Licorice Almond, Lemon Cranberry, Moccachino, Peanut Butter, Raisin Spice | 220 | 8 |
| | **Kinni Betik**** Chunky Chocolate | 220 | 8 |
| **KINGSMILL** | Chocolate Chip | 110 | 4 |
| | Cinnamon, Coconut, Orange | 125 | 4.4 |
| **OAKLAND DIETETIC BAKERY** | Banana Surprise, Butterscotch Chip, Fudge Mound, Molasses Sugar, Old Fashioned Chocolate Chip, Peanut Butter Chocolate Chip, Peanut Butter – Peanut Butter Chip | 454 | 16 |

| Company | Product | In Canada | In USA |
|---|---|---|---|
| **PAMELAS** | **Biscotti** Almond Anise, Chocolate Walnut, Lemon Almond | 113 | 4 |
| | **Shortbread** Butter, Chocolate Chip Pecan, Chunky Chocolate Chip, Lemon, Pecan, Simply Chocolate, Swirl | 150 | 7.25 |
| | Carob Hazelnut | 150 | 7.25 |
| | Chocolate Chip Walnut | 150 | 7.25 |
| | Chocolate Double Chip | 150 | 7.25 |
| | Ginger | 150 | 7.25 |
| | Peanut Butter | 150 | 7.25 |
| **PANNE RIZO**<br><br><br>*Gluten-Free/Casein-Free | Biscotti (Chocolate Dipped) | 140 | 4.9 |
| | Chocolate-Rolled Rum Balls | 56 | 2 |
| | Chocolate Nut Cookie | 192 | 6.8 |
| | Frosted Raspberry Swirls | 160 | 5.5 |
| | Grammas Cinnamon Dots | 80 | 2.8 |
| | Macaroons – Chocolate Dipped | 160 | 5.6 |
| | Macaroons – Plain* | 100 | 3.5 |
| | Pecan Snowballs | 160 | 5.6 |
| | Shortbread (Buttery or Pecan) | 170 | 6 |
| | Tollhouse Cookie | 180 | 6.3 |

# CRACKERS AND RICE CAKES

❖ Most crackers contain wheat, rye, oats, and/or barley. Read labels carefully,
    e.g., **SnackWell Potato Thins** (oat fiber)
        **Health Valley Amaranth Crackers** (wheat).

❖ The majority of large and mini rice cakes are gluten-free, however, some multigrain
    rice cakes may contain barley and/or oats and are **NOT** gluten-free.

## GLUTEN-FREE CRACKERS

| Company | Product | Grams | Ounces |
|---|---|---|---|
| **BI-AGLUT** | Snack Crackers | 150 | 5.3 |
| | Fette Tostate (Crackerbread) | 240 | 8.5 |
| | Grissini (Bread Sticks) | 150 | 5.3 |
| | Grissini with Sesame (Bread Sticks) | 150 | 5.3 |
| **BLUE DIAMOND** | **Nut Thins**       Almond, Hazelnut, Pecan | 120 | 4.25 |
| **DR. SCHAR** | Bread Sticks (Grissini) | 150 | 5.3 |
| | Cracker Toast (Fette Croccanti) | 150 | 5.3 |
| | Crackers | 200 | 7 |
| | Crispbread (Fette Biscottate) | 250 | 8.8 |
| | Pizzirilli Crackers | 150 | 5.3 |
| **EDWARD & SONS** | **Brown Rice Snaps** Cheddar, Onion & Garlic, Tamari Seaweed, Tamari Sesame, Toasted Onion, Unsalted Plain, Unsalted Sesame, Vegetable | 100 | 3.5 |
| **ENER-G FOODS** *Enriched with thiamin, riboflavin, niacin, iron and folic acid. | Broken Melba Toast | 454 | 16 |
| | Cheese Crackers (low protein) | 372 | 13.1 |
| | Cinnamon Crackers | 168 | 5.9 |
| | Garlic Crackers* | 300 | 10.6 |
| | Gourmet Crackers (low protein) | 200 | 7 |
| | Onion Crackers | 250 | 8.8 |
| | Seattle Crackers | 125 | 4.4 |
| | Sesame Crackers* | 300 | 10.6 |
| **GLUTAFIN** | **Crackers**       Plain, High Fiber | 200 | 7 |
| | Savoury Biscuits | 125 | 4.4 |
| **GLUTANO** | Crackers | 150 | 5.3 |
| | Crispbread | 125 | 4.4 |
| | Wafers | 100 | 3.5 |
| **HEALTH VALLEY** | Rice Bran Crackers | 200 | 7.0 |
| **HOL•GRAIN** | **Brown Rice Crackers** Lightly Salted, Lightly Salted Onion & Garlic, Lightly Salted Sesame, Unsalted | 127 | 4.5 |
| **PANNE RIZO** * Gluten-Free/Casein-Free | Crostini* | 112 | 4 |

# GLUTEN-FREE RICE CAKES – LARGE

| Company | Product | | Grams | Ounces |
|---|---|---|---|---|
| LIFESTREAM<br>*Brown rice, buckwheat, millet | Multigrain (salted)* | | 195 | 6.9 |
| | Whole Brown Rice - Original (salted or unsalted) | | 195 | 6.9 |
| | Whole Brown Rice - Sesame (salted or unsalted) | | 195 | 6.9 |
| LUNDBERG FAMILY FARM | Nutra – Farmed Rice Cakes | Apple Cinnamon | 241 | 8.5 |
| | | Brown Rice | 241 | 8.5 |
| | | Brown Rice (salt-free) | 241 | 8.5 |
| | | Buttery Caramel | 241 | 8.5 |
| | | Honey Nut | 241 | 8.5 |
| | | Mochi Sweet | 241 | 8.5 |
| | | Sesame Tamari | 241 | 8.5 |
| | | Toasted Sesame | 241 | 8.5 |
| | | Wild Rice | 241 | 8.5 |
| | Organic Brown Rice Cakes | Brown Rice | 241 | 8.5 |
| | | Brown Rice (salt free) | 241 | 8.5 |
| | | Koku Sesame | 241 | 8.5 |
| | | Koku Seaweed | 241 | 8.5 |
| | | Mochi Sweet | 241 | 8.5 |
| | | Popcorn | 241 | 8.5 |
| | | Sesame Tamari | 241 | 8.5 |
| | | Tamari Seaweed | 241 | 8.5 |
| | | Wild Rice | 241 | 8.5 |
| PLUM-M-GOOD | Organic Rice Cakes | Brown Rice(salted) | 185 | 6.5 |
| | | Brown Rice (unsalted) | 185 | 6.5 |
| | | Brown Rice Sesame (salted) | 185 | 6.5 |
| | | Brown Rice Sesame (unsalted) | 185 | 6.5 |
| | | Multigrain (salted)* | 185 | 6.5 |
| *Brown rice, buckwheat, millet | | Multigrain (unsalted)* | 185 | 6.5 |
| | Regular Rice Cakes | | 185 | 6.5 |
| PRESIDENT'S CHOICE | Brown Rice with Basmati | | 170 | 6 |
| | Brown Rice with Wild Rice | | 170 | 6 |
| QUAKER (CANADA) | Butter Popcorn | | 127 | 4.5 |
| | Caramel Corn | | 186 | 6.6 |
| | Caramel Chocolate Chip | | 199 | 7 |
| | Savory Tomato and Basil | | 173 | 6.1 |
| | White Cheddar | | 140 | 4.9 |
| | Original | | 127 | 4.5 |
| QUAKER (USA) | Apple Cinnamon, Caramel Apple, Caramel Corn | | 185 | 6.5 |
| | Butter Popcorn | | 127 | 4.5 |
| | Caramel Chocolate Chip | | 214 | 7.5 |
| | Chocolate Crunch, Peanut Butter | | 205 | 7.2 |
| | Lightly Salted and Salt Free | | 127 | 4.5 |
| | White Cheddar | | 140 | 4.9 |

# GLUTEN-FREE RICE CAKES – MINI

| Company | Product | | Grams | Ounces |
|---|---|---|---|---|
| HAIN | Apple Cinnamon, Plain, Ranch, Strawberry | | 113 | 4 |
| PRESIDENT'S CHOICE | Apple Cinnamon, Caramel, White Cheddar | | 113 | 4 |
| QUAKER (CANADA) | Crispy Mini Rice Chips | All Dressed, BBQ, Caramel, Cheddar, Crunchy Dill, Ketchup, Nacho, Ranch, Salt and Vinegar, Sea Salt, Sour Cream | 100 | 3.5 |
| (USA) | Crispy Mini Rice Snacks | Apple Cinnamon, Cheddar Cheese, Caramel Corn, Chocolate, Creamy Ranch, Nacho, Sour Cream and Onion | various sizes | various sizes |

# BAKING MIXES

- ❖ Many gluten-free cookbooks (see pages 164,165) have recipes for baking mixes.
- ❖ Several recipe ideas are found on page 60-68, 71-73.
- ❖ Tips for tasty gluten-free baking are found on pages 48-52.
- ❖ All-Purpose Flour and Baking Mixes are also listed on page 110 and 111.

# GLUTEN-FREE BAKING MIXES

| Company | Product | | Grams | Ounces |
|---|---|---|---|---|
| ABSOLUTELY GOOD  *Also available in bulk. | All Purpose Quick Bread Mix | | 454 | 16 |
| | Brown Rice Bread Mix* | | 660 | 23.3 |
| | Cake and Pastry Mix | | 300 | 10.6 |
| | Rice Dinner Roll Mix | | 454 | 16 |
| | Rice Pizza Crust Mix | | 330 | 11.6 |
| ARROWHEAD MILLS | All Purpose Baking Mix | | 794 | 28 |
| | Brownie Mix | | 496 | 17.5 |
| | Cookie Mix | Chocolate Chip | 366 | 12.9 |
| | Pancake and Waffle Mix | | 794 | 28 |
| | Pancake and Waffle Mix (Wild Rice) | | 907 | 32 |
| AUTHENTIC FOODS  *Dairy-Free | White Bread Mix* | | 567 | 20 |
| | Cinnamon Bread Mix* | | 567 | 20 |
| | Pancake and Baking Mix* | | 681 | 24 |
| | Pancake and Baking Mix* | | 3.18 kg | 7 lbs. |
| | Falafel Mix* | | 681 | 24 |
| | Cake Mixes | Chocolate*, Lemon* | 312 | 11 |
| | | Vanilla* | 341 | 12 |
| BARKAT | Bread Mix | | 500 | 17.6 |
| BOB'S RED MILL | Biscuit and Baking Mix | | 680 | 24 |
| | GF Brownie Mix | | 595 | 21 |
| | GF Pancake Mix | | 623 | 22 |
| | Homemade Wonderful GF Bread Mix | | 454 | 16 |

# GLUTEN-FREE BAKING MIXES CONT'D.

| Company | Product | | Grams | Ounces |
|---|---|---|---|---|
| CAUSE YOU'RE SPECIAL | Biscuit Mixes | Regular | 510 | 18 |
| | | Economy | 1.02 kg | 36 |
| | Bread Mixes | Traditional French | 595 | 21 |
| | | Cinnamon Raisin | 737 | 26 |
| | | Homestyle White | 595 | 21 |
| | | Mock Rye | 609 | 21.5 |
| | Cake Mixes | Rich Chocolate – Small | 397 | 14 |
| | | Rich Chocolate – Large | 794 | 28 |
| | | Moist Lemon – Small | 419 | 14.8 |
| | | Moist Lemon – Large | 839 | 29.6 |
| | | Moist Yellow – Small | 419 | 14.8 |
| | | Moist Yellow – Large | 839 | 29.6 |
| *All products are Gluten-Free/Casein-Free | | Golden Pound | 553 | 19.5 |
| | | Chocolate Pound | 541 | 19.1 |
| | Chocolate Fudge Brownie Mix | | 519 | 18.3 |
| | Cookie Mixes | Brownies | 519 | 18.3 |
| | | Chocolate Chip | 428 | 15.1 |
| | | Classic Sugar | 360 | 12.7 |
| | | Roll Out Sugar | 360 | 12.7 |
| | Muffin Mixes | Classic Muffin and Quickbread | 394 | 13.9 |
| | | Lemon Poppyseed | 396 | 13.9 |
| | Scone Mixes | Regular | 638 | 22.5 |
| | | Economy | 1.28 kg | 45 |
| | Pancake and Waffle Mixes | Regular | 553 | 19.5 |
| | | Economy | 1.11 kg | 39 |
| | Pie Crust Mix | | 221 | 7.8 |
| | Pizza Crust Mix | | 368 | 13 |
| CHEBE  *Also available in 5.5 lb. bags | Bread Mix | Regular* | 213 | 7.5 |
| | | Cinnamon | 213 | 7.5 |
| | Cinnamon Roll-Up Mix | | 213 | 7.5 |
| | Garlic Onion Bread Sticks Mix | | 213 | 7.5 |
| | Pizza Dough Mix | | 213 | 7.5 |
| DIETARY SPECIALTIES | Bread Mix | Apple, Banana | 598 | 21.1 |
| | | White | 500 | 17.6 |
| | Brownie Mix | | 680 | 24 |
| *All mixes are Casein-Free | Cake Mix | Chocolate | 740 | 26.1 |
| | | White | 750 | 26.4 |
| | Cornbread Mix | | 530 | 18.7 |
| | Muffin Mix | Blueberry | 567 | 20 |
| | | Bran | 480 | 16.9 |
| | Pancake Mix | | 485 | 17.1 |
| DR. SCHAR | Bread Mix (Mix B) | | 1 kg | 2.2 lbs. |
| | Cake Mix (Margherita) | | 500 | 17.6 |
| | Pastry Mix (Mix C) | | 1 kg | 2.2 lbs. |
| EL PETO  *Also available in Corn-Free | Bread Maker Mixes | Brown Rice, White Rice, Italian, Potato | 350, 700 g, 2.45 kg | 12, 24.5 oz., 5.4 lbs. |
| | Brownie Mix* | | 500 | 17.5 |

# GLUTEN-FREE BAKING MIXES CONT'D.

| Company | Product | | Grams | Ounces |
|---------|---------|---|-------|--------|
| **EL PETO** CONT'D. | **Cake Mixes** | Chocolate*, Lemon*, White* | 500 g<br>1 kg | 17.5 oz.<br>2.2 lbs. |
| | **Cake Mixes** | Marble* | 500 | 17.5 |
| *Also available in Corn-Free. | Old Fashioned Cookie Mix | | 750 | 26.5 |
| | Muffin Mix* | | 500 g<br>1 kg<br>2.5 kg<br>10 kg | 17.5 oz.<br>2.2 lbs.<br>5.5 lbs.<br>22 lbs. |
| | Pancake Mix* | | 500 g<br>1 kg<br>2.5 kg<br>10 kg | 17.5 oz.<br>2.2 lbs.<br>5.5 lbs.<br>22 lbs. |
| | Perfect Pie Dough Mix | | 500 | 17.5 |
| **ENER-G FOODS** | Corn Mix | | 454 | 16 |
| | Potato Mix (low protein) | | 567 | 20 |
| | Rice Mix | | 567 | 20 |
| **GLUTAFIN** | GFWF Fibre Mix | | 500 | 17.6 |
| | GFWF White Mix | | 500 | 17.6 |
| **GLUTEN-FREE COOKIE JAR** | **Bread Mixes** | Primo White* | 400 | 14.0 |
| | **Bread/Muffin Mixes** | Banana* | 590 | 20.8 |
| | | Blueberry* | 450 | 16.0 |
| | | Corn* | 500 | 17.6 |
| | | Pumpkin* | 550 | 19.4 |
| | | Strawberry* | 495 | 17.6 |
| *Dairy-Free | Bagel/Soft Pretzel Mix* | | 830 | 29.4 |
| | Scone Mix | | 330 | 11.6 |
| | Donut & Donut Hole Mix* | | 570 | 20.2 |
| | Buttermilk Pancake Mix | | 575 | 20.4 |
| | Brownie Mix* | | 720 | 25.2 |
| | **Cake Mixes** | Chocolate* | 780 | 27.6 |
| | | Orange*, White* | 905 | 32.0 |
| | **Cookie Mixes** | Chocolate Chip* | 455 | 16.0 |
| | | Italian Ricotta Cheese | 885 | 31.4 |
| | | Orange* | 975 | 34.4 |
| | | Peanut Butter* | 735 | 26.0 |
| | | Pumpkin* | 975 | 34.4 |
| | | Brown Sugar Wafer* | 735 | 26.0 |
| | | Cookie Jar Cut-Outs* | 720 | 25.2 |
| **GLUTEN-FREE DELIGHTS** | Chocolate Cake Mix (Dairy-Free) | | 340 | 12 |
| | White Bread Mix | | 482 | 17 |
| **GLUTEN-FREE PANTRY** *Lactose-Free/Casein-Free **Also available as "Dairy-Free" Sandwich Bread Mix. | Bagel, Breadstick & Pretzel Mix* | | 454 | 16 |
| | **Bread Mixes** | Country French Bread Mix* | 624 | 22 |
| | | Delicious Slicing Bread Mix | 482 | 17 |
| | | French Bread & Pizza Mix** | 2.27 kg | 5 lbs. |
| | | Favorite Sandwich Bread Mix** | 624 g, 2.27 kg | 22 oz., 5 lbs. |
| | | Light Rye-Style Bread Mix | 624 | 22 |

# GLUTEN-FREE BAKING MIXES CONT'D.

| Company | Product | | Grams | Ounces |
|---|---|---|---|---|
| **GLUTEN-FREE PANTRY** CONT'D.<br><br>* Lactose-Free/Casein-Free | **Bread Mixes** | Multi-Grain with Seeds Bread Mix | 580 | 20.5 |
| | | Tapioca Bread Mix* | 624 | 22 |
| | | Whole Grain Bread Mix | 500 | 17.6 |
| | Blueberry Buckwheat Muffin and Pancake Mix | | 425 | 15 |
| | Buttermilk Brown Rice Pancake Mix | | 454 | 16 |
| | Chocolate Chip Cookies, Squares & Cake Mix* | | 540 | 19 |
| | Chocolate Truffle Brownie Mix* | | 738 | 26 |
| | Coconut Macaroon Mix* | | 454 | 16 |
| | Cranberry Orange Bread/Muffin Mix | | 481 | 17 |
| | Crisp & Crumble Topping* | | 227 | 8 |
| | Danielle's Decadent Chocolate Cake Mix* | | 425 | 15 |
| | Luscious Angel Food Cake Mix* | | 454 | 16 |
| | Muffin, Scone & Quick Bread Mix* | | 425 g, 2.27 kg | 15 oz., 5 lbs. |
| | Nice 'n' Spicy Cake & Gingerbread Mix* | | 397 | 14 |
| | Old Fashioned Cake & Cookie Mix* | | 709 g, 2.27 kg | 25 oz., 5 lbs. |
| | Perfect Pie Crust* | | 454 | 16 |
| | Yankee Cornbread, Muffin, Corncake Mix* | | 340 | 12 |
| **GLUTINO**<br><br>* Gluten-Free/Casein-Free | All Purpose Corn Mix | | 1 kg | 35.3 |
| | All Purpose Rice Mix* | | 1 kg | 35.3 |
| | **Cake Mix** | Chocolate*, White* | 1.2 kg | 42.3 |
| | Muffin Mix* | | 1 kg | 35.3 |
| | Pancake Mix* | | 1.2 kg | 42.3 |
| | Pie Crust Mix | | 1 kg | 35.3 |
| **GOOD 'N EASY** | Pastry Mix, Quick Bread Mix | | 1.8 kg & bulk | 4 lbs. & bulk |
| **GRAIN PROCESS ENTERPRISES LTD.** | Gluten-Free Bean Flour Bread Mix | | 2.5 kg, 10 kg | 5.5 lb., 22 lbs. |
| | Grain Pro Rice Loaf Mix | | 2.5 kg, 10 kg | 5.5 lb., 22 lbs. |
| **HOL•GRAIN** | Chocolate Brownie Mix and Pancake & Waffle Mix | | 454 | 16 |
| **KAYBEE** | Basic Bread Mix | | 520 | 18.3 |
| | Basic Cookie Mix | | 370 | 13.1 |
| | Basic Muffin Mix | | 375 | 13.2 |
| | Chocolate Brownie Mix | | 360 | 12.7 |
| | Corn Muffin Mix | | 240 | 8.5 |
| | Cottage Pudding | | 270 | 9.5 |
| | Deluxe Pancake Mix | | 360 | 12.7 |
| | No-Knead Bun Mix | | 320 | 11.3 |
| | Pizza Crust Mix | | 245 | 8.6 |
| | Pyrogy Dough Mix | | 230 | 8.1 |
| | Super Easy Cake Mix | | 260 | 9.2 |
| | Wild Rice Pancake Mix | | 370 | 13 |
| **KINGSMILL** | Rice Bread and Baking Mix | | 800 | 28.2 |
| | Rice Cake and Cookie Base | | 600 | 21.2 |
| **KINNIKINNICK**<br><br>* Alta products:<br>Gluten-Free/Casein-Free | | **KINNI-KWIK MIXES** | | |
| | **Bread and Bun Mixes** | Plain*, Sunflower and Flax*, True Fibre* | 1000 | 33.5 |
| | **Cake Mixes** | Chocolate*, White* | 1000 | 33.5 |

# GLUTEN-FREE BAKING MIXES cont'd.

| Company | Product | | Grams | Ounces |
|---|---|---|---|---|
| **KINNIKINNICK** CONT'D. | **KINNI-KWIK MIXES** | | | |
| | **Cookie Mixes** | Chocolate Chip*, Ginger* | 1000 | 33.5 |
| *Alta products: Gluten-Free/Casein-Free | **Muffin Mixes** | Blueberry*, Cranberry*, Chocolate Chip* | 1000 | 33.5 |
| | Pastry and Pie Crust Mix* | | 1000 | 33.5 |
| | Pizza Crust Mix* | | 1000 | 33.5 |
| | **REGULAR MIXES** | | | |
| NOTE: Kinni-Kwik Mixes | **Bread Mixes** | Candadi Yeast Free Rice Bread* | 650 | 23 |
| require only the addition | | Tapioca Rice Bread* | 650 | 23 |
| of water. | | Tapioca Rice Brown Bread (Bread Maker)* | 650 | 23 |
| | | Tapioca Rice White Bread (Bread Maker)* | 650 | 23 |
| | | White Rice Bread* | 650 | 23 |
| All mixes are enriched with | | Yeast Free Brown Rice Bread* | 650 | 23 |
| thiamin, riboflavin, niacin, | **Muffin Mixes** | Regular*, Cornbread and Muffin* | 650 | 23 |
| folic acid and iron. | **Pancake Mixes** | Regular*, Buckwheat* | 650 | 23 |
| | Cookie Mix* | | 650 | 23 |
| | **Cakes Mixes** | Angel Food Cake* | 450 | 16 |
| | | Chocolate*, Lemon*, White*, Sponge* | 500 | 18 |
| | Pastry and Pie Crust Mix*, Pizza Crust Mix* | | 650 | 23 |
| **LAUREL'S SWEET TREATS** | **Bread Mixes** | Bean Bread | 454 | 16 |
| | | Good Ol' Corn Bread | 425 | 15 |
| | **Cake Mixes** | Cameron's Vanilla | 425, 850 | 15. 30 |
| | | Cinnamon Spice | 425, 850 | 15, 30 |
| | | Mom's Chocolate | 354, 709 | 12.5, 25 |
| All mixes are | Chocolate Fudge Brownie Mix | | 553 | 19.5 |
| Gluten-Free/Casein Free | **Cookie Mixes** | Chocolate Chip | 850 | 30 |
| | | Double Chocolate Chip | 850 | 30 |
| | | Roll 'Em Out Sugar | 652 | 23 |
| | Dinner Roll Mix | | 567 | 20 |
| | Pancake Mix | | NA | NA |
| | Pizza Dough Mix | | 340 | 12 |
| **MADE BY MONA** | **Bread Mixes** | French Bread* | 605 | 21.3 |
| | | Golden Goddess Bread** | 650 | 22.9 |
| | | Milk and Honey Brown Bread | 600 | 21.2 |
| * Gluten-Free/Casein Free | Happy Day Cake Mix* | | 685 | 24.2 |
| ** Gluten-Free/Casein Free/ | Mona's Bread, Roll & Pastry Mix | | 600 | 21.2 |
| Sugar-Free | Multi Mix* | | 680 | 24 |
| Mixes also available in 4.4 lbs. | Pancake & Waffle Mix | | 385 | 13.6 |
| (2 kg) and 11.2 lbs.(5 kg) | Sunny Bun & Pizza Mix* | | 410 | 14,5 |
| **MANISCHEWITZ** | Homestyle Potato Latke Mix | | 170 | 6 |
| | Mini Potato Knish Mix | | 170 | 6 |
| | Potato Kugel Mix | | 170 | 6 |
| | Potato Pancake Mix | | 85, 170 | 3, 6 |
| | Sweet Potato Pancake Mix | | 170 | 6 |

# GLUTEN-FREE BAKING MIXES CONT'D.

| Company | Product | | Grams | Ounces |
|---|---|---|---|---|
| **MISS ROBEN'S** | **Bagel Mixes** | Plain (12) | 624 | 22 |
| | **Biscuit Mixes** | Plain (12) | 38.6 | 13.6 |
| | **Bread Mixes** | Andi Wunderbread* – small | 635 | 22.4 |
| | | Andi Wunderbread* – large | 830 | 29.3 |
| *Corn-Free | | Dinner Bread – small | 406 | 14.3 |
| | | Homestyle Bread – small | 401 | 14 |
| **Also available in | | Noah's Bread Mix* | 462 | 16.3 |
| Corn-Free mixes | | Potato Bread – large | 542 | 19.1 |
| | | White Sandwich Bread – small | 573 | 20.2 |
| | **Cake Mixes** | Angel Food – One Step | 361 | 12.7 |
| | | Carrot Cake* | 618 | 21.8 |
| NOTE: Many of the mixes | | Chocolate** | 800 | 28.2 |
| are low in sugar. | | Gingerbread Mix (seasonal) | 595 | 21 |
| | | Pound Cake | 586 | 20.7 |
| | | White | 895 | 31.6 |
| | | Yellow** | 722 | 25.5 |
| | Chewy Brownie Mix** | | 423 | 14.9 |
| | **Cookie Mixes** | Animal Cookie* | 369 | 13 |
| | | Crunchy Chocolate Chip** | 864 | 30.5 |
| | | Crunchy Chocolate Sugar | 518 | 18.3 |
| Makes 48 cookies | | Crunchy Sugar** | 528 | 18.6 |
| | | Crunchy Versatile | 682 | 24 |
| | | Mock Graham Cracker* | 369 | 13 |
| | | Mock Oatmeal Raisin | 851 | 30 |
| | | Roll & Cut Gingerbread (seasonal) | 620 | 21.9 |
| | | Roll & Cut Sugar** | 572 | 20.5 |
| | **Muffin Mixes** | Versatile** (24) | 710 | 25 |
| | Pancake & Waffle Mix (36 P. or 10 W.) | | 363 | 12.8 |
| | Pie Crust Mix (2 crusts) | | 355 | 12.5 |
| | Pizza Crust Mix (12") | | 360 | 12.7 |
| | Pizza Crust Mix (18") | | 529 | 18.7 |
| | Soft Pretzel Mix** (36 sticks) | | 393 | 13.9 |
| | Corn-Free Soft Pretzel | | 421 | 14.9 |
| | Traditional Cornbread Mix | | 397 | 14 |
| **NELSON DAVID OF** | Apple Cinnamon Cake and Muffin Mix | | 415 | 14.6 |
| **CANADA** | Batter Coating Mix | | 240 | 8.5 |
| **(CELIMIXES)** | **Bread Mixes** | Flax Bread, Rice Bread, White Bread | 2 kg | 4.4 lbs. |
| | **Cake Mixes** | Dutch Chocolate Supreme | 350 | 12.3 |
| | | White | 415 | 14.6 |
| | Carob Cake & Loaf Mix | | 415 | 14.6 |
| | **Cookie Mixes** | Regular | 300 | 10.6 |
| | | Shortbread | 170 | 6 |
| | Dutch Chocolate Supreme Brownie Mix | | 400 | 14.1 |
| | Hamburger Bun Mix | | 190 | 6.7 |
| | Lemon Loaf & Muffin Mix | | 415 | 14.6 |
| | Muffin Mix | | 430 | 15.2 |
| | Pancake Mix – Regular or Brown Rice | | 600 | 21.2 |

# GLUTEN-FREE BAKING MIXES CONT'D.

| Company | Product | | Grams | Ounces |
|---|---|---|---|---|
| **NELSON DAVID OF CANADA** CONT'D. | Pastry Mix | | 900 | 1.98 lbs. |
| | Pizza Crust Mix | | 350 | 12.3 |
| | Tea Biscuit Mix | | 420 | 14.8 |
| | Yorkshire Pudding Mix | | 300 | 10.6 |
| **PAMELA'S** | Pancake & Baking Mix | | 680 | 24 |
| | Pancake & Baking Mix | | 2.27 kg | 5 lbs. |
| | Ultra Chocolate Brownie Mix | | 454 | 16 |
| **PANNE RIZO** * Gluten-Free/Casein-Free | Pancake Mix* | | 695 | 24.5 |
| | White Cake Mix* | | 640 | 22.6 |
| **SYLVAN BORDER FARM** | Bread Mix | | 454 | 16 |
| | Bread Mix (Non-Dairy) | | 454 | 16 |
| | Classic Dark Bread Mix | | 454 | 16 |
| | Pancake & Waffle Mix | | 341 | 12 |
| | Lemon Cake Mix | | 757 | 26.7 |
| **THE REALLY GREAT FOOD COMPANY** | **Bread Mixes** | Biscuit Loaf | 496 | 17.5 |
| | | Brown Rice Bread | 595 | 21 |
| | | Buttermilk Biscuit | 425 | 15 |
| | | Cinnamon Bread | 567 | 20 |
| | | Dark Euro Bread | 595 | 21 |
| | | French Bread Country Farm Bread | 369 | 13 |
| | | Home-Style Cornbread | 794 | 28 |
| | | Irish Soda Bread | 709 | 25 |
| | | Rye-Style Bread | 539 | 19 |
| | | White Bread (Original) | 567 | 20 |
| | | Zesty Cornbread | 794 | 28 |
| | **Muffin Mixes** | Apple Spice | 369 | 13 |
| | | Cornbread | 369 | 13 |
| | | English Muffin | 397 | 14 |
| | | Maple Raisin | 369 | 13 |
| | | Spinach Muffin | 284 | 10 |
| | | Sweet Muffin | 369 | 13 |
| | | Vanilla | 340 | 12 |
| | **Pancake Mixes** | Brown Rice Flour, Classic | 425 g, 1.28 kg | 15, 45 |
| | Pizza Crust Mix | | 454 | 16 |
| | Pie Crust Mix | | 369 | 13 |
| | **Cake Mixes** | Aunt Tootsie's Brownie | 624 | 22 |
| | | Banana Bread | 539 | 19 |
| | | Butter | 425 | 15 |
| | | Chocolate | 650 | 23 |
| | | Cinnamon | 425 | 15 |
| | | Colonial Spice | 709 | 25 |
| | | Gingerbread | 539 | 19 |
| | | Golden | 650 | 23 |
| | | Grandma's Pound | 567 | 20 |
| | | Lemon Poppy | 650 | 23 |
| | | Orange | 650 | 23 |

# Gluten-Free Baking Mixes cont'd.

| Company | Product | | Grams | Ounces |
|---|---|---|---|---|
| **The Really Great Food Company** cont'd. | **Cake Mixes** | Pineapple | 567 | 20 |
| | | Pumpkin Bread | 539 | 19 |
| | | White | 397 | 14 |
| | | Yellow | 650 | 23 |
| | **Cookie Mixes** | Anise Biscotti | 482 | 17 |
| | | Chocolate Crinkle | 454 | 16 |
| | | Lemon | 567 | 20 |
| | | Lemon Poppyseed Biscotti | 482 | 17 |
| | | Versatile | 425 g, 1.28 kg | 15, 45 |
| **Shiloh Farms** | Bread & Pizza Crust Mix | | 482 | 17 |
| | Cake & Muffin Mix | | 567 | 20 |
| | Cookie Mix | | 600 | 21 |
| | Pancake & Waffle Mix | | 425 | 15 |

# Flours

❖ Some "wheat-free" flours (e.g., kamut and spelt) are **NOT** gluten-free.

❖ Some buckwheat mixes contain wheat flour and buckwheat flour.

❖ When purchasing bulk-bagged gluten-free flours be aware of the possibility of cross contamination with other gluten-containing flours. Ask the store what procedures they use when bagging their various flours.

❖ A variety of gluten-free all-purpose flour mixes and flours are listed below and on the following pages. Each flour has unique properties, therefore follow recipes closely!

## Gluten-Free All-Purpose Flour Mixes

**Amazing grains**
- **Montina™ All Purpose Baking Flour Blend**
  - white rice flour, tapioca starch flour and Montina™ Pure Flour

**Authentic Foods**
- **Bette's Gourmet Featherlight Rice Flour Blend**
  - white rice flour, tapioca flour, cornstarch, potato flour
- **Bette's Gourmet Four Flour Blend**
  - garfava flour, sorghum flour, cornstarch, tapioca flour

**Bob's Red Mill**
- **GF All Purpose Baking Flour**
  - garbanzo flour, potato starch, tapioca flour, sorghum flour, fava flour

**El Peto**
- **All Purpose Flour Mix**
  - cornstarch, white rice flour, xanthan and/or guar gum
- **All Purpose Flour Mix (Corn-Free)**
  - potato starch, white rice flour, xanthan and/or guar gum

# GLUTEN-FREE ALL-PURPOSE FLOUR MIXES CONT'D.

### ENER-G FOODS
- **Gluten Free Gourmet Blend**
  - white rice flour, potato starch, tapioca starch
- **Four Flour Blend (from Authentic Foods)**
  - cornstarch, tapioca starch, garfava flour, sorghum flour

### GLUTANO
- **Flour Mix**
  - rice flour, pregelatinized rice flour, maize flour, mono and diglycerides, guar gum

### GLUTEN FREE PANTRY
- **All Purpose Sugar Free Baking Mix**
  - buckwheat flour, soy flour, potato starch, tapioca starch, white rice flour, guar gum, salt

### KINNIKINNICK
- **All Purpose Celiac Flour**
  - white rice flour, potato starch, tapioca starch, sodium carboxymethylcellulose, guar gum
- **All Purpose Mix**
  - white rice flour, tapioca starch, sugar, fructooligosaccharide, gluco delta lactone, dextrose, whole egg powder, sodium bicarbonate, egg white powder, pea fiber, soy lecithin, sodium carboxymethylcellulose, pea protein, fructose

### LAUREL'S SWEET TREATS
- **Gluten Free Baking Flour Mix**
  - white rice flour, potato starch, tapioca flour

### MADE BY MONA
- **Multi Mix**
  - organic brown rice flour, white rice flour, potato starch, tapioca starch, sorghum flour, xanthan gum

### MISS ROBENS
- **Bette Hagman's Original Flour Mix**
  - white rice flour, potato starch, tapioca starch

### PANNE RIZO
- **Gluten Free Flour**
  - white rice flour, potato starch, tapioca flour

### THE REALLY GREAT FOOD COMPANY
- **All Purpose Rice Flour Mix**
  - white rice flour, potato starch, cornstarch, xanthan gum

### SYLVAN BORDER FARM
- **General Purpose Flour Mix**
  - potato flour, white rice flour, brown rice flour, amaranth, quinoa flour, white cornmeal, garbanzo bean flour, soy flour

# GLUTEN-FREE BEAN, CHICKPEA, LENTIL AND PEA FLOURS

**BEANS 'R US BEAN FLOUR** (navy beans, black-eyed peas, soybeans)
- Gluten-Free Pantry

**BETTE'S GOURMET FOUR FLOUR BLEND**
(garfava flour, sorghum flour, cornstarch, tapioca starch)
- Authentic Foods
- Ener-G Foods

**BLACK BEAN FLOUR**
- Bob's Red Mill

**CHICKPEA FLOUR** (garbanzo bean flour)
- Authentic Foods
- Bob's Red Mill
- Gluten-Free Pantry
- Glutino
- Northern Quinoa Corporation

**EASY WHITE FIBRE MIX** (pea fibre, inulin, cellulose)
- Kinnikinnick

**GARBANZO BEAN FLOUR** (see chickpea flour)

**GARBANZO BEAN FLOUR AND FAVA BEAN FLOUR**
- Authentic Foods (developed original mixture called "Garfava Flour")
- Bob's Red Mill
- El Peto
- Ener-G Foods ("Garfava")
- Grain Process Enterprises Ltd.
- Kinnikinnick
- Miss Roben's ("Garfava")

**GREEN LENTIL FLOUR**
- Northern Quinoa Corporation

**GREEN PEA FLOUR**
- Bob's Red Mill
- Northern Quinoa Corporation

**ROMANO BEAN FLOUR** (cranberry bean or whole bean)
- El Peto
- Glutino
- Grain Process Enterprises Ltd.
- Kinnikinnick

**WHITE BEAN FLOUR**
- Bob's Red Mill

**YELLOW PEA FLOUR**
- Northern Quinoa Corporation

# GLUTEN-FREE FLOURS

**ALMOND FLOUR**
- Authentic Foods
- Bob's Red Mill
- Gluten-Free Pantry
- Kinnikinnick

**AMARANTH FLOUR**
- Arrowhead Mills
- Bob's Red Mill
- El Peto
- Grain Process Enterprises Ltd.
- Northern Quinoa Corporation
- Nu-World Amaranth/Nu-World Foods (also carry Toasted Amaranth Bran Flour, Puffed Amaranth, Amaranth Pre-Gel Powder)
- Shiloh Farms

**ARROWROOT STARCH**
- Authentic Foods
- Bob's Red Mill
- El Peto
- Glutino
- Grain Process Enterprises Ltd.
- Kinnikinnick
- Miss Roben's
- Nelson David

**BUCKWHEAT FLOUR**
- Arrowhead Mills
- The Birkett Mills
- Bob's Red Mill
- Glutino
- Grain Process Enterprises Ltd.
- Kinnikinnick
- Minn-Dak Growers Ltd.
- New Hope Mills
- Nelson David
- Shiloh Farms

**CHESTNUT FLOUR**
- Hammermühle

**CORN BRAN**
- Glutino
- Grain Process Enterprises Ltd.

**CORN FLOUR**
- Authentic Foods
- Bob's Red Mill
- El Peto
- Glutino
- Grain Process Enterprises Ltd.
- Kinnikinnick
- Nelson David
- Shiloh Farms

**CORNMEAL**
- Arrowhead Mills
- Bob's Red Mill
- El Peto
- Glutino
- Grain Process Enterprises Ltd.
- Kinnikinnick
- Shiloh Farms

**FLAX SEED FLOUR** (flax seed meal)
- Bob's Red Mill
- El Peto
- Gluten-Free Pantry
- Glutino
- Gold Top Organics
- Grain Process Enterprises Ltd.
- Kinnikinnick
- Nelson David
- Omega Nutrition ("Nutri-Flax")

# GLUTEN-FREE FLOURS CONT'D.

## HAZELNUT FLOUR
- Bob's Red Mill
- Kinnikinnick

## MILLET FLOUR
- Arrowhead Mills
- Bob's Red Mill
- El Peto
- Grain Process Enterprises Ltd.
- Shiloh Farms

## MONTINA™ FLOUR
- Amazing Grains

## POTATO FLOUR
- Authentic Foods
- Bob's Red Mill
- Club House
- El Peto
- Ener-G Foods
- Glutino
- Grain Process Enterprises Ltd.
- Kinnikinnick
- Shiloh Farms

## POTATO STARCH FLOUR
- Authentic Foods
- Bob's Red Mill
- Casco
- Cause You're Special
- El Peto
- Ener-G Foods
- Gluten-Free Cookie Jar
- Gluten-Free Pantry
- Glutino
- Grain Process Enterprises Ltd.
- Kinnikinnick
- Manischewitz
- Miss Roben's
- Nelson David
- The Really Great Food Company

## QUINOA FLOUR
- Ancient Harvest
- Bob's Red Mill
- El Peto
- Grain Process Enterprises Ltd.
- Kinnikinnick
- Northern Quinoa Corporation – "NorQuin" brand
- Shiloh Farms

## RICE BRAN
- Bob's Red Mill
- El Peto
- Ener-G Foods
- Glutino
- Grain Process Enterprises Ltd.
- Kinnikinnick

## RICE FLOUR (Brown)
- Arrowhead Mills
- Authentic Foods
- Bob's Red Mill
- El Peto
- Ener-G Foods
- Glutino
- Grain Process Enterprises Ltd.
- Kinnikinnick
- Miss Roben's
- Nelson David
- The Really Great Food Company
- Shiloh Farms

## RICE FLOUR (Sweet)
- Authentic Foods
- Bob's Red Mill
- El Peto
- Ener-G Foods
- Gluten-Free Pantry
- Grain Process Enterprises Ltd.
- Kinnikinnick
- Miss Roben's
- The Really Great Food Company

# GLUTEN-FREE FLOURS CONT'D.

## RICE FLOUR (White)
- Arrowhead Mills
- Authentic Foods
- Bob's Red Mill
- Cause You're Special
- Club House
- Cybro's
- El Peto
- Ener-G Foods
- Gluten-Free Cookie Jar
- Gluten-Free Pantry
- Glutino
- Grain Process Enterprises Ltd.
- Kinnikinnick
- Miss Roben's
- Nelson David
- The Really Great Food Company
- Shiloh Farms

## RICE POLISH
- Ener-G Foods

## SORGHUM FLOUR
- Authentic Foods
- Bob's Red Mill
- El Peto
- Ener-G Foods
- Grain Process Enterprises Ltd.
- Kinnikinnick
- Made By Mona
- Miss Roben's
- Twin Valley Mills, LLC.

## SOY FLOUR
- Arrowhead Mills
- Bob's Red Mill
- Dixie Diners' Club
- Eden Foods
- El Peto
- Glutino
- Grain Process Enterprises Ltd.
- Hilton
- Kinnikinnick
- Nelson David
- Shiloh Farms
- Sylvan Border Farms

## SWEET POTATO FLOUR
- Ener-G Foods

## TAPIOCA STARCH FLOUR
- Authentic Foods
- Bob's Red Mill
- Cause You're Special
- Canasoy
- Cybro's
- El Peto
- Ener-G Foods
- Gluten-Free Cookie Jar
- Gluten-Free Pantry
- Glutino
- Grain Process Enterprises Ltd.
- Kinnikinnick
- Miss Roben's
- Nelson David
- The Really Great Food Company
- Shiloh Farms

## TEFF FLOUR
- Bob's Red Mill
- Kinnikinnick
- Shiloh Farms
- The Teff Company

**NOTE:** **The following distributors also carry many of the flours from the companies listed above:**

- Gluten-Free Mall
- Gluten-Free Trading Company
- Gluten Solutions
- Liv-N-Well Distributors
- Specialty Food Shop
- Various Health Food Stores – e.g., Whole Foods Market, Wild Oats Family of Markets

# GRAINS AND BEANS

- Gluten-free grains (amaranth, buckwheat, flax, millet, quinoa, sorghum and teff) are available in most health food stores and gluten-free specialty companies.
- Legumes (Pulses) – Dried beans, peas, chickpeas and lentils – are excellent sources of protein, dietary fiber, vitamins and minerals.
- Avoid soup mixes containing dried bean/peas as they usually contain barley and/or wheat.
- Some commercial ready-to-eat canned baked beans contain wheat/flour.

***See Eat Well Be Well* (see page 158), Clan Thompson Resources (page 163) or Co-operative GF Commercial Product Listing (page 160) for a listing of gluten-free products.**

## AMARANTH
- Arrowhead Mills
- Bob's Red Mill
- El Peto
- Grain Process Enterprises Ltd.
- Health Food Store Brands
- Kinnikinnick
- Northern Quinoa Corporation
- Nu-World Amaranth
- Shiloh Farms

## BUCKWHEAT (Whole Groats, Roasted Groats [Kasha], or Grits)
- Arrowhead Mills
- The Birkett Mills (Pocono Kasha, Wolff's Kasha, Pocono Wild Groats)
- Bob's Red Mill
- Grain Process Enterprises Ltd
- Health Food Store Brands
- Kinnikinnick
- Minn-Dak Growers Ltd.
- New Hope Mills
- Northern Quinoa Corporation
- Shiloh Farms

## FLAX (Whole Seed or Ground, Milled Meal)
- Arrowhead Mills
- Bob's Red Mill
- El Peto
- Gluten-Free Pantry
- Gold Top Organics
- Grain Process Enterprises Ltd.
- Health Food Store Brands
- Kinnikinnick
- Nelson David
- Northern Quinoa Corporation
- Omega Nutrition
- Vita Health

## MILLET
- Arrowhead Mills
- Bob's Red Mill
- Grain Process Enterprises Ltd.
- Health Food Store Brands
- Northern Quinoa Corporation
- Shiloh Farms

## QUINOA (Golden or Black Seed)
- Ancient Harvest
- Arrowhead Mills
- Bob's Red Mill
- Eden Foods
- Grain Process Enterprises Ltd.
- Health Food Store Brands
- Kinnikinnick
- Northern Quinoa Corporation – "NorQuin" brand
- Shiloh Farms

## SORGHUM (Grain)
- Authentic Foods
- Grain Process Enterprises Ltd.
- Twin Valley Mills, LLC.

## TEFF (Grain)
- Bob's Red Mill
- Kinnikinnick
- Shiloh Farms
- The Teff Company

# PASTA

❖ Some so-called **"wheat-free"** pastas are made from **spelt** or **kamut** and are **NOT** gluten-free.

❖ Some buckwheat pastas contain buckwheat flour and **wheat flour** and are **NOT** gluten-free – e.g., **Canasoy Buckwheat Noodles** ("Soba" noodles) and **Annie Chun's**.

❖ Gluten-free pastas are made from corn, legumes, potato, quinoa, rice or soy. However, check ingredient labels to make sure that no wheat, spelt or kamut has been added to these gluten-free ingredients.

## GLUTEN-FREE PASTAS

| Company | Product | Grams | Ounces |
|---|---|---|---|
| **ANCIENT HARVEST**<br>* Quinoa and corn flour pasta | Elbows, Garden Pagodas, Linguine, Rotelle, Shells, Spaghetti, Veggie Curls | 227 g, 4.5 kg | 8 oz., 10 lbs. |
| **ANNIE CHUN'S** | **Rice Noodles** (Angel Hair) — Original, Hunan, Thai Basil | 227 | 8 |
| | **Pad Thai Rice Noodles** (Fettuccine) — Original, Thai Basil | 227 | 8 |
| **APROTEN**<br>* Low-protein pasta | Anellini, Ditalini, Fettuccine, Fusilli, Penne, Rigatini, Spaghetti, Tagliatelle | 250, 500 | 8.8, 17.6 |
| | Lasagna | 250 | 8.8 |
| **BI-AGLUT** | Ditalini, Fusilli, Lasagna, Macaroni, Penne, Sedani, Spaghetti | 250, 500 | 8.8, 17.6 |
| **CAFE BONJOUR**<br>* Brown rice pasta | Penne, Spaghetti, Spirals | 454 g, 2.2 kg | 16 oz., 5 lbs. |
| **CANASOY** | Rice Noodles | 227 | 8 |
| | Rice Vermicelli | 400 | 14.1 |
| | Brown Rice, Macaroni | 400 g, 6 kg | 14.1 oz., 13 lb. |
| | Mung Bean Noodles | 227, 454 | 8, 16 |
| **CELIMIX (NELSON DAVID OF CANADA)** | Brown Rice Elbows, Spaghetti White Rice Spaghetti | 350 g, 2.27 kg | 12.3 oz., 5 lbs. |
| **DE BOLES** | Corn Elbows | 340 | 12 |
| | Corn Spaghetti | 227 | 8 |
| | Rice – Angel Hair, Fettuccine, Penne, Spaghetti, Spirals | 227 | 8 |
| | Rice – Lasagna | 284 | 10 |
| | Rice – Macaroni & Cheese, Shells & Cheese | 206 | 7.25 |
| **DIETARY SPECIALTIES** | Elbows, Spaghetti, Spirals, Tri-Alphabets | 500 | 17.6 |
| | Herb and Garlic Ziti, Tri-Color Shells | 250 | 8.8 |
| | Lasagna | 100 | 3.5 |
| **DR. SCHAR** | Alphabet, Anellini, Capelli (Angel Hair), Conchigliette (Small Shells), Lasagna | 250 | 8.8 |
| | Ditalini, Fusillli, Penne, Pipette, Rigatini, Spaghetti | 500 | 17.6 |
| | Fettuccine (eggs & bacon) | 100 | 3.5 |
| | Fusilli (with mushrooms & tomatoes) | 100 | 3.5 |
| | Maccheroni (cheese noodles) | 100 | 3.5 |

# Gluten-Free Pasta cont'd.

| Company | Product | | Grams | Ounces |
|---|---|---|---|---|
| **Eden Foods** | Bifun (Rice Pasta) | | 100 | 3.5 |
| | Harusame (Mung Bean Pasta) | | 70 | 2.4 |
| **Ener-G Foods** | **Brown Rice** | Lasagna, Macaroni | 454 | 16 |
| | | Spaghetti | 446 | 15.8 |
| | **White Rice** | Cannelloni | 335 | 11.8 |
| | | Garden Rotini | 454 | 16 |
| | | Lasagna | 454 | 16 |
| | | Macaroni | 454 | 16 |
| | | Small or Large Shells | 454 | 16 |
| | | Spaghetti | 446 | 15.8 |
| | | Tagliatelle | 397 | 14 |
| | | Vermicelli | 285 | 10.1 |
| | **Low Protein/G.F.** (cornstarch/potato starch) | Lasagna, Macaroni | 454 | 16 |
| | | Small or Large Shells | 454 | 16 |
| | | Spaghetti | 454 | 16 |
| **Food For Life Baking Company** | Rice Elbows | | 454 | 16 |
| **Foods By George** | Egg Noodles | | 369 | 13 |
| | Elbows, Gnocchetti, Macaroni, Radiatore, Spaghetti | | 369 | 13 |
| **Glutafin** | Macaroni (Penne), Shells, Spaghetti, Spirals | | 500 | 17.6 |
| | Lasagna, Tagliatelle Nests | | 250 | 8.8 |
| **Glutano** | Animal Shapes, Macaroni, Spaghetti, Spirals, Tagliatelle | | 250 | 8.8 |
| **Glutino** | **Brown Rice Pasta** | Fusilli, Macaroni, Penne, Spaghetti | 454 | 16 |
| **Lundberg Family Farms** | **Organic Brown Rice Pasta** | Penne | 340 | 12 |
| | | Rotini, Spaghetti | 284 | 10 |
| **Mrs. Leeper's** * Available in bulk | **Brown Rice Pasta** | Alphabets, Elbows*, Garlic Parsley Twists*, Penne*, Shapes for Kids, Spaghetti, Vegetable Twists | 340 | 12 |
| | **Corn Pasta** | Elbows*, Penne, Rotelli*, Spaghetti*, Vegetable Radiatore* | 340 | 12 |
| **Natural Noodles** * Also available in organic. | Lentil Noodles* | | 250 | 8.8 |
| | Wild Rice and Pea Flour Noodles* | | 250 | 8.8 |
| | Brown Rice Lentil Noodles | | 250 | 8.8 |
| | Mung Bean Noodles | | 250 | 8.8 |
| | Pea Noodles* | | 250 | 8.8 |
| **Norquin** *Organic brown rice & quinoa pasta | Elbows, Fettucine | | 341 | 12 |
| | Spaghetti | | 454 | 16 |
| | Spirals | | 227 | 8 |
| **Orgran** | Corn and Vegetable Shells | | 300 | 10.5 |
| | Brown Rice Spirals | | 250 | 8.8 |
| | Brown Rice Millet Spirals | | 250 | 8.8 |
| **Papadini** | **Pure Lentil Bean** | Cavatappi (elbows), Conchigliette (shells), Orzo (rice shaped), Rotini (twists) | 227 | 8 |

# GLUTEN-FREE PASTA CONT'D.

| Company | Product | | Grams | Ounces |
|---|---|---|---|---|
| **PASTATO**<br><br>Potato and organic brown rice pasta | Elbows*, Penne*, Spaghetti* | | 284 | 10 |
| | Shells | | 200 | 7 |
| | **Pasta and Cheese Dinners** (White or Yellow Cheddar) | Mac & Cheese, Mini Shells, Mini Spaghetti* | 190 | 6.8 |

\* Also contains quinoa flour, ground flax, psyllium, FOS, Vitamins B1, B2, B3, B6, folic acid, pantothenic acid, iron and magnesium

| Company | Product | | Grams | Ounces |
|---|---|---|---|---|
| **PASTARISO**<br><br>Organic brown rice pasta | **Rice** | Angel Hair, Elbows(Mini), Shells, (Regular & Mini), Spirals | 200 | 7 |
| | | Elbows (Regular), Fusilli, Penne, Spaghetti | 284 | 10 |
| | | Fettucine, Lasagna, Vermicelli | 227 | 8 |
| | **Fortified Rice** | Spaghetti* | 284 | 10 |
| | **Rice Spinach** | Elbows, Penne, Spaghetti | 284 | 10 |
| | | Fettucine | 227 | 8 |
| | | Spirals | 200 | 7 |
| | **Rice Vegetable** | Penne | 284 | 10 |
| | | Shells, Spirals | 200 | 7 |
| | **Rice Tomato** | Penne | 284 | 10 |
| | | Spirals | 200 | 7 |
| | **Rice Pasta & Cheese Dinners** (white Cheddar) | Macariz Mac & Cheese | 190 | 6.8 |
| | | Rice Mini Shells & Cheese | 190 | 6.8 |
| | | Rice Mini Spaghetti & Cheese | 190 | 6.8 |
| | | Rice Spinach Pasta & Cheese | 190 | 6.8 |
| | **Rice Pasta & Cheese Dinners** (yellow Cheddar) | Rice Fettucine & Cheese | 190 | 6.8 |
| | | Rice Mac & Cheese | 190 | 6.8 |
| | | Rice Mini Spaghetti & Cheese | 190 | 6.8 |
| | | Rice Spinach Pasta & Cheese | 190 | 6.8 |

\* Brown rice flour, quinoa flour, ground flax, psyllium husks, FOS, vitamins B1, B2, B3, B6, folic acid, pantothenic acid, iron & magnesium.

Most products available in bulk.

| Company | Product | | Grams | Ounces |
|---|---|---|---|---|
| **PRESIDENT'S CHOICE** | Thai Rice Sticks | | 227 | 8 |
| **THAI KITCHEN** | **Rice Noodles** (plain) | Stir Fry, Thin, Wide Style | 200 | 7 |
| | **Stir-Fry Rice Noodles** (with sauce) | Original Pad Thai, Thai Peanut | 155 | 5.5 |
| | | Pad Thai with Chili | 170 | 6 |
| **TINKYADA**<br><br>\* Brown rice with rice bran<br>\*\* Organic brown rice<br>\*\*\* White rice<br><br>All pasta available in bulk 4.54 kg (10 lbs.). | Elbows*, Fusilli*, Penne*, Rigatoni*, Shells*, Spaghetti*, Spirals* | | 454 | 16 |
| | Lasagna* or Lasagna** | | 280 | 10 |
| | Spinach Rice Spaghetti*, Vegetable Rice Spirals* | | 340 | 12 |
| | Elbows**, Penne**, Spaghetti**, Spirals** | | 340 | 12 |
| | Spaghetti*** | | 454 | 16 |
| | Fettuccini*, Linguine*, Rigatoni* | | 397 | 14 |
| **WESTBRAE**<br>Corn pasta | Angel Hair, Garden Twists, Spaghetti | | 227 | 8 |

# Gluten-Free Entrées and Side Dishes

| Company | Product | | Grams | Ozs. | Serves |
|---|---|---|---|---|---|
| **AlpineAire Foods**<br><br>NOTE: Also have many other products. | **Side Dishes** | Brown Rice, Instant | 57 | 2 | 2 |
| | | Corn, Sweet, Freeze-Dried | 43 | 1.5 | 2 |
| | | French Cut Green Beans Almondine | 50 | 1.75 | 2 |
| | | Garden Vegetables | 43, 85 | 1.5, 3 | 2, 4 |
| | | Mashed Potatoes, Instant | 50, 100 | 1.75, 3.5 | 2, 4 |
| | | Peas, Freeze-Dried | 43 | 1.5 | 2 |
| | | Potatoes & Cheddar with Chives | 113 | 4 | 2 |
| | | Vegetable Mix | 43, 85 | 1.5, 3 | 2, 4 |
| **Amy's Kitchen**<br><br>* Casein-Free | **Bowls** | Brown Rice and Vegetables*, Santa Fe Enchilada, Teriyaki* | 284 | 10 | |
| | **Chili** | Medium*, Medium Black Bean*, Medium with Vegetables*, Spicy* | 417 | 14.7 | |
| | **Enchiladas** | Black Bean Vegetable* | 269 | 9.5 | |
| | | Black Bean Whole Meal* | 284 | 10 | |
| | | Cheese | 255 | 9 | |
| | | Cheese Whole Meal | 255 | 9 | |
| | **Stir-Fries** | Asian Noodle* | 284 | 10 | |
| | | Indian Matlar Paneer | 284 | 10 | |
| | | Thai* | 269 | 9.5 | |
| | **Miscellaneous** | Garden Vegetable Lasagna | 291 | 10.3 | |
| | | Mexican Tamale Pie* | 227 | 8 | |
| | | Rice Crust Cheese Pizza | 340 | 12.0 | |
| | | Rice Mac & Cheese | 255 | 9 | |
| | | Shepherd's Pie* | 227 | 8 | |
| **Barkat** | Mexican Rice Pot Meal | | 79 | 2.8 | 1 |
| | Rice & Tomato Pot Meal | | 71 | 2.5 | 1 |
| **Dietary Specialties**<br><br>* Casein-Free | **Entrées** | Chicken Nuggets* | 454 | 16 | |
| | | Ravioletti Primavera | 340 | 12 | |
| | | Lasagna with Meat Sauce | 340 | 12 | |
| | | Macaroni and Cheese | 340 | 12 | |
| | **Filled Pasta** | Cheese Ravioli, Meat Ravioli*, Stuffed Shells | 454 | 16 | |
| | **Pizzas** | Cheese (8") | 340 | 12 | 3 |
| | | Vegetable (8") | 391 | 13.8 | 3 |
| **Foods By George** | Lasagna | | 340 | 12 | |
| | **Manicotti** | Cheese, Spinach & Cheese | 397 | 14 | |
| | Pizza | Cheese | 255 | 9 | 1 |
| **Gluten-Free Pantry** | **Meal in a Cup** | Hearty Chicken Primavera | 104 | 3.7 | |
| | | Santa Fe Black Beans & Rice | 92 | 3.2 | |
| | | Stroganoff Style with Beef | 92 | 3.2 | |
| | | Zesty Chicken Gumbo | 78 | 2.8 | |
| **Glutino** | Tomato and Cheese Pizza | | 12.4 | 4 | |

# GLUTEN-FREE ENTRÉES AND SIDE DISHES CONT'D.

| Company | Product | | Grams | Ozs. | Serves |
|---|---|---|---|---|---|
| HEALTH VALLEY | Chilies | Burrito Flavor, Enchilada Flavor, Fajita Flavor, Lentil (regular and no salt), Mild (regular and no salt), Mild with Black Bean, Mild with 3 Beans, Spicy (regular and no salt), Spicy Black Bean, Turkey with Beans | 425 | 15 | |
| INSTANT GOURMET | Meal in a Cup | Hearty Mountain Chili | 94 | 3.3 | 1 |
| | | N'Orleans Chicken Gumbo | 78 | 2.75 | 1 |
| | | Santa Fe Chicken | 118 | 4.2 | 1 |
| | | Stroganoff with Beef & Rice | 107 | 3.8 | 1 |
| | | Texas BBQ Chicken | 116 | 4.1 | 1 |
| LEGUMES PLUS | Mexicali Lentil Salad | | 177 | 6.25 | 4 |
| | Herbed Lentil Casserole | | 234 | 8.25 | 4 |
| | Meatless Lentil Chili | | 234 | 8.25 | 4 |
| LUNDBERG FAMILY FARMS | One Step Rice & Lentil Entrées | Chili, Curry, Garlic Basil, | 255 | 9 | |
| | | Olde World Pilaf | 1.14 kg | 25 lbs. | |
| | Organic Quick Brown Rice | Hearty Harvest Brown (Plain) | 170 | 6 | |
| | | Picante Spanish Fiesta | 142 | 5 | |
| | | Roasted Garlic Pesto | 142 | 5 | |
| | | Savory Vegetarian Chicken | 142 | 5 | |
| | Risotto | Creamy Parmesan, Tomato Basil | 156 | 5.5 | |
| MANISCHEWITZ | Lentil Pilaf Mix, Spanish Pilaf Mix | | 191 | 6.75 | 4 |
| NATURE'S HILIGHTS | Rice Crust Pizza (Soy Cheese Style) | | 312 | 11 | 2 |
| | Tostada (Cheese & Vegetarian Beans) | | 369 | 13 | 2 |
| | Tostada (Soy Cheese & Vegetarian Beans) | | 369 | 13 | 2 |
| PANNE RIZO | Chicken Pot Pie (5") | | 300 | 10.6 | 1 |
| | Macaroni and Cheese | | 390 | 13.8 | 1 |
| | Mini Pizzola | Ham & Pineapple, Mushroom & Olive | 170 | 6 | 1 |
| | Panini | Tuna Melt | 310 | 11 | 1 |
| | | Oven Roasted Turkey | 225 | 8 | 1 |
| PRIVATE RECIPE | Frozen Entrées | Apple Braised Pork | 225 | 8 | 1 |
| | | Beef and Vegetable Casserole | 275 | 10 | 1 |
| | | Country Chicken, Lemon Herb Fish | 255 | 9 | 1 |
| | | Pot Roast with Rice & Peas | 255 | 9 | 1 |
| | | Sweet and Sour Chicken | 295 | 10.5 | 1 |
| | | Turkey Dinner | 265 | 9.5 | 1 |
| TAMARIND TREE  NOTE: Ready to eat in 5 minutes.  No preservatives or MSG.  Shelf stable for 2 years. | Vegetarian Side Dishes: (microwave trays with precooked long-grain brown rice) | | | | |
| | | Creamy Vegetable Medley with Nuts | 262 | 9.25 | 1 |
| | | Garden Peas & Sautéed Mushrooms | 262 | 9.25 | 1 |
| | | Golden Lentils with Vegetables | 262 | 9.25 | 1 |
| | | Curried Garbanzos and Potatoes | 262 | 9.25 | 1 |
| | | Savory Spinach with Indian Cheese | 262 | 9.25 | 1 |
| | | Tender Spinach & Garbanzos | 262 | 9.25 | 1 |
| | | Spicy Garden Vegetables | 262 | 9.25 | 1 |
| | | Aromatic Lentil Chili | 262 | 9.25 | 1 |

# GLUTEN-FREE ENTRÉES AND SIDE DISHES CONT'D.

| Company | Product | | Grams | Ozs. | Serves |
|---|---|---|---|---|---|
| TASTE ADVENTURE | Quick Cuisine "Entrées" | Black Beans & Rice Santa Fe Fiesta | 170 | 6 | 4 |
| | | Lentil & Rice Bombay Curry | 170 | 6 | 4 |
| | | Louisiana Red Bean Jambalaya | 170 | 6 | 4 |
| | Quick Cooking Chilies | Black Bean | 156 | 5.5 | 2 |
| | | Five Bean | 156 | 5.5 | 2 |
| | | Lentil | 156 | 5.5 | 2 |
| | | Red Bean | 156 | 5.5 | 2 |

# SNACKS

## Candy, Chips, Nuts, Seeds, Pretzels

❖ Read labels carefully. Many snack foods contain wheat, rye oats or barley: e.g., flavored tortilla chips, potato chips, soy nuts, snack bars.

❖ **Soy nuts:** Whole soybeans that have been soaked in water and then baked or roasted in oil or by dry heat.

Plain soy nuts are available whole or crumbled.

# GLUTEN-FREE SNACKS

| Company | Product | | Grams | Ounce |
|---|---|---|---|---|
| ALLENS<br><br>* Gold package | Belgian Chocolate Licorice* "Wheat-Free/Gluten-Free" | | 32 | 1.1 |
| | Gourmet Licorice* "Wheat-Free/Gluten-Free" | | 32 | 1.1 |
| | NOTE: Also makes a Belgian chocolate and Gourmet Licorice that contains wheat. Read label carefully and purchase "Wheat-Free/Gluten-Free products" only. | | | |
| BARBARA'S BAKERY | Cheese Puffs | Original (Natural) | 30, 200 | 1, 7 |
| | | Original Bakes | 155 | 5.5 |
| | | Jalapeño | 200 | 7 |
| | | White Cheddar | 155 | 5.5 |
| CANASOY | Soy Nuts (Organic Dry Roasted) | | 227 | 8 |
| CHEECHA KRACKLES<br><br>* Potato Pasta Chips | Puffed Chips | Luscious Lime, Original, Sea Salt & Vinegar | 75 | 2.7 |
| | Unpuffed Chips (GF label only) | | 350 | 12.3 |
| | NOTE: Also make Puffed (Nacho Cheese) and Unpuffed (Regular Label) which contain wheat-flour which are not gluten-free. | | | |
| CLOCKIT CROC' DOR | Soybean Snack | BBQ, Regular, Sea Salt | 200 | 7 |
| DIXIE DINERS' CLUB | Soy Beanits™ | Salted, Lightly Salted | 454 | 16 |
| ENER-G FOODS | Crisp Pretzels (low protein) | | 75 | 2.7 |
| | Sesame Pretzel Rings | | 75 | 2.7 |
| GENISOY | Soy Nuts | Salted, Unsalted, BBQ, Hickory Smoked | 99 | 3.5 |
| GLUTANO | Pretzels | | 75 | 2.6 |
| GLUTINO | Pretzels | | 76, 116 | 2.7, 14.1 |

# GLUTEN-FREE SNACKS CONT'D.

| Company | Product | | Grams | Ounces |
|---|---|---|---|---|
| HILTON | Toasted Soy Crisps | BBQ, Onion and Garlic, Lightly Sea Salted, Unsalted | 13.6 kg | 30 lbs. |
| LUNDBERG | Rice Chips | Pico De Gallo, Santa Fe BBQ, Sea Salt, Sesame & Seaweed | 170 | 6 |
| NATURE'S HILIGHTS | Rice Sticks | Salted, Unsalted | 85 | 3 |
| NU-WORLD Amaranth | Nu-World Foods Amaranth Snackers | BBQ Hot & Spicy, BBQ Sweet & Sassy, Chili Lime, French Onion, Garden Burst | 170 | 6 |
| PUMPKORN® * Seasoned with wheat-free tamari | Pumpkorn* (Pumpkin Seeds) | Caramel, Chili, Curry, Maple Vanilla, Mesquite, Original, Mild Original | 78 | 2.75 |
| ROBERT'S GOURMET | Potato Flyers (Puffed Potato Chips with potato/rice) | Original, Basalmic Vinegar, Pesto Parmesan | 43, 113 | 1.5, 4 |
| | Fruity Booty (Fruit Snack with rice, corn and soy) | | 30, 113 | 1, 4 |
| | Pirates Booty (Rice and Cheese Snack) | | 30, 113 | 1, 4 |
| | Pirates Booty with Caramel (Rice Snack) | | 78, 156 | 2.75, 5.5 |
| | Plundered Booty (Potato Crisps) | | 30, 85 | 1, 3 |
| | Veggie Booty (Vegetable Snack with rice, corn & soy) | | 30, 113 | 1, 4 |
| SKINNY | Corn Chips (Original Flavor) | | 21, 113 | 0.75, 4 |
| | "Sticks" (Garden Vegetable, Original Spud) | | 227 | 8 |
| TERRA | Terra Chips Original (taro, sweet potato, yucca batata, parsnip, oils and salt) | | 28, 213 | 1, 7.5 |
| | Terra Stix (Original) | | 227 | 8 |
| | Taro Chip (Original Taro) | | 170 | 6 |
| | Sweet Potato Chips (Original No Salt) | | 34, 170 | 1.2, 6 |

# GLUTEN-FREE SNACK BARS

| Company | Product | | Grams | Ounces |
|---|---|---|---|---|
| ENER-G FOODS * Also available in bulk. | Granola Bar (10/package)* | | 393 | 13.9 |
| ENJOY LIFE FOODS | Snack Bars* | Apple Cinnamon, Cranberry | 50 | 1.7 |
| | *Enriched with thiamin, riboflavin, niacin, Vit. B6, B12, folate, calcium, iron, magnesium and zinc. | | | |
| GENISOY | Soy Protein Bars | Chunky Peanut Butter Fudge, Creamy Peanut Yogurt | 61.5 | 2.2 |
| | Xtreme Bars | Peanut Butter Fix | 45 | 1.6 |

# GLUTEN-FREE SNACK BARS CONT'D.

| Company | Product | Grams | Ounces |
|---|---|---|---|
| **GLUTANO** | Chocolate Covered Hazelnut Wafer Bars (3/package) | 125 | 4.4 |
| **GOVINDA FITNESS FOODS**<br><br>*All bars are gluten-free except "Pistachio Planet" which contains barley malt. | **Bliss Bars** (nuts, seeds, dried fruits, puffed amaranth)* | | |
| | Almond Cashew Sublime | 50 | 1.75 |
| | Brazil Pine Divine | 50 | 1.75 |
| | Cosmic Combo | 50 | 1.75 |
| | Fig Date Delight | 50 | 1.75 |
| | Heavenly Hazelnut | 50 | 1.75 |
| | Macadamia Madness | 50 | 1.75 |
| | Omega Bar | 50 | 1.75 |
| | Peanut Perfection | 50 | 1.75 |
| | Pumpkin Pleasures | 50 | 1.75 |
| | Sesame Sensation | 50 | 1.75 |
| | Sunflower Power | 50 | 1.75 |
| | Walnut Date the Great | 50 | 1.75 |
| **KINNIKINNICK**<br><br>*Alta Products: Gluten-Free/Casein-Free | **Crispy Rice Bars** | | |
| | Chocolate Covered | 95 | 3.5 |
| | Peanut Butter* | 60 | 2.5 |
| | Raisin* | 80 | 3 |
| | Regular* | 60 | 2.5 |
| | **Granola Bar** Cranberry*, Blueberry* | 50 | 2 |
| | Kin-Etic Energy Bar | 50 | 2 |
| **NATURE'S PATH** | **EnviroKidz Crispy Rice Bars** | | |
| | Berry, Chocolate, Peanut Butter | 28 | 1 |
| **OMEGA SMART** | **Nutritional Bars** | | |
| | Apricot Almond, Carrot Cake, Chocolate Nut, Cinnamon & Apple, Orange & Pineapple, Raisin & Spice | 67 | 2.35 |
| **PANNE RIZO** | Honey Cranberry Granola Bar | NA | NA |
| **WHOLE FOODS MARKET** | **365 Everyday Value Nutrition Bars** | | |
| | Chocolate Fudge, Chocolate Raspberry, Honey Peanut, Honey Peanut Yogurt | 50 | 1.76 |

# GLUTEN-FREE MISCELLANEOUS SNACKS

| Company | Product | Grams | Ounces |
|---|---|---|---|
| **BARKAT** | Ice Cream Cones (24) | 70 | 2.5 |
| **ENER-G FOODS** | Communion Wafers (made with "Soyquick" and rice flour) | 50/box | 50/box |
| | Waffle Ice Cream Cones (3 large) | 117 | 4.1 |

# SOUPS

❖ Most canned soups are **NOT** gluten-free as they contain wheat flour, barley, noodles, hydrolyzed plant or vegetable protein (HPP or HVP) made from wheat.

❖ Bouillon cubes and soup broths often contain wheat flour or HPP or HVP made from wheat and are **NOT** gluten-free.

❖ Soup stock can be made from meat or poultry bones and a variety of vegetables.

## GLUTEN-FREE SOUPS

| Company | Product | | Grams | Ounces |
|---|---|---|---|---|
| **ALPINEAIRE FOODS** | "Kernel's" Corn Chowder | | 113 | 4 |
| **AMY'S KITCHEN** <br><br> * Casein-Free | **Organic Canned** <br><br> **Soups** | Black Bean* | 411 | 14.5 |
| | | Chunky Tomato Bisque | 411 | 14.5 |
| | | Cream of Tomato | 411 | 14.5 |
| | | Lentil* | 411 | 14.5 |
| | | Lentil Vegetable* | 411 | 14.5 |
| | | Split Pea* | 400 | 14.1 |
| **CELIFIBR** <br> * 6 cubes/box | **Bouillon Cubes** | Vegetable Medley | 60 | 2 |
| | | Vegetarian Beef | 60 | 2 |
| | | Vegetarian Chicken | 60 | 2 |
| **COOK IN THE KITCHEN** | **Dried Soup Mixes** | Harvest Garden Vegetable | 156 | 5.5 |
| | | Mediterranean Lentil Soup | 156 | 5.5 |
| | | Dilled Tomato | 156 | 5.5 |
| | | Welsh Potato | 156 | 5.5 |
| **DIXIE DINERS' CLUB** <br> * Dried soup mixes (96 servings) | Beef (Not!) Official Broth | | 454 | 16 |
| | Chicken (Not!) Official Broth | | 454 | 16 |
| **EDWARD & SONS** <br><br><br><br><br><br><br><br><br> * 2 cubes/box | **Heritage Soups** <br> (Organic Instant) | Potato Leek | 60 | 2.1 |
| | | Tomato Basil | 60 | 2.1 |
| | | Vegetable | 60 | 2.1 |
| | **Miso-Cup** <br> (Organic Instant) | Organic Reduced Sodium | 28 | 1.0 |
| | | Organic Traditional with Tofu | 37 | 1.3 |
| | | Original Golden | 70 | 2.5 |
| | | Savory Seaweed | 70 | 2.5 |
| | **Organic Country Bouillon Cubes** | Herb Medley* | 20 | 0.7 |
| | | Vegetable Harvest* | 20 | 0.7 |
| **EL PETO** | **Soup Concentrates** | Beef Flavor, Onion, Tomato, Tomato Vegetable | 300 | 10.5 |
| | | Chicken Flavor, Vegetable | 280 | 9.9 |
| **ENER-G FOODS** | Cream of Mushroom Soup (dry mix) | | 25 | 0.88 |
| **GLUTINO** | Beef Flavoured Soup Mix | | 160 | 5.6 |
| | Chicken Flavoured Soup Mix | | 160 | 5.6 |
| | Cream of Mushroom Soup Mix | | 160 | 5.6 |
| | Onion Soup Mix | | 160 | 5.6 |

# GLUTEN-FREE SOUPS CONT'D.

| Company | Product | | Grams | Ounces |
|---|---|---|---|---|
| **HEALTH VALLEY** | Chicken Rice Soup | | 425 | 15 |
| | **Fat-Free Soups** | Black Bean & Vegetable, Country Corn & Vegetable, Five Bean Vegetable, 14 Garden Vegetable, Lentil & Carrots, Split Pea & Carrots, Supper Broccoli, Tomato Vegetable | 425 | 15 |
| | **Organic Soups** (No Salt) | Black Bean, Lentil, Potato Leek, Split Pea, Tomato, Vegetable | 425 | 15 |
| | **Organic Soups** (Regular) | Black Bean, Lentil, Potato Leek Split Pea, Tomato, Vegetable | 425 | 15 |
| **IMAGINE** | **Natural Garden Vegetable Soups** (Organic) | Creamy Broccoli | 443, 946 mL | 15, 32 |
| | | Creamy Butternut Squash | 443, 946 mL | 15, 32 |
| | | Creamy Mushroom (non-organic) | 443, 946 mL | 15, 32 |
| | | Creamy Potato Leek | 443, 946 mL | 15, 32 |
| | | Creamy Sweet Corn | 443, 946 mL | 15, 32 |
| | | Creamy Tomato | 443, 946 mL | 15, 32 |
| | | Vegetable Broth | 443, 946 mL | 15, 32 |
| | | Free Range Chicken Broth | 443, 946 mL | 15, 32 |
| | | No-Chicken Broth | 443, 946 mL | 15, 32 |
| **INSTANT GOURMET** | **Soup in a Cup** | Bay Shrimp Bisque, | 28 | 1 |
| | | Broccoli Cheddar | 28 | 1 |
| **LEGUMES PLUS** | **Soup Mixes** | Country Vegetable Lentil | 276 | 9.75 |
| | | Gourmet Herb Lentil | 276 | 9.75 |
| | | Green Split Pea | 305 | 10.75 |
| | | Olde World Lentil | 269 | 9.5 |
| | | Red Curry Lentil | 326 | 11.6 |
| | | Wild Rice & Herbs Lentil | 269 | 9.5 |
| | | Zesty Tomato Lentil | 305 | 10.75 |
| **MANISCHEWITZ** | **Borscht** | Clear, No Sodium, Reduced Sodium, Reduced Calorie, Shredded Beets | 936 | 33 |
| | Schav | | 936 | 33 |
| **PACIFIC FOODS** | **Natural Broths** | Beef, Free Range Chicken | 946 mL | 32 |
| | **Organic Broths** | Free Range Chicken, Mushroom, Vegetable | 946 mL | 32 |
| | **Soups** | Creamy Butternut Squash, Roasted Red Pepper & Tomato | 454, 946 mL | 16, 32 |
| | **Organic Soups** | French Onion, Creamy Tomato | 454, 946 mL | 16, 32 |
| **TASTE ADVENTURE** | **Dried Soups** | Black Bean | 130 | 4.6 |
| | | Curry Lentil | 170 | 6 |
| | | Golden Pea | 142 | 5 |
| | | Navy Bean | 156 | 5.5 |
| | | Split Pea | 142 | 5 |
| | | Sweet Corn Chowder | 142 | 5 |

# GLUTEN-FREE SOUPS CONT'D.

| Company | Product | | Grams | Ounces |
|---|---|---|---|---|
| THAI KITCHEN | Coconut Ginger Soup , Hot & Sour Soup (can) | | 397 | 14 |
| | **Instant Rice Noodle Soups** | Bangkok Curry, Garlic & Vegetable, Lemon Grass & Chili, Spring Onion, Thai Ginger & Vegetable | 45 | 1.6 |
| | **Rice Noodle Soups** | Curry | 139 | 4.9 |
| | | Hot & Sour | 120 | 4.25 |
| | **Rice Noodle Bowls** | Mushroom Medley, Roasted Garlic, Spring Onion | 50 | 1.75 |
| WHOLE FOODS MARKET | **365 Everyday Value Homestyle Soups** | Corn Chowder, Split Pea, Three Bean Chili, Tomato | 425 | 15 |

# GLUTEN-FREE COATINGS AND CRUMBS

| Company | Product | Grams | Ounces |
|---|---|---|---|
| DIETARY SPECIALTIES | Rice Crumbs | 454 | 16 |
| DR. SHAR | Gluten-Free Bread Crumbs (Pangrati) | 250 | 8.8 |
| EL PETO | Gluten-Free Bread Crumbs | 500 | 17.5 |
| | Gluten-Free Stuffing | 300 | 10.5 |
| ENER-G FOODS | Bread Crumbs (Stuffing) | 227 | 8 |
| GILLIAN'S FOODS | Bread Crumbs | 340 | 12 |
| GLUTEN-FREE COOKIE JAR | Bread Crumbs (Plain or Fresh Herb) | 454 | 16 |
| GLUTEN-FREE DELIGHTS | Graham Cracker Crumbs | 227 | 8 |
| | Seasoned Croûtons | 142 | 5 |
| | Stuffing | 142 | 5 |
| HOL•GRAIN | Brown Rice Bread Crumbs | 113 | 4 |
| KINNIKINNICK * Alta Products: Gluten-Free/Casein-Free | Crispy Chicken Coating Mix* | 500 | 18 |
| | General Coating Mix* | 500 | 18 |
| | Graham Style Cracker Crumbs* | 200 | 7 |
| LAUREL'S SWEET TREATS | Onion Ring Batter | 326 | 11.5 |
| MISS ROBEN'S | Breading Batter Coating Mix (Mild) | 170, 510 | 6, 18 |
| NU-WORLD AMARANTH | Amaranth Breading Crumbs | 170 | 6 |
| PANNE RIZO | Plain Rice Crumbs | 142 | 5 |
| | Herb Croutons | 213 | 7.5 |

# GLUTEN-FREE GRAVY MIXES

| Company | Product | Grams | Ounces |
|---|---|---|---|
| **GLUTINO** | Brown Gravy Mix (casein-free) | 159 | 5.6 |
| **KINNIKINNICK** | Brown Gravy Mix | 113 | 4 |
| | Chicken Gravy Mix | 113 | 4 |

# GLUTEN-FREE SAUCES

| Company | Product | Grams | Ounces |
|---|---|---|---|
| **GLUTINO**<br>* Gluten-Free/Casein-Free | BBQ Sauce | 125 | 4.4 |
| | **All Natural Dressings and Marinades**<br>Classic Caesar, Fine Herbs & Basalmic*,<br>Peppercorn Garlic*, Naturally Italian* | 340 | 12 |
| **LAUREL'S SWEET TREATS** | Rib It On | 454 | 16 |
| **MR. SPICE** | Garlic Steak Sauce, Ginger Stir Fry Sauce, Honey<br>BBQ Sauce, Honey Mustard Sauce, Indian Curry Sauce,<br>Sweet & Sour Sauce, Tangy Bang! Hot Sauce,<br>Thai Peanut Sauce | 298 | 10.5 |
| **THAI KITCHEN** | Lemon Grass Salad Splash | 200 | 7 |
| | Light Plum Spring Roll Sauce | 200 | 7 |
| | Original Recipe Peanut Satay Sauce | 227 | 8 |
| | Pad Thai Sauce | 227 | 8 |
| | Red Chili Dipping Sauce | 200 | 7 |
| | Spicy Thai Chili Sauce | 200 | 7 |
| | Spicy Thai Peanut Satay Sauce | 227 | 8 |
| | Thai Barbecue Sauce | 200 | 7 |

# GLUTEN-FREE SOY SAUCES

| Company | Product | Grams | Ounces |
|---|---|---|---|
| **LIFESOY** | **Wheat-Free/Gluten-Free Soy Sauce** | | |
| | Original, Oriental Ginger, Shitake Mushroom, Spicy Garlic | 500 | 17.6 |
| **SAN J**<br>NOTE: San J regular tamari and lite tamari soy sauces contain wheat. | Organic Wheat-Free Tamari Soy Sauce (Gold Label) | 142, 284 & 567 mL | 5, 10 & 20 |
| | Organic Lite Tamari Soy Sauce (25% less salt)*<br>* In USA called "Reduced Sodium Wheat Free Tamari". | 284, 567 mL | 10, 20 |

# GLUTEN-FREE SPREADS

| Company | Product | Grams | Ounces |
|---|---|---|---|
| **KETTLE FOODS** | California Almond Butter | 310 | 11 |
| | Cashew Butter, Hazelnut Butter, Organic Peanut<br>Butter, Sesame Butter, Sunflower Butter | 322 | 11.5 |

# DAIRY/NON-DAIRY SUBSTITUTES

❖ Some people with celiac disease (newly diagnosed) have a temporary lactose intolerance (see page 37-40). However, once the gastrointestinal villous function returns to normal (after following a strict gluten-free diet) most people can re-introduce lactose into their diet.

❖ **Some non-dairy beverages are NOT gluten-free:**

## RICE BEVERAGES (NOT GLUTEN-FREE):

**Imagine Foods "Rice Dream" Non-Dairy Beverage** is made from rice but the enzymatic process utilizes a barley enzyme. Even though this enzyme is discarded after use, the final beverage may contain a minute residual amount of barley protein (0.002%).

## SOY BEVERAGES (NOT GLUTEN-FREE):

Many contain barley, barley malt extract or oats and are **NOT** gluten-free,

**e.g.:** ◆ **EdenSoy** – all contain gluten except "Eden Blend"

  ◆ **Nutrisoy** – Original, Vanilla
  ◆ **President's Choice** – Fortified, Lite
  ◆ **Vitasoy**
  ◆ **Westbrae Westsoy** • 100% Organic – Original*
                • Low-Fat – Plain*, Vanilla*, Chocolate*

*Westbrae uses two types of brown rice syrup in their Westsoy Soy Beverages and Westbrae Rice Drinks. The brown rice syrup in the 100% Organic Original Soy Beverage and Low-Fat Soy Beverages contain a barley enzyme. The Westsoy Lite, Non Fat, Plus Soy Beverages and Westbrae Rice Drinks brown rice syrup does not contain a barley enzyme.

## OTHER BEVERAGES (NOT GLUTEN-FREE):

  ◆ **Pacific Foods** • Non-Dairy Multigrain Beverage – Original
             • Non-Dairy Oat Beverage – Original, Vanilla

# GLUTEN-FREE LACTOSE-REDUCED DAIRY PRODUCTS

**Lacteeze Ice Cream**
- ◆ Cartons (1 litre) – Chocolate, Mango, Strawberry, Vanilla

**Lactaid Milk (CANADA)**
- ◆ Shelf stable (1 litre) – 2%
- ◆ Refrigerated (1 and 2 litres) – skim and 2%

**Lactaid Milk (USA)**
- ◆ Refrigerated (half gallon)
- ◆ Fat-Free, Low-Fat (1%), Reduced Fat (2%), Whole, Calcium Fortified (Fat-Free)

**Lacteeze Milk**
- ◆ Refrigerated (1 litre) – Skim, 1% and 2%

# GLUTEN-FREE SOY BEVERAGES

**Ener-G Foods "Soyquik"**
- ◆ Powder (16 oz/454g)

**Imagine Foods "Soy Dream" Non-Dairy Beverages**
- ◆ Shelf Stable (8 oz. and 32 oz./240 mL and 946 mL)
  - Soy Dream Regular – Original, Vanilla, Carob
  - Soy Dream Enriched – Original*, Vanilla*, Chocolate*
- ◆ Refrigerated (32 oz.)
    Soy Dream Enriched – Original*, Vanilla*, Chocolate*
- ◆ Refrigerated (64 oz.)
  - Soy Dream Enriched – Original*, Vanilla*
  - *  Enriched with Calcium and Vitamins A, D, E and B12 in USA
  - *  Enriched with Calcium and Vitamins A, D, B2, B12 and Zinc in Canada

**Pacific Foods "Non-Dairy Soymilk Drinks" (USA)**
- ◆ Shelf Stable (32 oz./946 mL)
  - Organic Original Soy – Unsweetened
  - Enriched Organic Soy – Plain*, Cocoa*, Coffee*, Strawberry*, Vanilla*
  - Fat Free Soy – Plain**, Vanilla**
  - Select Soy – Plain, Vanilla
  - Ultra Soy – Plain***, Vanilla***
    - *  Enriched with Calcium and Vitamins A, D, E, B2, B6, B12
    - **  Enriched with Calcium and Vitamins A and D
    - ***  Enriched with Calcium and Vitamins A, D, E, B2, B6 and B12

## Soya World "So Good Fortified" (CANADA)*

- ◆ Shelf Stable (1 litre) – Original, Chocolate, Vanilla, Fat Free
- ◆ Fresh (946 mL) – Original, Chocolate, Strawberry, Vanilla, Fat Free Vanilla, Soyaccino
- ◆ Fresh (1.89 litres) – Original, Chocolate, Vanilla, Fat Free, Omega**

  * Fortified with Calcium, Iron, Phosphorus, Potassium, Zinc and Vitamins A, C, D, B1, B2, B3, B6, B12, Folacin and Pantothenate.
  ** Contains flax seed oil

## Soya World "So Nice Soyganic" (CANADA AND USA)*

- ◆ Shelf Stable (946 mL/32 oz.) – Natural**, Original, Chocolate, Vanilla
- ◆ Fresh (946 mL/32 oz.) – Natural**, Original, Chocolate, Mocha, Vanilla, Noel Nog
- ◆ Fresh (1.89 litres/64 oz.) – Original, Chocolate, Vanilla

  * All flavors except natural fortified/enriched with Calcium, Iron, Zinc and Vitamins A, C, D, B1, B2, B3, B6, B12, Folacin and Pantothenate.
  ** Natural is non-fortified/enriched

## Sunrise Soya Beverage (CANADA)

- ◆ Shelf Stable (250 mL) – Sweetened*
- ◆ Fresh (1, 2 and 4 litres) – Sweetened*
- ◆ Fresh (2 and 4 litres) – Natural*
- ◆ Fresh (1.89 litres) – Enriched Original**, Enriched Unsweetened**

  * Non-fortified
  ** Fortified with Calcium, Phosphorous, Iron, Zinc and Vitamins A, C, D, B1, B2, B3, B6, B12, Folacin and Pantothenate.

## Westbrae Westsoy Non-Dairy Soy Beverages (USA)

- ◆ Shelf Stable
  - • Non Fat (32 oz. and 64 oz.) – Plain*, Vanilla*
  - • Lite (6.3 oz. and 64 oz.) – Plain, Vanilla
  - • Lite (32 oz.) – Plain, Vanilla, Cocoa
  - • Plus (6.3 oz. and 64 oz.) – Plain**, Vanilla**
  - • Plus (32 oz.) – Plain**, Vanilla**, Cocoa**

  * Enriched with Calcium, Vitamins A and D
  ** Enriched with Calcium, Vitamins A, D and B2

## White Wave Silk Soy Beverages (CANADA)*

- ◆ Fresh (946 mL and 1.89 litres) – Plain, Vanilla, Chocolate

  * Fortified with Calcium, Zinc and Vitamins A, D, B2 and B12.

## White Wave Silk Soy Milk (USA)*

- ◆ Fresh (64 oz.) – Plain, Chocolate, Vanilla
- ◆ Fresh (32 oz.) – Plain, Chai, Chocolate, Coffee Soylatte, Mocha, Nog, Vanilla, Unsweetened
- ◆ Fresh (11 oz. single serve) – Plain, Chocolate, Coffee Soylatte, Spice Soylatte, Vanilla
- ◆ Shelf Stable (32 oz.) – Plain, Vanilla

  * All flavors (except Nog) enriched with Calcium, Vitamins A, D, B2 and B12.

# Gluten-Free Soy Yogurts

### Soya World "So Nice" Yogurts (CANADA)
- ◆ Fresh Carton (175 g) – Peach, Strawberry, Vanilla
- ◆ Fresh Carton (440 g) – Plain, Strawberry

### White Wave Silk Cultured Yogurts*
- ◆ Fresh Carton (32 oz./908 g) – Plain, Vanilla
- ◆ Fresh Carton (6 oz./170 g) – Apricot-Mango, Banana-Strawberry, Black Cherry, Blueberry, Key Lime, Lemon, Peach, Raspberry, Strawberry and Vanilla

　* Enriched with Calcium

# Gluten-Free Rice Beverages

### Lundberg "Drink Rice" Non-Dairy Beverage*
- ◆ Shelf Stable (32 oz.) – Original, Vanilla
  * Enriched with Calcium, Vitamins A and D

### Pacific Foods Non-Dairy Rice Drinks (USA)
- ◆ Shelf Stable (32 oz.)
  - Fat Free Rice – Plain*, Cocoa*, Vanilla*
  - Low Fat Rice – Plain*, Cocoa*, Vanilla*
  - Organic Low Fat Rice – Plain**, Vanilla**

　* Enriched with Calcium and Vitamins A and D with added L. Acidophilus and L. Bifidus
　** Enriched with Calcium and Vitamins A, D, E, B6 and B12 with added L. Acidophilus and L. Bifidus

### Pacific Foods Non-Dairy Rice Drinks (CANADA)*
- ◆ Shelf Stable (946 mL)
  - Fat Free Rice – Plain, Vanilla
  * Non-fortified

### Westbrae Rice Drink (USA)*
- ◆ Shelf Stable (32 oz. and 64 oz.) – Plain and Vanilla
  * Enriched with Calcium and Vitamins A, D, and B2

### Westbrae Rice Drinks (CANADA)
- ◆ Shelf Stable (946 mL) – Plain, Vanilla

# OTHER GLUTEN-FREE BEVERAGES

**Blue Diamond "Almond Breeze" Non-Dairy Beverage***
- ◆ Shelf Stable (8 oz and 32 oz.) – Chocolate, Original, Vanilla
    - \* Enriched with Vitamins A, D, and E and Calcium

**Eden Foods "EdenBlend" Brown Rice & Soy Beverage**
- ◆ Shelf Stable (8.45 and 33.8 oz./250 mL and 1L)

**Ener-G Foods "Nutquik"**
- ◆ Powdered Almonds (15oz./425 g)

**Pacific Foods "Almond Low-Fat Non-Dairy Beverage" (USA)***
- ◆ Shelf Stable (32 oz.) – Original, Vanilla
    - \* Enriched with calcium, Vitamins A, B2, B12 and D

**Pacific Foods Almond Low Fat Non-Dairy Drink (CANADA)**
- ◆ Shelf Stable (946 mL) – Vanilla flavor only

**Pacific Foods Hazelnut Non-Dairy Beverage (USA)***
- ◆ Shelf Stable (32 oz.) – Original
    - \* Enriched with calcium, Vitamins A, B2, B12 and D

**Tayo Foods Non-Dairy Drink (POTATO BASED SUBSTITUTE) ***
- ◆ Fresh (2 L) – Original, Chocolate
    - \* Fortified with Calcium, Folic Acid, Zinc, Vitamins A, B2, B6, B12 and D

**Vances DariFree Non-Dairy Beverage (POTATO BASED SUBSTITUTE) USA***
- ◆ Dry Mix Potato Based Milk Substitute – Original, Chocolate
    - • 21 oz. Carton yields 6 quarts
    - • 25 lb. Box yields 115 quarts
    - \* Enriched with Calcium, Vitamins A, D, E, C, B1, B2, B3, B6, B12, Folic Acid and Biotin

# GLUTEN-FREE COMPANIES/DISTRIBUTORS

## ✦ = Products can be ordered directly from company

**Absolutely Good**, JJB Naturals, Inc., Unit 135 – 12031 Horseshoe Way, Richmond, BC, Canada V7A 4V4
✦ Phone: 604-644-2588                     FAX: 604-271-3151
E-mail:jjbnaturals@telus.net              http://jjbnaturals.tripod.com

• Gluten-free specialty company.
• Gluten-free mixes (brown bread, cake & pastry, dinner roll, pizza crust and quick bread).

**Allen's Gourmet Candies,** 620 Lakeside Drive, Nelson, BC, Canada V1L 5S7
Phone: 250-352-3576                       FAX: 250-354-0125
E-mail: licorice@netidea.com

• Produce Belgian chocolate and gourmet licorice. Are available in wheat-free/gluten-free as well as regular varieties which contain wheat.

**AlpineAire Foods**, P. O. Box 1799, Rocklin, CA, USA 95677
Phone: 800-322-6325/916-624-6050         FAX: 916-624-1604
      866-322-6325
✦ E-mail: infor@aa-foods.com              www.aa-foods.com

• Gluten-free fully prepared meals, side dishes, vegetables, fruits, desserts, beverages, soups, rice and legumes that are freeze-dried and specially packaged for a long shelf life. No preservatives or MSG. These instant foods are in resealable, lightweight, foil pouches (stable for 1 year) and prepared in the pouch. Also available in cans (stable for 5-20 years).
• Order direct by phone, fax or internet; also available in retail stores.
• Shipping based on product weight; ships via UPS Ground.

**Amazing Grains Grower Cooperative,** 405 Main St. SW, Ronan, MT, USA 59864
Phone: 877-278-6585/406-676-3536          FAX: 406-676-3537
✦                                         www.montina.com

• Specialize in Montina™ products made from Indian rice grass that is grown by its members and milled, processed and packaged in a gluten-free facility.
• Montina™ flour and all purpose baking flour blend.
• Order direct by phone, fax or internet; ships via UPS.

**Amy's Kitchen Inc.**, Box 7868, Santa Rosa, CA, USA 95407
Phone: 707-578-7188                       FAX: 707-578-7995
E-mail: amy@amyskitchen.net               www.amyskitchen.com

• Organic, vegetarian, prepared natural meals (e.g., pot pies, entrées, pizzas, whole meals, Asian meals, skillet meals, burritos, pocket sandwiches, veggie burgers, snacks, toaster pops, soups, chilies, refried beans, pasta sauces and salsas.
• A variety of products are gluten-free and some are also casein-free.

**Ancient Harvest Quinoa Corporation**, Box 279, 222 E. Redondo Beach Blvd. Unit B, Gardena, CA, USA 90248
✦ Phone: 310-217-8125                     FAX: 310-217-8140
E-mail: quinoacorp@aol.com                www.quinoa.bigstep.com

• Organic quinoa products include quinoa grain, flour, cereal flakes and pastas (quinoa flour and corn flour) which are gluten-free.
• Regular supergrain organic pasta (whole-wheat and quinoa flour) is **NOT** gluten-free.

# GLUTEN-FREE COMPANIES/DISTRIBUTORS CONT'D.

**Annie Chun's Gourmet Food**, 54 Mark Dr., Suite 103, San Rafael, CA, USA 94903
Phone: 415-479-8272
E-mail: info@anniechun.com          www.anniechun.com

• Asian sauces, noodles (chow mein, rice, soba) and meal kits (noodles and sauces).
• Rice noodles (original and flavored) are gluten-free.

**Arrowhead Mills**, Hain-Celestial Group, Box 2059, Hereford, TX, USA 79045
Phone: 800-749-0730/806-364-0730     FAX: 806-364-8242

• Wide variety of products (cereals, flours, mixes, legumes, seeds, pastas). Many are gluten-free.
• They test a large number of their products for gluten.

**Authentic Foods**, 1850 W. 169th St., Suite B, Gardena, CA, USA 90247
Phone: 800-806-4737/310-366-7612     FAX: 310-366-6938
E-mail: sales@authenticfoods.com     www.authenticfoods.com

• Gluten-free specialty company.
• Produce wheat-free and gluten-free baking mixes, flours and natural flavors.
• Mixes contain "garfava flour" (chickpeas and fava beans) developed by founder of this company.
• Order direct by phone, fax, or internet. Also available in retail stores and GF e-commerce companies via internet.
• Shipping based on weight and destination; ships via UPS Ground.

**Banducci & Daughters**, 627 Webster St., Palo Alto, CA, USA 94301
Phone: 888-207-1429/650-529-9336     FAX: 650-323-5825
E-mail: angel@angelkisscookies.com     www.angelkisscookies.com

• Meringue cookies made without additives or preservatives.
• Available in canisters (2.25 and 5 oz.) and tub (11 oz.).
• Order by phone. Also available in retail stores.

**Barbara's Bakery**, 3900 Cypress Dr, Petaluma, CA, USA 94954
Phone: 707-765-2273     FAX: 707-765-2927
E-mail: info@barbarasbakery.com     www.barbarasbakery.com

• Produce a line of natural cereals and snacks (chips, crackers, cookies and snack bars).
• Several cereals and snack foods are gluten-free.

### Barkat (see Glutano)

**The Birkett Mills**, Box 440A, Penn Yan, NY, USA 14527
Phone: 315-536-3311     FAX: 315-536-6740
E-mail: service@thebirkettmills.com     www.thebirkettmills.com

• One of the world's largest millers of buckwheat products.
• Process all buckwheat products in a self-contained mill dedicated solely to buckwheat grain. No other substances are processed in their buckwheat milling systems. After milling, buckwheat products are packaged on totally dedicated equipment.
• They also do random testing for gluten in their products using the enzyme immunoassay that tests at sensitivity levels of 20 ppm.
• Order direct by phone, fax, mail or internet.

# GLUTEN-FREE COMPANIES/DISTRIBUTORS CONT'D.

**Blue Diamond Growers**, 1802 C Street, Sacramento, CA, USA 95814
  Phone: 800-987-2329/916-442-0771        FAX: 916-446-8461
                                     www.bluediamond.com

- World's largest tree nut processing and marketing company specializing in a variety of almond products (nuts, nut thins and "Almond Breeze" non-dairy beverage).

**Bob's Red Mill Natural Foods, Inc.**, 5209 SE International Way, Milwaukie, OR, USA 97222
  Phone: 800-553-2258/503-654-3215      FAX: 503-653-1339
                                 www.bobsredmill.com

- Mill and manufacture a very extensive line of whole-grain natural foods using flint-hard quartz millstones.
- Produce a large variety of products (baking ingredients, cereals, dried fruits, flours, mixes, nuts, legumes, seeds, soup mixes, spices/herbs and sweeteners). Many of these products are gluten-free. They also sell baking equipment and books.
- Recently developed a line of gluten-free specialty products that are milled separately from gluten-containing products and are batch-tested using the Elisa test for gluten in Bob's Red Mill laboratory.
- In addition to the gluten-free specialty products, a large number of their other products, which are also gluten-free, are tested regularly for gluten.

**Breadshop's Natural Foods**, Hain-Celestial Group, 16007 Camino de la Cantera, Irwindale, CA, USA 91706
  Phone: 800-423-4846/626-334-3421      FAX: 626-633-1084
  E-mail: consumeraffairs@hain-celestial.com  www.hain-celestial.com

- Produce ready-to-eat cereals and granola bars.
- "Puffs n' Honey" cereal is gluten-free.

**Café Bonjour**, Rice Innovations, Inc./Maplegrove Foods, 8175 Winston Churchill Blvd., Norval, ON, Canada L0P 1K0
  Phone: 905-451-7423             Fax: 905-453-8137
  E-mail: info@maplegrovefoods.com      www.maplegrovefoods.com

- Gluten-free specialty company
- Produce brown rice pasta in a variety of shapes.

**Canasoy Enterprises (Canada) Ltd.**, 57 Lakewood Dr., Vancouver, BC, Canada V5L 4W4
  Phone: 604-255-1304           FAX: 604-255-5659
  E-mail: info@canasoy.com         www.canasoy.com

- Variety of nutritional health food products (baking supplies, beverages, cereals, dried fruits, herbs, legumes, pastas and spreads). Also distribute Ener-G Foods products.
- Some products are gluten-free.

**Casco**, Unilever Best Foods Canada, Ltd., Loch Lomond Place 120 McDonald St. John, NB, Canada E2J 1M5
  Phone: 800-858-2511           www.bestfoods.com

- Casco potato starch is one of many products from Unilever Best.
- Contact company for a listing of gluten-free products.

# GLUTEN-FREE COMPANIES/DISTRIBUTORS CONT'D.

**'Cause You're Special!**, P. O. Box 316, Phillips, WI, USA 54555
Phone: 866-NO-WHEAT/715-339-6959   FAX: 603-754-0245
E-mail: info@causeyourespecial.com   www.causeyourespecial.com
www.glutenfreegourmet.com

- Gluten-free specialty company.
- Produce a variety of "Cause You're Special" gluten-free, casein-free baking mixes (breads, biscuits, cakes, cookies, muffins, pancakes, pie crusts, pizza crusts, scones), flours and other baking ingredients. Also carry snack bars, books and other products.
- Order direct by phone, fax or internet, also available in some retail stores.
- Shipping based on amount purchased; ships via UPS (all available services) and USPS Priority Mail.

**CelifibR**, Rice Innovations, Inc./Maplegrove Foods,
8175 Winston Churchill Blvd., Norval, ON, Canada L0P 1K0
Phone: 905-451-7423   Fax: 905-453-8137
E-mail: info@maplegrovefoods.com   www.maplegrovefoods.com

- Gluten-free bouillon cubes (vegetable medley, vegetarian beef, vegetarian chicken).
- Made with organic vegetables and cold pressed sunflower oil.
- No GMOs, MSG or Sulphites.

**Celimix (see Nelson David)**

**Chebe**, Prima Provisions Co., P. O. Box 991, Newport, VT, USA 05855
Phone: 800-217-9510/802-334-8272   FAX: 802-334-5343
E-Mail: info@chebe.com   www.chebe.com

- Products made from manioc flour and manioc starch (also known as tapioca, yucca, cassava or namdioca).
- Mixes (bread, bread sticks, cinnamon rolls, pizza dough) and frozen dough (bread, sticks, pizza and sandwich buns) are gluten-free.

**Cheecha Krackles**, CadCan Marketing and Sales, Inc., 3412 9th St. SE., Calgary, AB, Canada T2G 3C3
Phone: 877-243-3242/403-287-6731   FAX: 403-287-6732
E-mail: cadcan@cheecha.ca   www.cheecha.ca

- Hot-air puffed potato and unpuffed potato pasta chips that are low in fat.
- Puffed (Luscious Lime, Original and Salt/Vinegar flavors are gluten-free).
- Unpuffed chips (gluten-free label only).

**Clock It**, Croc'Dor, 177 Loyola Schmidt St., Vaudreuil-Dorion, QC, Canada J7V 8P2
Phone: 877-459-4410/450-424-0228   FAX: 450-424-0292
E-mail: crocdor@rocler.qc.ca   www.crocdor.com

- Soybean snacks (3 flavors are gluten-free).

**Club House**, McCormick Canada, P. O. Box 5788, London, ON, Canada N6A 4Z2
Phone: 800-265-2600/519-432-1166   www.clubhouse-canada.com

- Large variety of products (baking ingredients, food extracts and colors, dry sauces and seasoning mixes, spices).
- Many products are gluten-free (e.g., potato flour, rice flour).
- Contact company for a listing of gluten-free products.

# GLUTEN-FREE COMPANIES/DISTRIBUTORS CONT'D.

**Cook in the Kitchen**, P. O. Box 3, Post Mills, VT, USA 05058
✦ Phone: 800-474-5518/802-333-4141          FAX: 802-333-4624
E-mail: chef@cookinthekitchen.com          www.cookinthekitchen.com

• Soups (4 flavors) are gluten-free.

---

**Cream of The Crop**, Aliments Trigone, Inc., 93 Aqueduc, St.Francois-de-la Riviere, QC, Canada G0R 3A0
Phone: 418-259-7414          FAX: 418-259-2417

• Organic buckwheat hot cereal is gluten-free.

---

**Cybros Inc.**, P. O. Box 851, Waukesha, WI, USA 53187-0851
✦ Phone: 800-876-2253/262-547-1821          FAX: 262-547-8946
E-mail: sales@cybrosinc.com          www.cybrosinc.com

• Produce gluten-free breads, buns, rolls, cookies.
• Available in retail outlets and also order direct by phone or fax.
• Shipping charges based on weight and destination; ships via UPS Ground.

---

**De Boles**, Hain-Celestial Group, Box 2059, Hereford, TX, USA 79045
Phone: 800-749-0730/806-364-0730          FAX: 806-364-8242

• Produce a variety of pastas (wheat, rice and corn).
• Corn and rice pastas in a variety of shapes and the macaroni/cheese and shells/cheese rice pasta are gluten-free.

---

**Dietary Specialties**, 10 Leslie Court, Whippany, NJ, USA 07981
✦ Phone: 888-640-2800/973-895-4446          FAX: 973-895-3742
E-mail: info@dietspec.com          www.dietspec.com

• Gluten-free specialty company.
• Wide variety of "Dietary Specialties" products such as baking mixes (bread, cake, muffin, pancake), breads, cookies and crackers, as well as ready-to-eat frozen products (e.g., chicken nuggets, desserts, English muffins, pie shells, pizza, ravioli).
• Also carry gluten-free products from other companies such as Aproten and Bi-Aglut.
• Also carry a variety of low protein products from Dietary Specialties and other companies.
• Order direct by phone, fax or internet.
• Shipping based on amount purchased.
• Grocery items shipped via UPS ground service and frozen items shipped express with dry ice within contiguous USA.

---

**Dixie Diners' Club**, Dixie USA, Inc., P. O. Box 1969, Tomball, TX, USA 77377
✦ Phone: 800-233-3668/281-516-3535          FAX: 800-688-2507
E-mail: info@dixieusa.com          www.dixieusa.com

• Very extensive line of health food products, including a unique line of soy-based products.
• Dixie's exclusive products are produced in several plants throughout the USA.
• Also carry other companies' products.
• A number of products are gluten-free.
• Order direct by phone, fax, mail or internet; also available in retail outlets.
• Shipping based on amount purchased.

# GLUTEN-FREE COMPANIES/DISTRIBUTORS CONT'D.

**Dr. Schar**, Dr.Schar GmbH, Winkelau 9, I-39014 Postal (BZ)  Italy
  Phone: +39 0473 293300      FAX: +39 0473 293399
  E-mail: info@schaer.com      www.schaer.com

- Gluten-free specialty company.
- Wide variety of "Dr. Schar" gluten-free mixes (all-purpose, bread, cake), baked products (breads, baguettes, biscuits, cakes, pizza crusts, rolls), cereal and pasta.
- Available from gluten-free specialty companies in Canada and USA, pharmacies and health food stores in U.K. and Europe.

**Eden Foods, Inc.**, 701 Tecumseh Rd, Clinton, MI, USA  49236
  Phone: 800-248-0320/517-456-7424      FAX: 517-456-6075
  E-mail: info@edenfoods.com      www.edenfoods.com

- Large variety of organic, natural health food products (e.g., beans, condiments, crackers, oils, vinegars, pasta, quinoa, tomatoes, soy beverages and soy/rice beverages).
- Some products are gluten-free.

**Edward & Son's Trading Co.**, Box 1326, Carpinteria, CA, USA  93104
  Phone: 805-684-8500      FAX: 805-684-8220
  E-mail: info@edwardandsons.com      www.edwardandsons.com

- Organic vegetarian foods under brand names: Edward & Sons, Organic Country, Native Forest, Let's Do Organic and Edwards and Son's Organic Saucery Group.
- Brown rice snaps, instant soups, bouillon cubes and gummi bears are gluten-free.

**El Peto Products Ltd.**, 41 Shoemaker St., Kitchener, ON, Canada  N2E 3G9
  Phone: 800-387-4064/519-748-5211      FAX: 519-748-5279
  E-mail: sales@elpeto.com      www.elpeto.com

- Gluten-free specialty company.
- Wide variety of "El Peto" baked products (breads, buns, cakes, cookies, muffins, pies, pizza crusts), cereals, mixes, flours, grains, pasta and soups.
- Also produce gluten-free corn, yeast, sugar, soy and milk-free baked products.
- Also carry some European products (cookies, crackers) and North American products (pasta, sauces) as well as books.
- Order direct by phone, fax, internet or in the El Peto store. Also available in retail stores.
- 10% discount on orders over $80.00.
- Shipping based on weight and destination; ships via UPS Ground or courier.

**Ener-G Foods**, Box 84487, Seattle, WA, USA  98124-5787
  Phone: 800-331-5222/206-767-6660      FAX: 206-764-3398
  E-mail: customerservice@ener-g.com      www.ener-g.com

- Gluten-free specialty company that is also Kosher certified.
- Very large variety of "Ener-G" shelf-stable gluten-free baked products (breads, rolls, buns, cakes, cookies, crackers), baking ingredients and mixes, cereals, flours, milk powders and substitutes, pastas, snacks and books.
- Also carry low-protein products.
- Order direct by phone, fax or internet. Also available in retail stores.
- Shipping based on amount purchased; ships via FedEx Ground, UPS or USPS.

# Gluten-Free Companies/Distributors cont'd.

**Enjoy Life Foods, LLC.**, 1601 N. Natchez, Chicago, IL, USA 60707
◆ Phone: 888-503-6569/773-889-5070      FAX: 773-889-5090
  E-mail: info@enjoylifefoods.com      www.enjoylifefoods.com

- Gluten-free specialty company making foods free from common allergens (no gluten, dairy, casein, egg, soy, peanut, tree nuts), corn, potato or additives.
- Produce bagels, cookies, snack bars, granola cereal and other items.
- 10% discount on sampler pack.
- Order direct by phone, fax or internet; also available in retail stores.
- Shipping based on weight; ships via UPS Ground.

**Erewhon**, US Mills Inc., 200 Reservoir St., Needham, MA, USA 02494
  Phone: 781-444-0440      FAX: 781-444-3411
                                    www.usmillsinc.com

- Cereals (five products) are gluten-free.

**Food For Life Baking Company**, 2991 E. Doherty St., Corona, CA, USA 91719
  Phone: 800-797-5090/909-279-5090      FAX: 909-279-1784
  E-mail: info@food-for-life.com      www.food-for-life.com

- Wholesale specialty bakery that produces gluten-free breads, muffins and pasta.
- Produces other baked products (organic, sprouted grain, low-sodium, low-fat, dairy-free and yeast-free).
- Available in retail stores.

**Foods By George**, 3 King St., Mahwah, NJ, USA 07430
◆ Phone: 201-612-9700      FAX: 201-684-0334
  E-mail: foodsbygeorge@aol.com      www.foodsbygeorge.com

- Gluten-free specialty company.
- Produce gluten-free baked products (brownies, cakes, cookies, muffins, tarts), pizza, lasagna, manicotti and pasta.
- Order direct by phone, fax or mail, also available in retail stores.
- Shipping based on amount purchased; ships via UPS Ground, 3 day select service or 2nd day air.

**Frookies**, Division of Parmalat, 2070 Maple St. Des Plaines, IL, USA 60018
  Phone: 800-272-2537/847-699-3200      FAX: 847-699-3201

- Produce a line of cookies of which three are gluten-free.

**GardenSpot's Finest**, 438 White Oak Rd.. New Holland, PA, USA 17557
◆ Phone: 800-829-5100      FAX: 877-829-5100
  E-mail: cs@gardenspotsfinest.com      www.gardenspotsfinest.com

- Natural, organic and specialty food distributor; carries a wide variety of gluten-free products.
- Exclusive distributor of Shiloh Farms products and Glutano products.
- Wholesale and retail divisions, order direct by phone, fax or internet.
- Shipping based on weight and destination; ships via UPS (Ground or Air).

# GLUTEN-FREE COMPANIES/DISTRIBUTORS CONT'D.

**Genisoy**, 2351 N.Watney Way, Suite C, Fairfield, CA, USA 94533
◆ Phone: 888-436-4769/707-399-2500    FAX: 707-399-2518
   E-mail: sales@mloproducts.com    www.genisoy.com

- A variety of soy protein products (bars, shakes, powders, soy milks, soy nuts and soy crisps).
- "Original Soy Protein Bars" (2 flavors), Xtreme Bars (1 flavor) and soy nuts (4 flavors) are gluten-free.

**Gillian's Foods, Inc.**, 82 Sanderson Ave., Lynn, MA, USA 01902
◆ Phone: 781-586-0086    FAX: 781-586-0087
   E-mail: chefbobo@aol.com    www.gilliansfoods.com

- Gluten-free specialty company.
- Gluten-Free/Lactose-Free baked products (French Rolls), pizza dough and bread crumbs.
- Order direct by phone, fax or internet, also available from some Gluten-Free e-commerce companies via internet.
- Ships via UPS (ground, next or 2nd day air and 3rd day select)

**Glutafin**, Nutricia Dietary Care, Newmarket Ave.,Trowbridge,Wiltshire BA14 OXQ, England
Phone: 01 225 711801    FAX: 01 225 711567
E-mail: glutenfree@nutricia.co.uk    www.glutafin.co.uk

- Gluten-free specialty company.
- Nutricia Dietary Care produces "Glutafin" products (breads, rolls, cakes, biscuits, crackers, pasta and mixes). Many of the products are gluten-free.
- Also produces a line of products containing wheat starch. None of which are listed in this guide, as wheat starch is not allowed on a gluten-free diet in Canada and the USA.

**Glutano**, Gluten-Free Foods Ltd., Unit 270 Centennial Park, Centennial Ave, Elstree, Borehamwood, Herts WD6 3SS, England
Phone: +44(0)20 8953 4444    FAX: +44(0)20 8953 8285
E-mail: info@glutenfree-foods.co.uk    www.glutano.com

- Gluten-free specialty company.
- Gluten-Free Foods produces "Glutano" line of gluten-free products (breads, cookies, crackers, cereals, pastas, pretzels and mixes) as well as "Barkat" gluten-free products (breads, pizza crusts, bread mix, cereal, pot meals, ice cream cones).
- They also sell "Odlums Tritamyl" products from Ireland which contain wheat starch, which is not allowed on a gluten-free diet in Canada and the USA.

**Gluten-Free Cookie Jar**, Box 52,Trevose, PA, USA 19053
◆ Phone: 888-458-8360/215-355-9403    FAX: 215-355-7991
   E-mail: dsutter@glutenfreecookiejar.com    www.glutenfreecookiejar.com

- Gluten-free specialty company.
- Produce "Gluten-Free Cookie Jar" gluten-free baked products (breads, bagels, rolls, cakes, and cookies), baking mixes (breads, bagels, cakes, cookies, muffins, scones) and flours.
- Order direct by phone, fax, or internet.
- Shipping based on amount purchased; ships via UPS Ground.

# Gluten-Free Companies/Distributors cont'd.

**Gluten-Free Delights**, Box 284 Cedar Falls, IA, USA 50613
◆ Phone: 888-403-1806/319-266-7167          FAX:319-268-7355
E-mail: diana@glutenfreedelights.com          www.glutenfreedelights.com

- Gluten-free specialty company. Also carry other companies' gluten-free products.
- Mail-order company that produces baked products (breads, cakes, cookies, doughnuts, pies, pizza crusts) and baking mixes (breads, buns, cakes, muffins).
- Order direct by phone, fax or internet.
- Shipping based on amount purchased; ships via UPS Ground or FedEx (2nd Day Air).

**Gluten-Free Mall**
◆ E-mail: info@glutenfreemall.com          www.glutenfreemall.com

- Gluten-free specialty company.
- Internet shopping mall carrying hundreds of gluten free products from dozens of companies from around the world.
- Low product and shipping costs, plus convenience of being able to choose from many products shipped in a single delivery.
- Shipping charges vary depending on each vendor's rates.

**Gluten-Free Pantry**, P. O. Box 840, Glastonbury, CT, USA 06033
◆ Phone: 800-291-8386/860-633-3826          FAX: 860-633-6853
E-mail: pantry@glutenfree.com          www.glutenfreepantry.com
                                        www.glutenfree.com

- Gluten-free specialty company.
- Produce "Gluten-Free Pantry" mixes (breads, cakes, cereals, cookies, muffins, pastry, pancakes and scones).
- Also carry other companies' gluten-free products (breads, cookies, cereals, crackers, condiments, flours, pasta, snacks, soups), as well as bread machines and cookbooks.
- Order direct by phone, fax or internet, also available in many retail outlets.
- Shipping based on amount purchased; ships via UPS (Ground, next day, 2nd or 3rd day) or Fed Ex Ground.

**Gluten-Free Trading Company**, 604 A, W. Lincoln Ave, Milwaukee, WI, USA 53215
◆ Phone: 888-993-9933/414-385-9950          FAX: 414-385-9915
E-mail: info@gluten-free.net          www.gluten-free.net

- Gluten-free specialty company.
- Retail store featuring over 1000 gluten-free items from around the world.
- New store address fall 2003.
- Purchase on-site or order by phone, fax or internet.
- Shipping charges are based on weight; ships via UPS Ground.

**Gluten Solutions, Inc.**, 3810 Riviera Dr., Suite 1, San Diego, CA, USA 92109
◆ Phone: 888-845-8836/858-483-8877
E-mail: info@glutensolutions.com          www.glutensolutions.com

- Gluten-free specialty company.
- Internet grocery store that sells over 300 of the most popular gluten-free products and books from 30 vendors.
- Ships all products from a central warehouse with one shipping charge based on weight; ships via UPS (Ground, Next Day, 2nd Day) or USPS Priority.

# GLUTEN-FREE COMPANIES/DISTRIBUTORS CONT'D.

**Glutino** (formerly **De-Ro-Ma**), 3750 Francis Hughes Ave., Laval, QC, Canada H7L 5A9
   Phone: 800-363-3438/450-629-7689     FAX: 450-629-4781
   E-mail: info@glutino.com     www.glutino.com

- Gluten-free specialty company.
- Wide variety of "Glutino" baked products (bagels, breads, buns, cakes, cookies, muffins, pie crusts, pizza crusts), mixes, flours, grains, salad dressings, pasta, pretzels, sauces and soups.
- Distributor of Aproten, Bi-Aglut, Dr. Schar and Glutafin (breads, cereals, crackers, cookies, mixes and pasta) in Canada and the US.
- Order direct by phone, fax, internet or in the Glutino store, also available in retail stores.
- Shipping based on weight and destination; ships via UPS Ground or UPS Air (in the US) or Purolator Ground (in Canada).

**Gold Top Organics**, 16831- 110 Ave., Edmonton, AB, Canada T5P 1G8
   Phone: 877-891-4019/780-483-1504
   E-mail: GoldTop@telusplanet.net     www.goldtoporganics.com

- Organic products (flax oil, ground flax seed, six-in-one oil and sunflower oil).

**Good 'n Easy**, JJB Naturals, Inc., Unit 135 – 12031 Horseshoe Way, Richmond, BC, Canada V7A 4V4
   Phone: 604-644-2588     FAX: 604-271-3151
   E-mail: jjbnaturals@telus.net     http://jjbnaturals.tripod.com

- Gluten-free specialty company.
- Gluten-free mixes (cake/pastry and quick bread).

**Govinda's Fitness Foods**, 2651 Ariane Dr., San Diego, CA, USA 92117
   Phone: 800-900-0108/858-270-0691     FAX: 858-270-0696
   E-mail: blissbar@earthlink.net     www.govindabars.com

- Snack bars made from dried fruits, nuts, seeds, puffed amaranth or other grains: "Bliss Bars", "Hemp Bars", "Raw Power".
- "Bliss Bars" (all are gluten-free except "Pistachio Planet").

**Grain Process Enterprises Ltd.**, 115 Commander Blvd., Scarborough, ON, Canada M1S 3M7
   Phone: 800-387-5292/416-291-4004     FAX: 800-437-4420/416-291-2159

- Wholesale food processing company with an extensive line of products (baking ingredients, cereals, confectionary items, flours, mixes, nuts, oils, pastas, sweeteners, spices and other products). A variety of products are gluten-free.
- Individual consumers can purchase items in their retail store or by phone, fax or mail.

**Hain Foods**, Hain-Celestial Group, 16007 Camino de la Cantera, Irwindale, CA, USA 91706
   Phone: 800-423-4846/626-334-3241     FAX: 626-633-1084
   E-mail: consumeraffairs@hain-celestial.com   www.hain-celestial.com

- A variety of natural food products (e.g., "kidz" food and snack products, expeller–pressed oils and crackers).
- "Mini Munchie" rice cakes (four flavors) are gluten-free.

# Gluten-Free Companies/Distributors cont'd.

**Health Valley**, Hain-Celestial Group, 16007 Camino de la Cantera, Irwindale, CA, USA 91706
    Phone: 800-423-4846/626-334-3241        FAX: 626-633-1084
    E-mail: consumeraffairs@hain-celestial.com   www.hain-celestial.com

- A variety of natural health-food products (e.g., chili, soups, broths, cereals, crackers, cookies, snack bars.)
- Some cereals, crackers and soups are gluten-free.

**Hilton Whole Grain Millers**, RR #2, Staffa, ON, Canada N0K 1Y0
◆ Phone: 800-835-9831              FAX: 519-345-2547
    E-mail: hilton@hilton.on.ca         www.hilton.on.ca

- Process soy and oat products (soy crisps, soy flour and several oat products).
- Several soy products are gluten-free.

**Hol•Grain**, Conrad Rice Mill Inc., P. O. Box 10640, New Iberia, LA, USA 70562
◆ Phone: 800-551-3245/337-364-7242     FAX: 337-365-5806
    E-mail: info@conradricemill.com      www.conradricemill.com

- Oldest rice mill in North America.
- "Konriko", "R.M. Quiggs" and "Hol•Grain" products.
- A variety of rice, spices, seasonings, soups, mixes, snack and wheat-free/gluten-free products.
- Brown rice crackers, brown rice bread crumbs, brownie mix, pancake/waffle mix and plain rice are gluten-free.

**Imagine Foods**, 1245 San Carlos Ave., San Carlos, CA, USA 94070
    Phone: 650-595-6300 ext. 1800       FAX: 650-327-1459
    E-mail: questions@imaginefoods.com    www.imaginefoods.com

- Natural food products include beverages ("Rice Dream", "Soy Dream", "Power Dream", "Soy Energy Drinks"), frozen desserts and novelties, "Imagine" products (broths, soups).
- Many products are gluten-free.

**Instant Gourmet**, AlpineAire Foods, P. O. Box 1799, Rocklin, CA, USA 95677
    Phone: 800-322-6325/866-322-6325/916-624-6050   FAX:916-624-1604
    E-mail: info@aa-foods.com        www.aa-foods.com

- Instant gluten-free meals in a ready-to-serve disposable bowl (entrées, soups).
- Order direct by phone, fax or internet; also available in retail stores.
- * Shipping based on product weight; ships via UPS Ground.

**Jennies (see Red Mill Farms Inc.)**

**JJB Naturals, Inc. (see Absolutely Good and Good 'n Easy)**

# GLUTEN-FREE COMPANIES/DISTRIBUTORS CONT'D.

**Kaybee**, Box 629, Cudworth, SK, Canada  S0K 1B0
✦ Phone: 306-256-3424             FAX: 306-256-3424
   E-mail: kaybee@sasktel.net

- Gluten-free specialty company.
- Variety of "Kaybee" gluten-free mixes (bread, buns, cakes, cookies, muffins, pancakes, pizza crusts, puddings, and perogies).
- Order direct by phone or fax, also available in retail stores.
- Shipping is free for orders of 24 packages or more.
- Shipping parcels under 24 packages, a flat rate of $6.00 in Canada and $10.00 (US funds) in USA.

**Kettle Foods**, P. O. Box 664, Salem,  OR, USA  97308
   Phone: 888-453-8853/503-364-0399      FAX: 503-371-1447
                                    www.kettlefoods.com

- Potato chips (Natural Gourmet; Baked), tortilla chips (organic), nuts and nut butters.
- Some products are gluten-free.

**Kingsmill Foods**, 1399 Kennedy Rd, Unit 17, Toronto,  ON, Canada  M1P 2L6
✦ Phone: 416-755-1124            FAX: 416-755-4486
   E-mail:kingsmill@kingsmillfoods.com     www.kingsmillfoods.com

- Gluten-free specialty company.
- Variety of products for special dietary needs (gluten-free, dysphagia, lactose intolerance and low protein).
- "Kingsmill" gluten-free breads, cookies, pizza crusts and baking mixes as well as "Egg Replacer".
- "Lacteeze" milk, ice cream, enzyme drops and tablets.
- Available in retail stores.

**Kinnikinnick Foods**, 10940 - 120 Street, Edmonton,  AB, Canada  T5H 3P7
✦ Phone: 877-503-4466/780-424-2900     FAX: 780-421-0456
   E-mail: info@kinnikinnick.com         www.kinnikinnick.com

- Gluten-free specialty company.
- Very large variety of "Kinnikinnick" baked products (breads, buns, bagels, cakes, cookies, doughnuts, loaves, muffins, pizza crusts, waffles), cereals, flours, mixes, sauces and soups.
- Majority of products are also casein-free labeled as "GFCF Alta".
- Also produce sugar-free products called "Kinni Betic".
- Carry a variety of other companies' products (cereals, crackers, pastas, snacks, soups).
- "CareFree" program (receive a variety of gluten-free baked goods on a regular basis).
- Order direct by phone, fax, internet or in the Kinnikinnick store, also available in retail stores.
- Shipping/handling is $10.00 flat rate for parcels in Canada.
- Also ship to USA for a $10.00 (US Funds) flat rate for products valued up to $200.

**Lactaid**, McNeil Consumer Health Care, Guelph,  ON, Canada  N1K 1A5
   Phone: 800-522-8243             www.lactaid.com

- "Lactaid" (lactose-reduced milk) is available in shelf-stable and refrigerated forms.
- "Lactaid drops", "Lactaid tablets" and "Lactaid caplets".
- All products are gluten-free.

# Gluten-Free Companies/Distributors cont'd.

**Lactaid**, McNeil Nutritionals, 7050 Camp Hill Rd., Ft. Washington, PA,
　　USA 19034
　Phone: 800-522-8243　　　　　　　FAX: 215-273-4070
　　　　　　　　　　　　　　　　　www.lactaid.com

- "Lactaid" (lactose-reduced milk) is available in refrigerated forms.
- "Lactaid tablets" and "Lactaid caplets".
- All products are gluten-free.

**Lacteeze**, Kingsmill Foods, 1399 Kennedy Rd., Toronto, ON, Canada M1P 2L6
◆ Phone: 416-755-1124　　　　　　FAX: 416-755-4486
　E-mail: kingsmill@kingsmillfoods.com　www.kingsmillfoods.com

- "Lacteeze" (lactose-reduced milk) is available in shelf stable and refrigerated forms.
- "Lacteeze" drops and tablets.
- "Lacteeze" ice cream available in four flavors.
- All products are gluten-free.

**Laurel's Sweet Treats, Inc.**, 16004 SW Tualatin – Sherwood Road, #123,
　　　　　　　　　　　Sherwood, OR, USA 97140
　Phone: 866-225-3432/503-625-3432　　FAX: 503-925-8190
　E-mail: sales@glutenfreemixes.com　　www.glutenfreemixes.com

- Gluten-free specialty company.
- Variety of baking mixes (bread, brownie, cake, cookie), spice mixes (Rib Rub), onion ring batter and gluten-free decorating supplies. Baking mixes are also casein-free.
- Order direct by phone, fax, email or internet.
- Shipping based on weight and destination; ships via UPS or USPS.

**Legumes Plus**, Dixie USA, Inc., P. O. Box 1969, Tomball, TX, USA 77377
◆ Phone: 800-233-3668/281-516-3535　　FAX: 800-688-2507
　E-mail: info@dixieusa.com　　　　　www.dixieusa.com

- Variety of soups, chilies, salads and main dishes.
- Mixes are packaged with ingredients needed to prepare them (the addition of liquids is all that is required for preparation, except salad mixes).
- Some lentil soups, salads and entrées are gluten-free.
- Order direct by phone, fax, mail or internet; also available in retail stores.

**LifeSoy**, LifeMax Natural Foods Distribution Inc., 1773 Bayly St.,
　　　Pickering, ON, Canada L1W 2Y7
　Phone: 905-831-5433　　　　　　　FAX: 905-831-4333

- Wheat-free, gluten-free tamari soy sauces, soup bases, pasta sauces and other products.

**Lifestream Natural Foods**, 7453 Progress Way, Delta, BC, Canada V4G 1E8
　Phone: 888-808-9505　　　　　　　FAX: 604-940-0522
　E-mail: consumer_service@naturespath.com　www.naturespath.com

- Organic rice cakes and waffles from whole grains with no preservatives or artificial flavors.
- Toaster waffles (two flavors) and rice cakes are gluten-free.

# GLUTEN-FREE COMPANIES/DISTRIBUTORS CONT'D.

**Liv-N-Well Distributors**, 7900 River Rd, Unit #1, Richmond, BC, Canada V6X 1X7
♦ Phone: 877-270-8479/604-270-8474     FAX: 604-270-8477
   E-mail: info@liv-n-well.com     www.liv-n-well.com

- Gluten-free specialty company.
- Specializes in wheat-free/gluten-free, low-protein, PKU, and dysphagia products.
- Very large selection of gluten-free baked products, flours, grains, mixes, cakes, cookies, crackers, pastas, sauces/condiments, snacks and soups from various companies (e.g., Aproten, Dr. Schar, El Peto, Ener-G Foods, Glutafin, Hol•Grain, JJB Naturals, Kingsmill, Rice Innovations).
- Books also available.
- Order direct by phone, fax, internet or in the Liv-N-Well retail store.
- Case lot volume discounts.
- Shipping based on weight and destination; ships via Courier or Canada Post.

**Lundberg Family Farms**, P. O. Box 369, 5370 Church St., Richvale, CA, USA 95974
♦ Phone: 530-882-4551     FAX: 530-882-4500
   E-mail: question@lundberg.com     www.lundberg.com

- Family-owned farm that grows and produces brown rice, specialty rice varieties and brown rice products.
- Most of their products are gluten-free.
- Brown rice syrup and tamari soy sauce are also gluten-free.

**Made By Mona Enterprises**, 1462 Jamaica Rd., Victoria, BC, Canada V8N 2C8
   Phone: 250-472-3672     FAX: 250-389-1780
   E-mail: mona@madebymona.com     www.madebymona.com

- Gluten-free specialty company.
- Produce a variety of mixes (breads, cakes, pancake/waffle, pastry, pizza, all purpose). Also carries sorghum flour.
- Products available in single units, case lots and bulk.
- Order direct by phone, fax or internet.
- US prices include shipping via USPS.
- Canadian orders: shipping charges based on weight and destination via Canada Post ground.

**Manischewitz**, 340 Marin Blvd., Jersey City, NY, USA 07302
   Phone: 201-333-3700     FAX: 201-333-9153
   E-mail: info@manischewitz.com     www.manischewitz.com

- Largest USA manufacturer of processed kosher foods (gefilte fish, pastas, soups and soup mixes, snack foods, tams and crackers, matzos, potato and other mixes).
- Also produce products especially for Passover.
- A variety of products are gluten-free.

# Gluten-Free Companies/Distributors cont'd.

**Med-Diet Laboratories, Inc.,** 3600 Holly Lane N., Suite 80, Plymouth, MN, USA 55447

Phone: 800-633-3438/763-550-2020      FAX: 763-550-2022
E-mail: meddiet@med-diet.com      www.med-diet.com

- A variety of products for special dietary needs (gluten-free, cardiac, critical care, diabetes, dysphagia, low protein).
- Gluten-free baking mixes, breads, cookies and pastas from Aproten, Dr. Schar, Ener G, Kingsmill and Med-Diet.
- Order direct by phone, fax or internet.
- Shipping based on weight and destination; ships via UPS Ground, FedEx (Overnight) or FedEx (2 Day Service).

**Minn-Dak Growers Ltd.,** Highway 81 North, P. O. Box 13276, Grand Forks, ND, USA 58208

Phone: 701-746-7453      FAX: 701-780-9050
E-mail: info@minndak.com      www.minndak.com

- Is a processor, contractor and marketer of buckwheat to the domestic and international food ingredients industry.
- Has the newest and largest dedicated buckwheat milling facility in North America.
- Buckwheat products include flour, Farinetta™ (buckwheat bran), groats, grits and kasha.
- Also processes safflower, sunflower seeds and mustard seeds.

**Miss Roben's,** Box 1149, Frederick, MD, USA 21702

Phone: 800-891-0083/301-665-9580      FAX: 301-665-9584
E-mail: info@missroben.com      www.missroben.com

- Gluten-Free specialty company.
- Gluten-free/wheat-free mail-order supplier of over 450 products including flours, cereals, cookies, crackers, pastas, sauces, snacks, soups, ready-to-eat dinners and side dishes.
- Also produce "Miss Roben's" gluten-free mixes (breads, cakes, cookies, pancakes, pie and pizza crusts).
- Order direct by phone, fax or internet.
- Shipping based on amount purchased; ships via UPS Ground.

**Mrs. Leepers, Inc.,** 14949 Eastvale Rd., Poway, CA, USA 92064

Phone: 800-848-5266/ 858-486-1101      FAX: 858-486-5115
E-mail: mlpinc@pacbell.net      www.mrsleeperspasta.com

- Mrs. Leeper's brown rice pastas and corn pasta are gluten-free.
- Also produce other pasta products under brand names ("Eddies" and "Michelle's") that contain wheat.

**Mr. Spice,** Lang Naturals, 850 Aquidneck Ave., Newport, RI, USA 02842

Phone: 800-728-2348/401-848-7700      FAX: 401-848-7701
E-mail: customerservice@MrSpice.com      www.mrspice.com

- Sauces do not contain any gluten, dairy, HVP, MSG, preservatives, salt or sulfites.
- Available in nine different flavors.

# GLUTEN-FREE COMPANIES/DISTRIBUTORS CONT'D.

**Natural Noodles**, Box 24006, Penticton, BC, Canada V2A 8L9
Phone: 800-556-3339      FAX: 800-556-3339
E-mail: natural@bc.sympatico.ca      www3.bc.sympatico.ca/noodles

• Wheat-free/gluten-free pastas (brown rice/lentil, lentil, mung bean, pea, wild rice mix and wild rice).
• Pastas are high in protein and fiber.

**Nature's Hilights, Inc.**, P. O. Box 3526, Chico, CA, USA 95927
Phone: 800-313-6454/530-342-6154      FAX: 530-342-3130
E-mail: gluten-free@natures-hilights.com      www.natures-hilights.com

• Gluten-free specialty company.
• Family owned business that produces only gluten-free products.
• Rice sticks, pizza crust, tostadas and frozen desserts.
• Order direct via phone, fax, mail; also available in retail stores.

**Nature's Path Foods, Inc.**, 7453 Progress Way, Delta, BC, Canada V4G 1E8
Phone: 888-808-9505      FAX: 604-940-0522
E-mail: consumer_services@naturespath.com    www.naturespath.com

• Produce a variety of organic products generally made from whole grains.
• 13 products (cereals, waffles and snack bars) are gluten-free.

**Nature's Path Foods, Inc.**, 2220 Nature's Path Way, Blaine, WA, USA 98230
Phone: 360-332-1111      FAX: 360-332-2266
E-mail: consumer_services@naturespath.com    www.naturespath.com

• Produce a variety of organic products generally made from whole grains.
• 13 products (cereals, waffles and snack bars) are gluten-free.

**Nelson David of Canada**, 66 Higgins Ave, Winnipeg, MB, Canada R3B 0A5
Phone: 866-989-0379/204-989-0379      FAX: 204-989-0384
E-mail: crennnie244@aol.com

• Gluten-free specialty company.
• "Celimix" brand products of gluten-free mixes (bread, biscuits, buns, cakes, cookies, muffins, pancakes, pastry, pizza crusts, Yorkshire pudding), flours, grains, pastas as well as some European products.
• Order direct by phone, fax; also available in retail stores and e-commerce companies (e.g., glutenfreemall.com).
• Celimix "Starter Kit" (14 items) 15% saving.
• Shipping based on weight and destination; ships via Canada Post.

**New Hope Mills, Inc.**, 5983 Glen Haven Rd., Moravia, NY, USA 13118
Phone: 315-497-0783      FAX: 315-497-0810

• Process a variety of grain products including buckwheat.
• Sell buckwheat flour (light, medium and dark), grits and groats (roasted and unroasted).
• Product available in the retail outlet at the mill, mail order and some grocery stores.

**New Morning**, US Mills, Inc., 200 Reservoir St., Needham, MA, USA 02494
Phone: 781-444-0440      FAX: 781-444-3411
www.usmillsinc.com

• One cereal is gluten-free.

# GLUTEN-FREE COMPANIES/DISTRIBUTORS CONT'D.

**Northern Quinoa Corporation**, Box 519, Kamsack, SK, Canada  S0A 1S0
✦ Phone: 866-368-9304/306-542-3949          FAX: 306-542-3951
E-mail: info@quinoa.com                            www.quinoa.com

- Process a variety of gluten-free products (quinoa, amaranth, buckwheat, flax, legumes, millet, spices and wild rice).
- Quinoa is available as whole grain, flakes, flour and pasta.
- Company has developed a process to remove the bitter-tasting saponin coating from quinoa, making it ready to use and fast cooking.

**nSpired Natural Foods,** 14855 Wicks Blvd., San Leandro, CA, USA, 94577
✦ Phone: 510-686-0116                              FAX: 510-686-0126
www.nspiredfoods.com

- Large variety of snack products under different brand names: Ah! Laska (cocoas and syrups), Cloud Nine (chocolates), Cool Fruits (freezer pops and fruit snacks), Loriva (culinary oils), Maranatha (nut/seed butters), nSpired (baking chips), Pumpkorn (pumpkin seeds), Skinny (chips and sticks), Speakeasy (organic mints and gum), Sunspire (bulk candies), Tropical Source (dairy-free chocolate).
- Many products are gluten-free.

**Nu-World Amaranth**, Nu-World Foods, P. O. Box 2202, Naperville, IL, USA  60567
✦ Phone: 630-369-6819                              FAX: 630-369-6851
E-mail: contactus@nuworldfamily.com               www.nuworldfoods.com

- Produce a variety of gluten-free, amaranth and amaranth-based products (flour, toasted bran flour, puffed cereals, snack foods, bread crumbs, flat breads, pre-gel powder and oil).
- Order direct by phone, fax or internet; also available in retail stores.

**Oakland Dietetic Bakery**, P. O. Box 180302, Utica, MI, USA  48318-0302
✦ Phone: 800-815-6280                              FAX: 800-815-6280
E-mail: jjfb@flash.net                            www.oaklanddieteticbakery.com

- Produce gluten-free cookies with no preservatives.
- Order direct by phone, fax or internet, also available from gluten-free e-commerce companies.
- Shipping based on amount purchased; ships via USPS Priority or UPS Ground.

**Omega Nutrition Canada**, 1695 Franklin. St, Vancouver, BC, Canada  V5L 1P5
✦ Phone: 800-661-3529/604-253-4677                FAX: 604-253-4228
E-mail: info@omeganutrition.com                   www.omeganutrition.com

- Over 400 natural health products such as specialty oils (flax, borage, sesame, sunflower, hazelnut, olive, pistachio, pumpkin, safflower), flavorings, nutritional supplements, flax seed meal and books.

**Omega Nutrition USA**, 6515 Aldrich Rd., Bellingham, WA, USA  98226
✦ Phone: 800-661-3529/360-384-1238                FAX: 360-384-0700
E-mail: info@omeganutrition.com                   www.omeganutrition.com

- Over 400 natural health products such as specialty oils (flax, borage, sesame, sunflower, hazelnut, olive, pistachio, pumpkin, safflower), flavorings, nutritional supplements, flax seed meal and books.

# GLUTEN-FREE COMPANIES/DISTRIBUTORS CONT'D.

**Omega Smart Inc.**, 4 Lancelot Dr., Hooksett, NH, USA 03106
Phone: 603-624-5924      FAX: 603-232-3571
E-mail: ginj@omegasmartbar.com      www.omegasmartbar.com

• Produce gluten-free, dairy-free whole food meal replacement bars made from organic dried fruits, nuts, ground flax seed, soy flour, soynuts and agave syrup.

**Orgran**, Roma Food Products, 47-51 Aster Ave., Carrum Downs, Vic 3201, Australia
Phone: +613 9776 9044      FAX: +613 9776 9055
E-mail: info@orgran.com      www.orgran.com

• Roma Food Products, Australia's major manufacturer of alternative grain, pasta and health foods produce the "Orgran" products (crispbread, cereals, pasta, sauces, snacks and mixes).
• Brown rice, corn and soy pastas are gluten-free.

**Pacific Foods**, 19480 SW 97th Ave., Tualatin, OR, USA 97062
Phone: 503-692-9666      FAX: 503-692-9610
E-mail: info@pacificfoods.com      www.pacificfoods.com

• Variety of non-dairy beverages (almond, grain, hazelnut, rice and soy).
• Natural and organic broths and soups.
• Many of their products are gluten-free.

**Pamela's Products**, 335 Allerton Ave., South San Francisco, CA, USA 94080
Phone: 650-952-4546      FAX: 650-742-6643
E-maiL: info@pamelasproducts.com      www.pamelasproducts.com

• A variety of cookies, biscotti and baking mixes (pancake/baking and chocolate brownie).
• All products are gluten-free, except oatmeal cookies.

**Panne Rizo**, 1939 Cornwall Ave., Vancouver, BC, Canada V6J 1C8
Phone: 604-736-0885      FAX: 604-736-0825
E-mail: info@pannerizo.com      www.pannerizo.com

• Gluten-Free Specialty bakery, deli and cafe.
• Produce their own gluten-free breads, buns, special occasion cakes, cookies, muffins, pies, pastries, pizza crusts, ready-to-eat entrées, granola cereal and snack bars.
• Also carry other companies' products (cereals, cookies, crackers, pasta, soup cubes).
• Order direct by phone, fax, internet or in the Panne Rizo Store.
• Also available from Liv-N-Well Distributors, Capers Markets and other retailers.
• USA customers: products shipped every Wednesday via FedEx (2 day delivery). Minimum order $50.00 US.

**Papadini**, Adrienne's Gourmet Foods, 849 Ward Dr., Santa Barbara, CA, USA 93111
Phone: 800-937-7010/805-964-6848      FAX: 805-964-8698
E-mail: info@adriennes.com      www.adriennes.com

• Pure lentil bean pasta in a variety of shapes (high in protein and fiber).
• All products are gluten-free.

# Gluten-Free Companies/Distributors cont'd.

**Pastariso**, Rice Innovations, Inc./Maplegrove Foods,
8175 Winston Churchill Blvd., Norval, ON, Canada L0P 1K0
Phone: 905-451-7423                    FAX: 905-453-8137
E-mail: info@maplegrovefoods.com          www.maplegrovefoods.com
- Gluten-free specialty company.
- Produce a large variety of organic rice pastas (brown rice, rice spinach, rice vegetable, rice and cheese dinners) and potato/organic rice pasta called "Pastato" (variety of shapes, as well as pasta and cheese dinners). Some products also available in bulk.
- Some of the pastas are fortified with fibre from ground flax and psyllium husks as well as FOS, vitamins and minerals.

## Pastato (see Pastariso)

**Plum-M-Good**, Van Rice Products, #8 -1350 Valmont Way, Richmond, BC, Canada V6V 1Y4
Phone: 604-273-8038                    FAX: 604-273-7324
- Variety of organic and regular rice cakes that are gluten-free.

**President's Choice**, 22 St.Clair Ave. East, Toronto, ON, Canada M4T 2S8
Phone: 416-967-2501

- Large grocery chain under the names Westfair Foods (Western Canada), Loblaws (Eastern Canada) and President's Choice International (USA).
- Ancient Grain's Golden Maize Multigrain Corn Flakes and mini rice cakes (three flavors) are gluten-free.
- Contact company for gluten-free status of their extensive product lines.

**Private Recipes**, 12 Indell Lane, Brampton, ON, Canada L6T 3Y3
◆ Phone: 800-268-8199/905-799-1022          FAX: 905-799-2666
                                            www.privaterecipes.com
- Specialty company with products for health care food service.
- Frozen products include entrées, soups, puréed, minced, vegetarian, thickened juices.
- Produce a line of gluten-free frozen ready to eat entrées (also suitable for lactose-free and renal diets).

## Pumpkorn (see nSpired Natural Foods)

**Quaker Oats Canada**, 14 Hunter St. East, Quaker Park, Peterborough, ON, Canada K9J 7B2
Phone: 800-267-6287                    www.quakeroats.ca
- Extensive line of products.
- A variety of large and mini rice cakes are gluten-free.

**Quaker Oats USA**, P. O. Box 049003, Chicago, IL, USA 60604
Phone: 800-856-5781                    www.quakeroats.com
                                       www.quakeroatmeal.com
- Extensive line of products.
- A variety of large and mini rice cakes are gluten-free.

# GLUTEN-FREE COMPANIES/DISTRIBUTORS CONT'D.

**The Really Great Food Company**, P. O. Box 2239, St. James, NY, USA 11780
Phone: 800-593-5377/631-361-3553     FAX: 631-361-6920
www.reallygreatfood.com

- Gluten-free specialty company.
- Produce their own gluten-free mixes (breads, cakes, cookies, muffin, pancake, pastry).
- Also carry other companies' products (cereals, crackers, cookies, flours, snacks, soups), books and cookware.
- Order direct by phone, fax or internet.
- Shipping based on amount purchased; ships via UPS Ground.

**Red Mill Farms, Inc.**, 290 S. 5th St, Brooklyn, NY, USA 11211
Phone: 718-384-2150     FAX: 718-384-2988

- Gluten-free coconut macaroons (six flavors) in single-serving sizes, as well as one flavor in a multi-pack labeled "Jennies".
- Gluten-free cakes (Banana Nut, Dutch Chocolate) that are vacuum packed, labeled "Red Mill Farms".

**Robert's American Gourmet**, 100 Roslyn Ave., Box 326, Sea Cliff, NY, USA 11579
Phone: 800-626-7557/516-656-4545     FAX: 516-759-2713
E-mail: info@robscape.com     www.robscape.com

- Large variety of snack products (e.g., potato crisps, corn/rice puffs, corn chips, corn sticks).
- Most products are gluten-free.
- Order direct by phone, fax, mail or internet; also available in many retail stores.

**San J International**, 2880 Sprouse Dr., Richmond, VA, USA 23231
Phone: 800-446-5500/804-226-8333     FAX: 804-226-8383
E-mail: sales@san-j.com     www.san-j.com

- Tamari soy sauces (liquid, powder, low salt/lite), sauces (Asian, barbecue) instant miso soups and rice crackers.
- Wheat-free tamari soy sauces (two varieties) are gluten-free.

**Shiloh Farms (see Garden Spot's Finest)**

- Large variety of products: breads, baking ingredients, flours, grains, legumes, dried fruits mixes, nuts, nut butters and snacks.
- Many products are gluten-free.

**Skinny (see nSpired Natural Foods)**

**Soya World, Inc.**, P. O. Box 3018, Vancouver, BC, Canada V6B 3X5
Phone: 888-401-0019/604-291-0910     FAX: 604-291-0981
E-mail: consumer@soyaworld.com     www.soyaworld.com

- One of North America's largest producers of fresh and shelf-stable soy beverages ("So Good Fortified Soy", "So Nice Soyganic", "Sunrise Soy") and soy yogurt.
- Beverages and yogurts are gluten-free.

# GLUTEN-FREE COMPANIES/DISTRIBUTORS CONT'D.

**Specialty Food Shop**, 555 University Ave., Toronto, ON, Canada M5G 1X8
◆ Phone: 800-737-7976/416-813-5294       FAX: 416-977-8394
E-mail: sfs@sickkids.ca                    www.specialtyfoodshop.com

• Owned by the Hospital For Sick Children.
• Carries over 1200 specialty products (gluten-free, low-protein, low-sodium, dysphagia, food allergies and intolerances, nutritional supplements, enteral feeding equipment, specialized infant feeding products/equipment and books).
• Large variety of gluten-free products from North American and European companies.
• Dietitians on staff for inquiries.
• Order direct via phone, internet or in the Specialty Food Shop.
• Shipping based on amount purchased, ships via Purolator Courier.

**Sunrise Soya Foods**, 729 Powell Street, Vancouver, BC, Canada V6A 1H5
Phone: 800-661-2326/604-253-2326       FAX: 604-251-1083
E-mail: consumer-info@sunrise-soya.com  www.sunrise-soya.com

• Canada's leading tofu company.
• Produce a variety of tofu products and soy beverages.
• Many are gluten-free.

**Sylvan Border Farm**, Mendocino Gluten-Free Products Inc. P. O. Box 277,
Willits, CA, USA 95490-0277
Phone: 800-297-5399/707-459-1854       FAX: 707-459-1834
E-mail: sylvanfarm@pacific.net          www.sylvanborderfarm.com

• Gluten-Free specialty company.
• Produce "Sylvan Border Farm" gluten-free baking mixes packed in oxygen-free pouches.
• Order direct by phone, fax, or internet; also available in many retail stores.
• Shipping charges based on product weight; ships via UPS or FedEx Ground.

**Tamarind Tree**, Annie's Homegrown, Inc., 26 Princess Street, Wakefield, MA, USA
01880
◆ Phone: 800-432-8733/781-224-1172     FAX: 781-224-9728
E-mail: bernie@annies.com               www.annies.com

• Shelf-stable, heat-and-serve vegetarian Indian cuisine entrées that are gluten-free.
• Some are low-fat and most are suitable for "vegan" diets.

**Taste Adventure**, Will-Pak Foods, Inc., 1448 - 240th St, Harbor City, CA, USA 90710
◆ Phone: 800-874-0883/310-325-3504     FAX: 310-325-7038
E-mail: taste_adv@earthlink.net         www.tasteadventure.com

• Low-fat soups, beans, quick cuisine entrées and chilies.
• A variety of products are gluten-free.

**Tayo Foods (Canada) Inc.**, Food Steps Inc., Box 48706, 595 Burrard St.,
Vancouver, BC, Canada V7X 1A6
Phone: 866-327-4373/250-545-8283       FAX: 250-545-8275
                                        www.tayofoods.com

• Potato-based, gluten-free, non-dairy substitute available in fresh, refrigerated containers.

# GLUTEN-FREE COMPANIES/DISTRIBUTORS CONT'D.

**The Teff Company**, P. O. Box A, Caldwell, ID, USA 83606
Phone: 208-455-0375
E-mail: teffco@earthlink.net          www.teffco.com

- Gluten-free specialty company.
- Grow and mill only teff grain (brown and ivory varieties).
- Grain and flour available in various sizes.

---

**Terra**, Hain-Celestial Group, Suite 205 – 58 South Service Road, Melville, NY, USA 11747
Phone: 1-800-434-4246/631-730-2200
E-mail: consumeraffairs@hain-celestial.com   www.terrachips.com

- Variety of chips made from exotic root vegetables (taro, sweet potato, yucca [cassava], batata and parsnip).
- Several products are gluten-free.

---

**Thai Kitchen**, Epicurean International, 1919 Market St. Suite 100,
          Oakland, CA, USA 94607
Phone: 800-967-7424/510-268-0209          FAX: 510-834-3102
E-mail: info@thaikitchen.com          www.thaikitchen.com

- Asian products include a variety of plain and flavored rice noodles, rice side dishes, sauces, soups and coconut milk.
- Many products are gluten-free.

---

**Tinkyada**, Food Directions, Inc., 120 Melford Drive, Unit 8, Scarborough, ON,
          Canada M1B 2X5
Phone: 416-609-0016          FAX: 416-609-1316
E-Mail: allen@tinkyada.com/jojo@tinkyada.com          www.tinkyada.com

- Gluten-free specialty company.
- Brown rice (with rice bran), organic brown rice and white rice pastas in a variety of shapes.
- All products are gluten-free.

---

**Twin Valley Mills**, LLC., RR #1, Box 45, Ruskin, NE, USA 68974
Phone: 402-279-3965
E-mail: sorghumflour@hotmail.com          www.twinvalleymills.com

- Gluten-free specialty company.
- Grow and mill only sorghum.
- Sorghum flour available in 1.41 kg (2.5 lbs.) and 11.4 kg (25 lb.) containers.

---

**Valpiform**, 1, Square du docteur Henri Laborit, ZAC de Merciere 1, Compiegne
          60200, France
Phone: +33(0)344.97.20.20          FAX: +33(0)344.86.87.89
E-mail: contact@valpiform.com          www.valpiform.com

- Gluten-free specialty company.
- Produce fresh baked products (8-10 day shelf life) available in France.
- Also produce shelf-stable par-baked bread, baguettes, rolls and cakes.
- Carry other companies gluten-free products such as Glutafin and Hammermühle.

# Gluten-Free Companies/Distributors cont'd.

**Vance's Foods**, P. O. Box 571563, Salt Lake City, UT, USA 84157-1563
◆ Phone: 800-497-4834     FAX: 800-497-4329
 E-mail: info@vancesfoods.com  www.vancesfoods.com

- Dairy substitutes ("SNO*E Tofu", "Darifree", "Not Milk" and "Soy Healthy")
- Available as dry powder beverage mixes.
- "Darifree" is a potato-based non-dairy substitute which is gluten-free.

**Van's International Foods**, 20318 Gramercy Place, Torrance, CA, USA 90501
 Phone: 310-320-8611     FAX: 310-320-8805
 E-mail: customerservice@vansintl.com  www.vansintl.com

- Frozen waffles (Belgian, organic, mini, regular and wheat-free) that are also kosher.
- Wheat-free waffles (four flavors) are gluten-free (made with brown rice flour, potato starch flour and rice bran).

**Westbrae**, Hain-Celestial Group, 16007 Camino de la Cantera, Irwindale, CA, USA 91706
 Phone: 800-434-4246     FAX: 626-633-1053
 E-mail: westbrae@aol.com  www.westbrae.com

- Variety of natural food products (pasta, soups, soy beverages, rice beverages).
- Some products are gluten-free.

**White Wave, Inc.**, 1990 N. 57th Court, Boulder, CO, USA 80301
 Phone: 800-488-9283/303-443-3470  FAX: 303-443-3952
            www.whitewave.com/www.silkissoy.com

- Soy products (milk, yogurt, tofu and tempeh).
- Soy milks and yogurts are gluten-free.
- Many of the tofu and tempeh products are also gluten-free.

**Whole Foods Market**, 601 North Lamar, Suite 300, Austin, TX, USA 78703
◆ Phone: 512-477-4455     FAX: 512-477-1301
            www.wholefoodsmarket.com

- World's largest retailer of organic and natural foods and operates the largest chain of natural food supermarkets under the names: Whole Foods Market, Fresh Fields, Bread & Circus and Wellspring Grocery.
- Carry an extensive line of products including a variety of gluten-free items.

**Wild Oats Markets, Inc.**, 3375 Mitchell Lane, Boulder, CO, USA 80301
◆ Phone: 800-494-9453/303-440-5220  FAX: 303-928-0022
 E-mail: info@wildoats.com  www.wildoats.com

- Second largest natural food supermarket chain (over 110 stores) in the USA and Canada.
- Operate stores under a family of trade names including: Wild Oats Community Markets, Alfalfa's Markets, Capers Markets, Oasis Fine Foods, Sunshine Grocery, Henry's Marketplace, Ideal Market, Nature's Northwest, Sun Harvest, Vitamin Expo and Uptown Whole Foods.
- Carry a very large selection of products, including a variety of gluten-free items.
- Corporate nutritionists are on staff in several locations.

# CELIAC ORGANIZATIONS

## CANADIAN CELIAC ASSOCIATION (CCA)

5170 Dixie Road, Suite 204
Mississauga, ON, Canada L4W 1E3
Phone: 1-800-363-7296/905-507-6208 FAX: 905-507-4673
E-mail: celiac@look.ca                www.celiac.ca

## FONDATION QUÉBÉCOISE DE LA MALADIE COELIAQUE

(Quebec Celiac Foundation)

4837 rue Boyer, Bureau 230,
Montreal, Quebec, Canada  H2J 3E6
Phone: 514-529-8806                FAX: 514-529-2046
E-mail: info@fqmc.org              www.fqmc.org

## GLUTEN INTOLERANCE GROUP OF NORTH AMERICA (GIG)

15110 – 10th Ave. SW, Suite A,
Seattle, WA, USA  98166-1820
Phone: 206-246-6652                FAX: 206-246-6531
E-mail: info@gluten.net            www.gluten.net
Executive Director: Cynthia Kupper, RD, CD

## CELIAC DISEASE FOUNDATION (CDF)

13251 Ventura Blvd., Suite #1,
Studio City, CA, USA  91604-1838
Phone: 818-990-2354                FAX: 818-990-2379
E-mail: cdf@celiac.org             www.celiac.org
Executive Director: Elaine Monarch

## CELIAC SPRUE ASSOCIATION/USA, INC. (CSA)

P. O. Box 31700,
Omaha, NE, USA  68131
Phone: 877-272-4272/402-558-0600    FAX: 402-558-1347
E mail: celiacs@csaceliacs.org       www.csaceliacs.org
Executive Director: Mary Schluckebier, MA

# GLUTEN-FREE RESOURCES

## CANADIAN CELIAC ASSOCIATION (CCA)
(Contact information on page 157)

### New Members Information Kit
❖ An 82-page handbook that includes:
  ◆ Medical information, gluten-free diet guidelines, nutritional information
  ◆ Lifestyle issues, resources

### Growing Up As A Celiac
❖ A booklet specifically designed for the celiac child
❖ Written and illustrated by children; can be used as a coloring book

### Managing Diabetes and Celiac Disease . . . Together
❖ 50 page book for individuals dealing with celiac disease and diabetes which includes:
  ◆ Information about both diseases
  ◆ Shopping, label reading, meal planning, sample menus
  ◆ Recipes with food choice values, recipe substitutions, carbohydrate content of gluten-free flours
  ◆ Games, resources

### Pocket Dictionary:
### Acceptability of Foods and Food Ingredients for the Gluten-Free Diet
❖ Provides a brief description of each item along with an assessment of its acceptability for the gluten-free diet
❖ Booklet is presented in pocket size so that it may be easily carried

### Eat Well Be Well: A Guide to Gluten-Free Manufacturer's Products – 2nd Edition
❖ 88-page pocket-sized coil-bound book listing Canadian commercial food products by company and product name as well as company phone numbers.

### Celiac Disease: Hidden and Dangerous
❖ Fact Sheet on the disease, symptoms, diagnosis and treatment

### Gluten-Free Diet Information Cards
  ◆ Wallet-sized restaurant card for use when eating out

### Translations of Restricted Diet Information
  ◆ Provided on looseleaf bond paper; one sheet per language, most languages available

### PAMPHLETS
❖ Celiac Disease: What Is It?
❖ Dermatitis Herpetiformis – A Skin Disorder
❖ Teacher's Information About Celiac Disease
❖ Myth vs. Fact Brochure
❖ CCA Information Bookmarks

### VIDEOS
❖ *Celiac Disease – A Diet for Life*

### NEWSLETTER – Published three times/year

### BOOKS
❖ *Gluten-Free Diet: A Comprehensive Resource Guide* by Shelley Case
❖ *No Grain, No Pain – How to Thrive not Just Survive Living Gluten-Free* by Shirley Hartung

### COOKBOOKS
❖ *Gluten-Free By The Sea Cookbook*
❖ *Together We're Better for Life: 25th Anniversary Cookbook*

# GLUTEN INTOLERANCE GROUP (GIG)
(Contact information on page 157)

*Quick Start Diet Guide for Celiac Disease*
- ❖ Developed by GIG and the Celiac Disease Foundation

*GIG Diet Instruction*

*Diabetes, Celiac Disease and Me!*
- ❖ 32-page book which is an introduction to managing both diseases

*Health Care Professional Update*

*Hospital Guide*
- ❖ For persons with celiac disease (CD) or dermatitis herpetiformis (DH) anticipating a hospital stay and includes explicit instructions for hospital dietitians

*Resource Guide*
- ❖ Celiac disease                    ❖ Dermatitis Herpetiformis

*Patient Packets*
- ❖ Resource Guide for Celiac Disease or Dermatitis Herpetiformis and GIG Diet Instruction, Bread Recipes and a copy of the GIG Newsletter

*Restaurant Cards*
- ❖ Wallet-sized card to help chef/server assist you in menu selections

*Restaurant Guide* (in several foreign languages)

*Quick Reference Ingredient Card*

*Bookmarks*
- ❖ Alternative Sweeteners, Dairy Substitutes, Egg Substitutes, Wheat-Free Flours

NEWSLETTER – Published quarterly

BOOKS & COOKBOOKS
- ❖ *Gluten-Free Diet: A Comprehensive Resource Guide*
- ❖ *The Gluten-Free Gourmet-Living Well Without Wheat*
- ❖ *More From The Gluten-Free Gourmet*
- ❖ *The Gluten-Free Gourmet Makes Desserts*
- ❖ *The Gluten-Free Gourmet Cooks Fast and Healthy*
- ❖ *The Gluten-Free Gourmet Bakes Bread*
- ❖ *Wheat-Free Recipes and Menus: Delicious Dining Without Wheat or Gluten*
- ❖ *Special Diet Solutions: Healthy Cooking Without Wheat or Gluten*
- ❖ *Special Diet Celebrations: No Wheat, Gluten, Dairy or Eggs*
- ❖ *Gluten-Free 101*
- ❖ *Cooking Gluten-Free!*
- ❖ *Incredible Edible Gluten-Free Foods For Kids*
- ❖ *Kids with Celiac Disease: A Family Guide to Raising Happy, Healthy Gluten-Free Children*

VIDEO TAPES
- ❖ Over 40 different tapes on a variety of topics and presented by various speakers (e.g., Celiac Disease, Dermatitis Herpetiformis, Associated Disorders, Children, Diet and Nutrition, Medications, Cooking/Dining)

FOOD PRODUCTS
- ❖ Also carry some flours, mixes, xanthum gum and other gluten-free products.

# CELIAC DISEASE FOUNDATION (CDF)
(Contact information on page 157)

### *Quick Start Diet Guide for Celiac Disease*
❖ Developed by CDF and Gluten Intolerance Group (GIG)

### *Celiac Disease Foundation Brochure*
❖ Overview of celiac disease including symptoms, diagnosis, treatment and the CDF
❖ Also available in Spanish

### *Guidelines for a Gluten-Free Lifestyle* – 3rd Edition
❖ Do's and Don'ts for a gluten-free diet

### *Guia de Dieta Para Enfermedad Celiaca*

**NEWSLETTER** – Published quarterly

**BOOKS**
by Danna Korn
❖ *Kids with Celiac Disease*
❖ *Wheat-Free, Worry-Free*
by Shelley Case
❖ *Gluten-Free Diet: A Comprehensive Resource Guide*

**COOKBOOKS**
by Bette Hagman
❖ *The Gluten-Free Gourmet – Living Well Without Wheat*
❖ *More From The Gluten-Free Gourmet*
❖ *The Gluten-Free Gourmet Cooks Fast and Healthy*
❖ *The Gluten-Free Gourmet Bakes Bread*
❖ *The Gluten-Free Gourmet Makes Desserts*
by Carol Fenster
❖ *Special Diet Solutions*
❖ *Wheat-Free Recipes & Menus* – 2nd Edition
by Beth Hillson
❖ *Gluten-Free Pantry Companion*

# CELIAC SPRUE ASSOCIATION/USA, INC. (CSA)
(Contact information on page 157)

**PAMPHLETS**
❖ Focus on Gluten-Free Food Choices          ❖ Patient Packet
❖ Grains and Flours

**COOKBOOK SERIES**
❖ Seven cookbooks compiled from CSA members' contributions. Each contains a section of cooking hints, information on adapting recipes, and a variety of special topics related to cooking gluten-free.

### *Co-operative Gluten-Free Commercial Products Listing*
❖ A listing of gluten-free products, including vendor information that is published annually.

**NEWSLETTER** – Published quarterly

# GLUTEN-FREE PUBLICATIONS

## *Gluten-Free Living* Magazine

- ❖ Bi-monthly national publication covering all aspects of gluten sensitivity and the gluten-free diet. Reviewed by a medical and dietitian advisory board with expertise in celiac disease and edited by a journalist who is a celiac herself.
- ❖ An excellent, reliable, in-depth source of information about all aspects of gluten sensitivity and the gluten-free diet. Publishes leading-edge articles on the diet and on current events surrounding the gluten-free life.
- ❖ Also publishes two booklets: *A Basic Guide to the Gluten-Free Diet* and *25 Ways to Eat Well and Stay Healthy on the Gluten-Free Diet*, each $2.95, and numerous reprints.
- ❖ Subscriptions are $32 for one year or $54 for 2 years in US funds. Add $10 per subscription for orders outside the USA. Send check, money order, or Visa or MasterCard number /expiration date to:

    **Gluten-Free Living**
    **P. O. Box 105**
    **Hastings-on-Hudson, NY, USA 10706**
    **Phone/FAX: 914-969-2018**
    **E-mail: gfliving@aol.com**          **www.glutenfreeliving.com**

## *Living Without* Magazine

- ❖ Quarterly lifestyle magazine for people with food and chemical sensitivities such as celiac disease, lactose intolerance, wheat intolerance, food allergies, anaphylaxis, multiple chemical sensitivities and other gastro-intestinal disorders. Edited and published by Peggy Wagener, who has celiac disease and reviewed by an advisory board (physicians, dietitians and directors of American Celiac Organizations).
- ❖ An excellent source of information about food sensitivities including celiac disease.
- ❖ Subscriptions are $23/1 year or $40/2 years in US funds. Send check, money order, or credit card number/expiration date to:

    **Living Without, Inc.**
    **P. O. Box 2126**
    **Northbrook, IL, USA 60065**
    **Phone: 847-480-8810**          **www.livingwithout.com**

## *Wheat-Free, Worry-Free: The Art of Happy, Healthy Gluten-Free Living*

- ❖ 393-page book written by Danna Korn
- ❖ Practical and inspirational guide to living a wheat-free, gluten-free lifestyle.
- ❖ Includes extensive medical information, tips for traveling and eating out, menu suggestions, shopping, recipes, nutritional aspects, as well as positive strategies for emotional issues and psychological implications of coping with dietary restrictions.
- ❖ Cost is $14.95 (US funds)
- ❖ ISBN 1-56170-991-3; published by Hay House

### Kids with Celiac Disease: A Family Guide to Raising Happy, Healthy, Gluten-Free Children

- ❖ 256-page book written by Danna Korn
- ❖ Provides parents with advice and strategies on how to deal with the diagnosis, cope with emotional turmoil, and help their child develop a positive and constructive attitude.
- ❖ Practical information on menu planning, grocery shopping, food preparation, recipes and "junk foods" as well eating outside the home (e.g., birthday parties, restaurants, camps, vacations).
- ❖ Cost is $17.95 (US funds)
- ❖ ISBN 1-89062-72-16; published by Woodbine House

### What? No wheat? A Lighthearted Primer to Living the Gluten-Free, Wheat-Free life

- ❖ 88-page illustrated book by LynnRae Ries
- ❖ Provides information and inspiration in a cartoon-style format for both children and adults.
- ❖ Includes supporting medical information, as well as positive personal stories of those who are living the gluten-free life. Basic bread recipes are also included.
- ❖ Cost is $9.95 (US funds)
- ❖ ISBN 0-9724154-0-8
- ❖ What No Wheat Publishing/Enterprises,
  4757 East Greenway Road, Suite 107B, #91, Phoenix, AZ, USA  85032
  Phone: 602-485-8751          www.whatnowheat.com

### Waiter, Is there Wheat in My Soup?

*Important Questions and Techniques To Make Gluten-Free, Wheat-Free, Lactose-Free Dining Out Choices Easier*

- ❖ New book written by LynnRae Ries; available December 2003
- ❖ A resource guide designed to help people make informed dining out decisions
- ❖ What No Wheat Publishing/Enterprises (see contact information above)

### Rise 'N Shine Newsletter

- ❖ Gluten-free cooking, baking and lifestyle newsletter written by LynnRae Ries
- ❖ Contributors: "Rock" parents, nutritionists, bakers, chefs and children
- ❖ Published three times a year. Third issue includes Holiday Bonus section.
- ❖ Cost $14.95 (US funds) includes postage. Arizona residents add $1.20 for sales tax
- ❖ What No Wheat Publishing/Enterprises (see contact information above)

## Celiac.com

- ❖ On-line resource providing information about celiac disease and the gluten-free diet
- ❖ Site provides a searchable database of over 1,000 articles on celiac disease, recipes, message board, celiac calendar and a bookstore.
- ❖ Quarterly newsletter *Celiac.com's Guide to a Scott-Free Life without Gluten* available by subscription
- ❖ Managed by Scott Adams, who has celiac disease
- ❖ info@celiac.com          www.celiac.com

## Clan Thompson Gluten-Free Resources

### *Pocket Guide to Gluten-Free Foods\**
- ❖ 62 page guide listing foods from major brands found in USA supermarkets, company phone numbers and gluten status of food additives.

### *Pocket Guide to Gluten-Free Prescription Drugs\**
- ❖ 44 page guide listing the most commonly used prescription drugs and toll-free directory of pharmaceutical companies in the USA.

### *Pocket Guide to Gluten-Free Over the Counter Drugs\**
- ❖ 44 page guide listing drugs from 54 different categories and phone directory of manufacturers in the USA.

\* Send check or money order for $4.95 plus $1.00 S/H for 1-2 books or $1.75 S/H for 3-4 books (Maine residents add $0.25 sales tax): **Clan Thompson**
**91 Maine St. Stoneham, ME, USA 04231**
**Ph: 207-928-3303   www.clanthompson.com**

### *Database of Gluten-Free Foods for Palm OS Handhelds or P.C's.\*\**
- ❖ Includes over 3,500 items in 67 different categories of major brands of foods found in USA supermarkets.
- ❖ Can search by name of food, category or manufacturer.

### *Database of Gluten-Free Drugs for Palm OS Handhelds or P.C's.\*\**
- ❖ Includes over 1,500 prescription and over the counter medicines found in the USA
- ❖ Can search by name of product, category or manufacturer.

\*\* Computer database of foods and drugs are self-contained and do not require extra software.

- • Free demo versions are also available.
- • Purchase by secure credit card line, fax or telephone at www.clanthompson.com
- • Database of Gluten-Free Foods or Drugs Basic Version $14.95
  Subscription Version (Full "Basic Version" plus quarterly updates for 1 year) $49.95.

### *Celiac Newsletter*
- ❖ Free monthly e-mail newsletter featuring a variety of articles including news about celiac research, lists of gluten-free drugs and foods, *Ask The Doctor* column by Dr. Cynthia Rudert and more.
- ❖ To subscribe send an e-mail to: **celiac@clanthompson.com**
  The word SUBSCRIBE must appear in the subject line.

NOTE: Clan Thompson verifies all products listed in their resources directly with the manufacturer.

---

## Glutenfreeda.com, Glutenfreeda, Inc.
- ❖ On-line gluten-free monthly cooking magazine
- ❖ Over 1,800 gluten-free archived recipes in a variety of categories
- ❖ Featured articles by guest contributors, gf product evaluations, shopping, resources, on-line cooking classes, menus, seasonal and holiday features
- ❖ Membership available, $30 (US) per year (includes complete recipe database, archived cooking classes and articles, gf menus and more)
- ❖ www.glutenfreeda.com
- ❖ 8900 Lissie Court, Glen Allen, VA, USA  23060
  Phone: 804-965-0014/360-378-3675      www.glutenfreeda.com

## Glutenfreeda Cooking School

- ❖ Specialized gluten-free cooking classes taught by Yvonne Gifford and Jessica Hale
- ❖ Located in San Juan Island, WA and Richmond, VA
- ❖ Classes cover a well-stocked gf pantry, avoiding cross contamination, gf cooking and more
- ❖ Phone: 804-965-0014                                  www.glutenfreeda.com

## Gluten-Free Cooking Club and School

- ❖ Professionally, nutritionally designed classes for adults and children in Phoenix, Arizona
- ❖ Instructors include: LynnRae Ries (Private Chef and Baker; Member of the International Association of Culinary Professionals; student in the American Dietetic Association DTR program and book author) as well guest chefs and cookbook authors
- ❖ Classes include gluten-free shopping tips, product testing and tasting sessions, gf cooking and more
- ❖ Phone: 602-485-8751                                  www.glutenfreecookingclub.com

# GLUTEN-FREE COOKBOOKS

Many cookbooks are available from various gluten-free specialty companies and distributors, celiac organizations and support groups, as well as bookstores and health food stores.

*The Gluten-Free Gourmet Makes Dessert*
*The Gluten-Free Gourmet – Living Well Without Wheat* (Revised Edition)
*More From The Gluten-Free Gourmet*
*The Gluten-Free Gourmet Cooks Fast and Healthy* (1996)
*The Gluten-Free Gourmet Bakes Bread*
    Bette Hagman
    Published by Henry Holt & Company

---

*Gluten-Free 101: Easy Basic Dishes Without Wheat*
*Wheat Free Recipes and Menus: Delicious Dining Without Wheat or Gluten*
*Special Diet Solutions: Healthy Cooking Without Wheat, Gluten, Dairy, Eggs, Yeast or Refined Sugar*
*Special Diet Celebrations: No Wheat, Gluten, Dairy or Egg*
    Carol Fenster, PhD
    Savory Palate Press, 8174 S. Holly - PMB #404, Littleton, CO, USA 80122-4004
    Phone: 1-800-741-5418                          www.savorypalate.com

---

*Wheat-Free, Gluten-Free Recipes for Special Diets*
*Wheat-Free, Gluten-Free Cookbook for Kids and Busy Adults*
*Wheat-Free, Gluten-Free Dessert Cookbook*
*Wheat-Free, Gluten-Free Reduced Calorie Cookbook*
    Connie Sarros
    Published by McGraw Hill, Contemporary Books
    Gluten-Free Cookbooks, 3270 Camden Rue, Cuyahoga Falls, OH, USA 44223
    Phone: 330-929-1651
    E-mail: gfcookbook@hotmail.com                www.homestead.com/gfkids/gf.html

---

*Gluten-Free Baking*
    Rebecca Reilly
    Published by Simon and Schuster

# GLUTEN-FREE COOKBOOKS cont'd

*Cooking Gluten-Free! A Food Lover's Collection of Chef and Family Recipes Without Gluten or Wheat.*
Karen Robertson
Celiac Publishing, P. O. Box 99603, Seattle, WA, USA 98199
Phone: 206-282-4822
Email: celiacpublishing@earthlink.net    www.cookingglutenfree.com

*Together We're Better for Life: 25 Years & Growing –*
*Gluten-Free Recipes from the Canadian Celiac Association*
Available from Canadian Celiac Association (see page 157).

*Discover the Pulse Potential*
Saskatchewan Pulse Growers
Published by Centax Books & Distribution
1150 Eighth Avenue, Regina, SK, Canada S4R 1C9
Phone: 306-359-7580 or 1-800-667-5595    FAX: 306-359-6443 or 1-800-823-6829
E-mail: centax@printwest.com    www.centaxbooks.com

*125 Best Gluten-Free Recipes*
Donna Washburn, P.H.Ec. and Heather Butt, P.H.Ec.
Published by Robert Rose Inc.
Quality Professional Services,
1655 County Road 2, Mallorytown, ON, Canada K0E 1R0
Phone/FAX: 613-923-2116    www.bestbreadrecipes.com

*Incredible Edible Gluten-Free Food for Kids*
Sheri L. Sanderson
Published by Woodbine House    www.woodbinehouse.com

*The Gluten-Free Kitchen*
Roben Ryberg
Published by Prima Publishing

*Wheat-Free, Gluten-Free: 200 Delicious Dishes to Make Eating a Pleasure*
Michelle Berriedale-Johnson
Published by Surrey Books

*Delicious Gluten-Free, Wheat-Free Breads*
LynnRae Ries and Bruce Gross
What No Wheat Publishing/Enterprises
4757 E. Greenway Rd., Suite 107B, #91, Phoenix, AZ, USA 85032–8510
Phone: 602-485-8751    FAX: 602-485-4411
E-mail: whatnowheat@whatnowheat.com    www.whatnowheat.com

*Muffins From the Heart*
Shirley Hartung
Edible Options, 32 Layton Street, Kitchener, ON, Canada N2B 1H2
Phone: 519-570-4912    www.edible-options.com

# APPENDIX – Nutrient Composition of Gluten-Free Flours, Grains, Legumes, Nuts & Seeds

| FOOD ITEM GRAINS & FLOURS | Weight in Grams 250 mL (1 cup) | VITAMINS Thiamin mg | Riboflavin mg | Niacin mg | Pyridoxine mg | Folate mcg | MINERALS Calcium mg | Iron mg | Magnesium mg | Zinc mg | DIETARY FIBER grams | PROTEIN grams |
|---|---|---|---|---|---|---|---|---|---|---|---|---|
| Amaranth Seed | 195 | 0.16 | 0.41 | 2.50 | 0.44 | 96 | 298 | 14.8 | 519 | 6.2 | 29.6 | 28.2 |
| Amaranth Flour | 120 | 0.10 | 0.25 | 1.55 | 0.26 | 59 | 184 | 9.1 | 319 | 3.8 | 18.2 | 17.3 |
| Arrowroot Flour | 128 | 0.00 | 0.00 | 0.00 | 0.01 | 9 | 51 | 0.4 | 4 | 0.1 | 4.4 | 0.4 |
| Buckwheat Bran (Farinetta™) | 137 | 0.14 | 0.58 | 9.6 | 0.29 | 41 | 58 | 6.8 | 317 | 3.3 | 9.9 | 35.9 |
| Buckwheat Groats (roasted, dry) | 164 | 0.37 | 0.44 | 8.4 | 0.58 | 69 | 28 | 4.1 | 362 | 4.0 | 16.9 | 19.2 |
| Buckwheat Groats (roasted, cooked) | 168 | 0.07 | 0.07 | 1.6 | 0.13 | 24 | 12 | 1.3 | 86 | 1.0 | 4.5 | 5.7 |
| Buckwheat Flour (whole groat) | 120 | 0.50 | 0.23 | 7.4 | 0.70 | 65 | 49 | 4.9 | 301 | 3.7 | 12 | 15.1 |
| Corn Bran (crude) | 76 | 0.01 | 0.08 | 2.1 | 0.12 | 3 | 32 | 2.1 | 49 | 1.2 | 65 | 6.4 |
| Corn Flour – yellow (whole grain) | 117 | 0.29 | 0.09 | 2.2 | 0.43 | 29 | 8 | 2.8 | 109 | 2.0 | 15.7 | 8.1 |
| Corn Flour – yellow (Masa, enriched) | 114 | 1.63 | 0.86 | 11.2 | 0.42 | 213 | 161 | 8.2 | 125 | 2.0 | NA | 10.6 |
| Corn Flour – yellow (degermed, unenriched) | 126 | 0.09 | 0.07 | 3.4 | 0.12 | 61 | 3 | 1.2 | 23 | 0.5 | 2.4 | 7.0 |
| Cornmeal – yellow (degermed, enriched) | 138 | 0.99 | 0.56 | 6.9 | 0.36 | 258 | 7 | 5.7 | 55 | 1.0 | 10.2 | 11.7 |
| Cornmeal – yellow (degermed, unenriched) | 138 | 0.19 | 0.07 | 1.4 | 0.36 | 66 | 7 | 1.5 | 55 | 1.0 | 10.2 | 11.7 |
| Flax Seed | 155 | 0.26 | 0.25 | 2.2 | 1.44 | 431 | 309 | 9.6 | 561 | 6.5 | 43.2 | 30.2 |
| Flax Seed Meal | 120 | 0.20 | 0.19 | 1.7 | 1.12 | 334 | 239 | 7.5 | 434 | 5.0 | 33.5 | 23.4 |
| Garbanzo Flour | 120 | 0.58 | 0.25 | 5.5 | 0.65 | 668 | 126 | 7.5 | 138 | 4.1 | 20.9 | 23.2 |
| Garfava Flour | 157 | NA | NA | NA | NA | NA | 104 | 7.9 | NA | NA | 12 | 34.9 |
| Millet (raw) | 200 | 0.84 | 0.58 | 9.4 | 0.77 | 170 | 16 | 6.0 | 228 | 3.4 | 17 | 22.0 |
| Millet (cooked) | 174 | 0.18 | 0.14 | 2.3 | 0.19 | 33 | 5.2 | 1.1 | 77 | 1.6 | 2.3 | 6.1 |
| Potato Flour | 160 | 0.37 | 0.08 | 5.6 | 1.23 | 40 | 104 | 2.2 | 104 | 0.9 | 9.4 | 11.0 |
| Potato Starch | 192 | NA | NA | NA | 0.02 | NA | 67 | 3.5 | 12 | 0.3 | 0 | 1.1 |
| Quinoa Grain | 170 | 0.34 | 0.67 | 5.0 | 0.38 | 83 | 102 | 15.7 | 357 | 5.6 | 10.0 | 22.3 |
| Quinoa Flour | 102 | 0.20 | 0.41 | 3.0 | 0.22 | 50 | 61 | 9.4 | 214 | 3.4 | 6.0 | 13.4 |
| Rice Bran (crude) | 118 | 3.25 | 0.34 | 40 | 4.8 | 74 | 67 | 21.9 | 922 | 7.1 | 24.8 | 15.8 |
| Rice, Brown – raw (long grain) | 185 | 0.74 | 0.17 | 9.4 | 0.94 | 37 | 43 | 2.7 | 265 | 3.7 | 6.5 | 14.7 |
| Rice, Brown – cooked (long grain) | 195 | 0.19 | 0.05 | 3.0 | 0.28 | 8 | 20 | 0.8 | 84 | 1.2 | 3.5 | 5.0 |

NA = Not available

| FOOD ITEM | Weight in Grams 250 mL (1 cup) | VITAMINS | | | | | MINERALS | | | | DIETARY FIBER grams | PROTEIN grams |
|---|---|---|---|---|---|---|---|---|---|---|---|---|
| GRAINS & FLOURS CONT'D. | | Thiamin mg | Riboflavin mg | Niacin mg | Pyridoxine mg | Folate mcg | Calcium mg | Iron mg | Magnesium mg | Zinc mg | | |
| Rice Flour – brown | 158 | 0.70 | 0.13 | 10.0 | 1.2 | 25 | 17 | 3.1 | 177 | 3.9 | 7.3 | 11.4 |
| Rice Flour – sweet | 120 | 0.05 | 0.10 | 3.0 | 0.04 | 0 | 20 | 1.3 | 6 | 0.5 | 0 | 8.3 |
| Rice Flour – white | 158 | 0.22 | 0.03 | 4.1 | 0.69 | 6 | 16 | 0.6 | 55 | 1.3 | 3.8 | 9.4 |
| Rice, White – raw (long grain, parboiled, enr.) | 185 | 1.10 | 0.13 | 6.7 | 0.65 | 427 | 111 | 6.6 | 57 | 1.8 | 3.1 | 12.6 |
| Rice, White – ckd. (long grain, parboiled, enr.) | 175 | 0.44 | 0.03 | 2.5 | 0.03 | 88 | 33 | 2.0 | 21 | 0.5 | 0.7 | 4.0 |
| Rice, Wild – raw | 160 | 0.18 | 0.42 | 10.8 | 0.63 | 152 | 34 | 3.1 | 283 | 9.5 | 9.9 | 23.6 |
| Rice, Wild – cooked | 164 | 0.09 | 0.14 | 2.1 | 0.22 | 43 | 5 | 1.0 | 53 | 2.2 | 3.0 | 6.5 |
| Sorghum Grain | 192 | 0.46 | 0.27 | 5.6 | 0.59 | NA | 54 | 8.5 | NA | NA | 12.9 | 21.7 |
| Sorghum Flour | 146 | NA | NA | NA | NA | NA | 9 | 4.7 | NA | NA | 8.2 | 11.5 |
| Soy Flour (full-fat) | 84 | 0.49 | 0.97 | 3.6 | 0.39 | 290 | 173 | 5.4 | 360 | 3.3 | 8.0 | 29.0 |
| Soy Flour (defatted) | 100 | 0.70 | 0.25 | 2.6 | 0.57 | 305 | 241 | 9.2 | 290 | 2.5 | 17.5 | 47.0 |
| Teff Grain | 180 | 0.54 | 0.32 | 4.5 | NA | NA | 286 | 10.4 | 306 | 3.6 | 5.4 | 19.8 |
| Teff Flour | 120 | 0.36 | 0.22 | 3.0 | NA | NA | 191 | 7.0 | 204 | 2.4 | 3.6 | 13.2 |
| GLUTEN-CONTAINING FLOURS | | | | | | | | | | | | |
| Wheat Bran | 58 | 0.30 | 0.34 | 7.9 | 0.76 | 46 | 42 | 6.1 | 354 | 4.2 | 24.8 | 9.0 |
| Whole-Wheat Flour | 120 | 0.54 | 0.26 | 7.6 | 0.41 | 53 | 41 | 4.7 | 166 | 3.5 | 14.6 | 16.4 |
| White Flour, All-Purpose (enriched) | 125 | 0.98 | 0.62 | 7.4 | 0.06 | 193 | 19 | 5.8 | 28 | 0.9 | 3.4 | 12.9 |

NA = Not available    ckd. = cooked    enr. = enriched

NOTES: ❖ Nutrient composition values can vary considerably depending on factors such as; (1) specific variety, growing conditions and processing of the grain, legume, nut or seed; (2) coarseness of the grind of the grain and sifting process used to produce the flour; (3) individual laboratory analytical methods and testing equipment used for nutrient analysis.

❖ Nutrient composition values for this Appendix are from: (1) USDA Nutrient Data Base, Release #13; (2) Authentic Foods (Garfava Flour); (3) ESHA Research (Potato Starch); (4) Minn-Dak Growers Ltd. (Buckwheat Bran [Farinetta™]) (5) Waniska, R.D. and L.L. Rooney 2000. *Structure and Chemistry of the Sorghum Caryopsis.* In C.W. Smith and R.A. Frederiksen (eds.) Sorghum: Origin, history, technology, and production. John Wiley & Sons Inc., New York, NY (Vitamin B6, Zinc and dietary fiber of sorghum grain) and R.A. Frederiksen (eds.) Sorghum: Origin, history, technology, and production. John Wiley & Sons Inc., New York, NY (Vitamin B6, Zinc and dietary fiber of sorghum grain) (6) Silliker Laboratories of Texas, Inc., Grand Prairie, Texas (Whole Grain Sorghum Flour) (7) *Lost Crops of Africa*, Vol. I (Grains), 1996 (ISBN 0-309-04990-3), National Academy Press, Washington (Teff Grain& Flour)

❖ The weight in grams for 250 mL (1 cup) of the following flours were provided by: (1) Bob's Red Mill (Amaranth, Flax Seed Meal, Garbanzo, Potato Starch, Sweet Rice, Teff Grain and Flour); (2) Northern Quinoa Corporation (Quinoa); (3) Twin Valley Mills (Sorghum).

| FOOD ITEM<br>BEANS, PEAS, NUTS & SEEDS | Weight in Grams 250 mL (1 cup) | VITAMINS | | | | | MINERALS | | | | DIETARY FIBER | PROTEIN |
|---|---|---|---|---|---|---|---|---|---|---|---|---|
| | | Thiamin mg | Riboflavin mg | Niacin mg | Pyridoxine mg | Folate mcg | Calcium mg | Iron mg | Magnesium mg | Zinc mg | grams | grams |
| **Cooked Beans** | | | | | | | | | | | | |
| Cranberry – Romano Bean | 177 | 0.37 | 0.12 | 0.9 | 0.14 | 366 | 89 | 3.7 | 89 | 2.0 | 17.7 | 16.5 |
| Fava – Broad Bean | 170 | 0.17 | 0.15 | 1.2 | 0.12 | 177 | 61 | 2.6 | 73 | 1.7 | 9.2 | 12.9 |
| Garbanzo – Chickpea | 164 | 0.19 | 0.10 | 0.9 | 0.23 | 282 | 80 | 4.7 | 78 | 2.5 | 12.5 | 14.5 |
| Kidney Beans – Red | 177 | 0.29 | 0.10 | 1.0 | 0.2 | 229 | 50 | 5.2 | 80 | 1.9 | 13.1 | 15.4 |
| Lentils | 198 | 0.34 | 0.15 | 2.1 | 0.35 | 358 | 38 | 6.6 | 71 | 2.5 | 15.6 | 17.9 |
| Navy Beans | 182 | 0.37 | 0.11 | 1.0 | 0.30 | 254 | 127 | 4.5 | 107 | 1.9 | 11.7 | 15.8 |
| Pinto Beans | 171 | 0.32 | 0.16 | 0.7 | 0.27 | 294 | 82 | 4.5 | 94 | 1.9 | 14.7 | 14 |
| Soybeans | 172 | 0.27 | 0.49 | 0.7 | 0.4 | 93 | 175 | 8.8 | 148 | 2.0 | 10.3 | 28.6 |
| Split Peas | 196 | 0.37 | 0.11 | 1.7 | 0.1 | 127 | 27 | 2.5 | 71 | 2.0 | 16.3 | 16.3 |
| White Beans | 179 | 0.21 | 0.08 | 0.3 | 0.17 | 144 | 161 | 6.6 | 113 | 2.5 | 11.3 | 17.4 |
| **Nuts** | | | | | | | | | | | | |
| Almonds (whole, blanched) | 145 | 0.29 | 0.81 | 5.3 | 0.17 | 44 | 313 | 5.4 | 399 | 4.5 | 15.1 | 31.8 |
| Brazil Nuts (dried, unblanched) | 140 | 1.4 | 0.17 | 2.3 | 0.35 | 6 | 246 | 4.8 | 315 | 6.4 | 7.6 | 20.1 |
| Peanuts | 146 | 0.93 | 0.20 | 17.6 | 0.51 | 350 | 134 | 6.7 | 245 | 4.8 | 12.4 | 37.7 |
| Pecans (halves) | 108 | 0.71 | 0.14 | 1.26 | 0.23 | 24 | 76 | 2.7 | 131 | 4.9 | 10.4 | 9.9 |
| Walnuts – English (shelled, halves) | 100 | 0.34 | 0.15 | 1.91 | 0.54 | 98 | 104 | 2.9 | 158 | 3.1 | 6.7 | 15.2 |
| **Seeds** | | | | | | | | | | | | |
| Pumpkin Seeds (kernels, dried) | 138 | 0.29 | 0.44 | 2.4 | 0.31 | 79 | 59 | 20.7 | 738 | 10.3 | 5.4 | 33.9 |
| Sesame Seeds (kernels, dried, decorticated) | 150 | 1.08 | 0.13 | 7.0 | 0.22 | 144 | 197 | 11.7 | 521 | 15.4 | 17.4 | 39.6 |
| Sunflower seeds (hulled kernels, dry roasted) | 128 | 0.14 | 0.32 | 9.0 | 1.0 | 304 | 90 | 4.9 | 165 | 6.8 | 14.2 | 24.7 |

# INDEX

# Send *THE GLUTEN-FREE DIET* to a Friend

*Gluten-Free Diet – A Comprehensive Resource Guide* is $21.95/CDN or $19.95/US per book plus $4.00 (total order) for shipping and handling.

No of copies _____ x $21.95 CDN/$19.95 US ............................................. = $ _____

Shipping and handling (total order)................................................. = 4.00

Subtotal ....................................................................................... = _____

In Canada add 7% GST OR 15% HST where applicable ........................... = _____

Total enclosed .............................................................................. = _____

U.S. and international orders payable in U.S. funds./ Price is subject to change.

NAME: _____

ORGANIZATION: _____

STREET: _____

CITY: _____ PROV./STATE _____

COUNTRY _____ POSTAL CODE/ZIP _____

E-mail: _____

Please make cheque or money order payable to:    **CASE NUTRITION CONSULTING**
     **Phone/FAX: 306-751-1000**    **1940 Angley Court**
     **Web: www.glutenfreediet.ca**    **Regina, Saskatchewan**
     **E-mail: info@glutenfreediet.ca**    **Canada  S4V 2V2**

For fund raising or volume discount prices, contact **Case Nutrition Consulting** for rates.
Please allow 3-4 weeks for delivery.

---

# Send *THE GLUTEN-FREE DIET* to a Friend

*Gluten-Free Diet – A Comprehensive Resource Guide* is $21.95/CDN or $19.95/US per book plus $4.00 (total order) for shipping and handling.

No of copies _____ x $21.95 CDN/$19.95 US ............................................. = $ _____

Shipping and handling (total order)................................................. = 4.00

Subtotal ....................................................................................... = _____

In Canada add 7% GST OR 15% HST where applicable ........................... = _____

Total enclosed .............................................................................. = _____

U.S. and international orders payable in U.S. funds./ Price is subject to change.

NAME: _____

ORGANIZATION: _____

STREET: _____

CITY: _____ PROV./STATE _____

COUNTRY _____ POSTAL CODE/ZIP _____

E-mail: _____

Please make cheque or money order payable to:    **CASE NUTRITION CONSULTING**
     **Phone/FAX: 306-751-1000**    **1940 Angley Court**
     **Web: www.glutenfreediet.ca**    **Regina, Saskatchewan**
     **E-mail: info@glutenfreediet.ca**    **Canada  S4V 2V2**

For fund raising or volume discount prices, contact **Case Nutrition Consulting** for rates.
Please allow 3-4 weeks for delivery.